MURDER

THE BIOGRAPHY

KATE MORGAN

MURDER

THE BIOGRAPHY

MUDLARK

Mudlark
An imprint of HarperCollins*Publishers*
1 London Bridge Street
London SE1 9GF

www.harpercollins.co.uk

HarperCollins*Publishers*
1st Floor, Watermarque Building, Ringsend Road
Dublin 4, Ireland

First published by Mudlark 2021
This edition published 2022

1 3 5 7 9 10 8 6 4 2

A catalogue record of this book is
available from the British Library

ISBN 978-0-00-840734-6

Printed and bound in the UK using 100% renewable
electricity at CPI Group (UK) Ltd

MIX
Paper from
responsible sources
FSC™ C007454
FSC
www.fsc.org

CONTENTS

INTRODUCTION

THOU SHALT NOT KILL

'Scarlet billows start to spread'

The recording begins with the crackle of a gramophone, before the barrel organ starts to grind out an eerie fairground melody. The reedy voice begins to sing in German, the tongue rolling over the letter 'r' with a sinister relish. Even for those who don't speak the language, the nursery-rhyme rhythm of the song sounds vaguely but disconcertingly familiar:

> *Und der Haifisch, der hat Zähne, Und die trägt er im Gesicht ...*

> *(And the shark, he has teeth, and he bears the scars of them in his face ...)*

The singer is Bertolt Brecht and the song is 'Der Moritat von Mackie Messer', the opening number from *The Threepenny Opera*, the 1928 musical written by Brecht and composer Kurt

1

Weil. The *Opera* tells the story of the gangs of beggars and thieves that inhabit the underworld of Victorian London. Chief among these is the villainous Macheath, notorious for his murderous deeds around the streets and alleyways of the city, which are listed in the song for the audience's benefit. In the 1950s a production of the show opened off Broadway, and in 1955 Louis Armstrong recorded a tightened translation of the song set to a jaunty jazz tune – 'Mackie Messer' had been transformed and given a new American identity as 'Mack the Knife'.

Bobby Darin released another cover version of the song a couple of years later and the tune has become a lounge singer standard, covered by Frank Sinatra, Ella Fitzgerald and countless others. But its creepy origins as a 20th-century take on the traditional '*moritat*', or 'murder ballad', are often overlooked. These pieces, popular for centuries throughout Germany and the rest of Europe, set stories of murder, vengeance and justice to simple tunes. Tom Jones's 'Delilah' is another modern song that owes a similar debt to the tradition, a brutal crime of passion told from the murderer's point of view, with an instantly recognisable tune and a memorable chorus.

Mackie, and later Mack, is the embodiment of the murderer as a kind of folk hero, reviled and revered in almost equal measure. The celebration of his exploits goes to the heart of our grisly fascination with murder; we are simultaneously intrigued and revolted. His deeds are listed with relish and the song congratulates him on his ability to evade detection. The Armstrong and Darin versions cleaned up Mack's antics considerably – the original German verses are much darker, accusing him of raping and killing several women – but there is still a thinly disguised admiration, even affection, for him underlying all of the modern versions of the song. Darin's swinging portrait of Mack, whom he had recast as a suave gangster, earned him a Grammy for the 1959 Record of the Year. But the minstrels who wrote and sang the original ballads would still recognise the tale of death and bloody vengeance in 'Mack the Knife'.

Throughout our history, violent death at the hands of another has been part of the songs that we sing, the names that we give things and the stories that we tell each other. In Scottish folklore, the *sluagh* is a swarm of malevolent spirits said to haunt the night sky. No longer earthbound, they fly across the Hebrides seeking out the living, particularly those who have sinned, snatching them up and dropping them back down to earth from a fatal height. In their rarely glimpsed physical form, they appear as a flock of black birds, usually crows. The coal-black bird has had a long career in folk tales as an omen or even a harbinger of death; it scavenged on the bodies of the dead, irresistibly drawing it to sites of death such as battlefields and graveyards. Nowhere is this grim association more apparent than in the collective noun for a flock of crows – a 'murder'.

The appetite for stories of terrible deeds and the people who commit them is an enduring part of human nature. It can be traced from the medieval *moritats*, through Victorian penny dreadfuls, right up to the true crime documentaries and podcasts that we consume so voraciously today. The medium may have changed from ballad sheets to Netflix, but beneath the surface the stories are the same. Whether in fact or fiction, murder can be all things to all people. At a basic level, it is a tale of good versus evil, where the roles of victim and villain are clearly laid out before us. More often than not, there is an element of mystery at its heart, a riddle to be solved. The glut of detective novels in the first half of the 20th century epitomised this appeal, with the victim and their death often simply a vehicle to get into the intellectually satisfying fun of collecting and analysing the clues to unmask the killer. Then there is of course the voyeuristic and vicarious chill we get from reading about horrible things happening to other people, whether real or imagined.

In the midst of life, we are in death – and that's exactly how we like it. In his 1946 essay *Decline of the English Murder*, George Orwell was adamant that murder had peaked in a golden age between 1850 and 1925, but over seventy-five years later it seems that his report of murder's terminal decline was greatly exaggerated. Whether in fiction or on the news, murder exerts a fascination unlike any other crime, and our appetite for the homicidal is robustly insatiable. We invite it into our homes every night on the television and we go to sleep with it on the bedside table between the covers of a paperback. There is now no small-town homicide or suburban slaying too obscure to be picked over in minute detail in a podcast or documentary. In drama, tales of murder recur as plot devices in everything from Shakespeare to soap operas. As a genre, crime fiction has been a literary behemoth ever since the Victorians popularised the detective story. Our fictional encounters still usually climax with the apprehension of the culprit and the tacit conclusion that justice will be done, but in real life the solving of the crime is only half the story. There are many hurdles to leap before the captured killer becomes the convicted murderer.

Aside from its dark appeal, the act of murder itself is a blank canvas onto which we can project all manner of meanings. It can be an act of straightforward revenge or rage, be prompted by mercenary motivations or by reasons known only to the killer. It has been used as a tool of political expediency and an expression of personal honour. While some kill seemingly at random, there are those who murder because their own life depended upon it. At the heart of all of this sits a very real, lethally complex and endlessly fascinating offence that is the most hallowed in the annals of the criminal law. The label of 'murderer' carries a stigma far and above that of any other crime. Murder is the only offence for which a court must impose a life sentence on conviction and, for many years over the 19th and 20th centuries, was the only crime that justified taking a life. The law is the cornerstone of all of this.

Despite the pervasiveness of this crime in all aspects of our culture, popular or otherwise, there is nothing black and white about it. The law relating to homicide is a complete jumble of antique rules, odd judicial decisions and ambiguous interpretations. When it comes to murder, we really don't know the half of it. But we're so used to watching and reading about it, we think we know more than we do – and a little knowledge can be a dangerous thing.

As I was putting the finishing touches to this book, a story was reported in the press that summed up all the contradictions and captivations of our relationship with murder. The names and details are unimportant, as it could be one of many similar tragedies that take place every year. A man had killed a woman in circumstances that, however improbably, he claimed were accidental. He was acquitted of murder and convicted of manslaughter. Although the news report itself was a reasonably even-handed summation of the case, a quick glance below the byline to the reader comments revealed a maelstrom of outrage, misunderstanding and divided opinion.

Some said the man had got away with murder and the case was a miscarriage of justice. Others, obviously trolls, blamed the victim for her own demise and openly sympathised with her killer's actions. But many of the comments revealed our collective ignorance of the legal realities of murder and manslaughter as they currently stand in this country. Plenty of armchair lawyers proclaimed that the killing could not possibly be considered murder because it was not planned in advance or otherwise apparently premeditated. Others offered authoritative statements on the law that were several degrees removed from reality.

Trivial as they may seem, these pronouncements from keyboard warriors matter – because here are the people who end up sitting on juries or answering opinion polls on criminal justice that drive government policy on law and order. These misapprehensions can have a very real effect on how the justice system ultimately works for all of us. If we're going to indulge our darker sides with gruesome stories and graphic deaths in print and on screen, then at the same time we have a duty to educate ourselves about the lethal reality of the crime that exerts such a spell over us.

Statistically speaking, our collective obsession with murder is out of all proportion to our likely encounters with it. Each year, the Office for National Statistics publishes reports on the whys, hows and wherefores of the country's death toll for the previous twelve-month period. Heart disease and cancers unsurprisingly top the charts year on year. But the ONS also gathers data on unnatural causes of death in the population, including the UK's 'murder rate'. According to their figures, in the twelve months up to March 2019, out of the 519,000 people that died in England and Wales, 671 were victims of homicide. Out of a population of around 58 million souls, this equates to a fatality rate for homicide of eleven per million population.

With such small numbers involved, tracking trends in murder at a population level can be difficult. The ONS counts the number of victims based on the year in which their death was officially recorded as a homicide, which can lead to some anomalous results. The country's murder rate spiked dramatically in 2003, when the 173 people believed to have been killed by Dr Harold Shipman were formally recorded as homicide victims by the public inquiry into the case, although the murders themselves dated back to the 1970s.

Similarly, the deaths of the ninety-six people killed in the 1989 Hillsborough stadium disaster did not appear in the statistics until almost thirty years later, when a new inquest verdict of manslaughter was recorded in respect of their deaths. A single incident involving a high death toll, such as a terrorist attack, will produce a similar jump in the rate for a particular year. 2017 to 2018 saw successive tragedies, including the

Manchester Arena bombing and the London Bridge attacks, contribute to a peak in the national homicide figures unseen in the preceding years.

But some broad conclusions can be drawn from the latest data. Men are overwhelmingly more likely to kill and be killed, making up 64 per cent of victims and 92 per cent of homicide suspects. For both men and women, the home is the deadliest place to be, with the vast majority of killings taking place in the victim's residence. Staggeringly, over 40 per cent of female victims were killed by their current or former partner, but men are most often murdered by a friend or acquaintance. While serial killers like Dr Shipman steal the headlines, stranger danger is not borne out by the statistics; only 6 per cent of female victims were killed by a stranger, although this rises to 22 per cent of male victims.

Age and ethnicity also produce some noticeable variations. Black people made up 14 per cent of all murder victims in the 2019 figures, the highest number in twenty years; but of those victims, almost half of them were under the age of twenty-four. This contrasted with a trend of decreasing numbers of younger victims across other ethnic groups. Female killers were likely to be older than male ones, outnumbering them by around half in all of the older age categories. A sharp instrument has been the method of choice for killers for several decades, and is still the most common weapon used in attacks on both men and women. Guns are involved in only 5 per cent of the deaths recorded.

The banality of murder when laid out in cold, hard statistics is a world away from our dramatic, even romantic, images of a Mack the Knife; but it is perhaps even more terrifying. Behind each headline and datapoint is a life and death of a real person. This book is about the true story of murder in this country, viewed through the prism of one of our oldest and most notorious laws. Since its inception almost a thousand years ago, this most infamous crime has been shaped above all by *real* people – the killers and victims whose cases are tried by the court; the judges, juries and lawyers who preside over their fate; and the politicians and monarchs who have held lives in their hands even after the law has taken its course. This homicidal history of Britain takes in big questions about when, if ever, taking a life can be justified or excused, and the allowances that we should make for those good people who sometimes do very bad things.

Hand in hand with this story of crime goes the question of punishment. For much of its history the law operated by the maxim of 'a life for a life', but homicide was far from unique in attracting a lethal punishment. Over the course of the 18th century, England entered the age of the so-called 'Bloody Code', as the use of the death penalty expanded exponentially, with statute after statute turning an ever-increasing list of offences into capital ones. Writing in 1826, just as the tide was beginning to turn, the editors of the *Newgate Calendar* (a popular compendium of notorious criminal trials) observed:

The penal laws of the British empire are, by foreign writers, charged with being too sanguinary in the cases of lesser offences. They hold that the punishment of death ought to be inflicted only for crimes of the highest magnitude; and

philanthropists of our own nation have accorded with their
opinion. Such persons as have had no opportunity of inquir-
ing into the subject will hardly credit the assertion that there
are above one hundred and sixty offences punishable by
death.

We are accustomed to murder having an exalted status above all other crimes. It is elevated above all other offences within the criminal law. From 1861 until the abolition of capital punishment just over a century later, murder was in effect the only crime punishable by death. The gruesome formalities of executions took place behind closed prison doors after 1868, lending an added layer of mystique to the convicted killer's final moments that didn't accompany other crimes.

When hanging was finally abolished in 1965 the capital sentence was replaced by one of life imprisonment, and murder is still the only offence for which the court must impose a life sentence upon conviction. But not all murders are created equal – and the question of whether all murderers should be treated equally has vexed the justice system for a long time. Imposing the same sentence, whether for life or death, does not take into account the infinitely variable shades of grey in the horror and culpability of the crimes caught by the same criminal offence. And as medical science and psychiatry advanced in the 19th century, so the courts had to recognise that some killers were as much in need of help as they were of punishment.

The truth of murder is stranger, darker and more compelling than any fiction. It is made up of a patchwork of stories, stories of crime and punishment but also of justice and injustice, of people, places and very personal tragedies; all taking place against a backdrop of perpetual social shifts and political cataclysms. In tracing this history, we can see the effect that these deaths have had on all of our lives today. After all, the scariest stories are always the ones that are true.

*   *   *

In the England of a thousand years ago, a rudimentary legal system was only just beginning to emerge and it was a time when life truly was nasty, brutish and short – and violent death was a fact of it. Each man carried his own *wergild*, which was the financial value placed upon his life. If he were to be killed, his killer was required to make *bot*, or compensation, to the deceased's kin to the value of his particular *wergild*. And that, by and large, was the end of the matter. The payment of *bot* had exculpated the killer's act and the law took no further interest.

Things began to change following the landing of the Vikings on English shores in the 9th century. The kingdom that they established here, which covered a swathe of eastern and northern England, was known as the Danelaw and was subject to the rules and customs of the occupying Norsemen. One of these outlawed the killing of a Dane on English soil. This was one of the earliest examples of a discrete category of killing being recognised by the law, and it would pave the way for the creation of a distinct crime of murder in the centuries that followed.

Around the 10th century, from a primordial soup of mud, woad, Old English and bastardised French, the concept of *mordor* emerged. This was the first time that the law acknowledged separate classes of homicide, although scholars are divided on the original meaning of *mordor*.* It was clearly related to, if not directly derived from, the French idea of *mordre* and the German word *morth*. Both of these denoted a killing with an element of secrecy of concealment, and it was the subterfuge, rather than the killing itself, that marked it out as a special category. By the reign of King Cnut in the early decades of the 11th century, *mord* or *mordor* was generally accepted as referring to a secret killing, and, importantly, one that could not be simply atoned for by the payment of *wergild*. Just a short time later, in the laws set down during Edward the Confessor's reign between 1042 and the Norman conquest in 1066, the offence had been renamed *murdrum* and was punishable by death. Unlawful killing was now a matter sanctioned by the state, rather than being simply a question of compensation between citizens. Murder's long and fascinating criminal career had begun.

The modern offence of murder is a direct descendant of *murdrum*, but there is a world of difference between the crimes they denote. *Murdrum* still retained the original sense of a secret slaying inherent in the original *mord*; other killings, even if deliberate, were treated as lesser homicides or may not have even been considered criminal at all. By medieval times, the meaning of the crime was undergoing a shift that remains

* It has been suggested that J. R. R. Tolkien borrowed the term when seeking a name for his fictional Middle Earth realm ruled over by the Dark Lord Sauron.

fundamental to our understanding of it even today. The focus had moved from the secret nature of the act to the malicious intention that had motivated the killing. Legal texts from the 13th century separated homicides into *voluntarium* (intentional) and *casuale* (accidental). *Murdrum* was generally included in the category of *voluntarium* killings. Through the 14th century, the term made increasingly frequent appearances in official records and legal documents, gradually becoming anglicised to 'murder'. The concept of manslaughter, as a secondary category of culpable homicide below murder, took a little longer to emerge. The word is first recorded in a legal tract from the early 1500s, and it wasn't until the middle of the century that lawyers and courts began to seriously concern themselves with the differences between these two types of homicide.

By the time the renowned jurist Sir Edward Coke was writing his voluminous and influential legal textbook *Institutes of the Lawes of England* in the first half of the 17th century, the law had become relatively sophisticated in its treatment of homicides. Coke's was the pre-eminent legal mind of his day. He was called to the bar in 1578, the start of an illustrious legal career that encompassed stints as attorney general and chief justice, serving both Elizabeth I and James I. As attorney general, Coke was the main prosecutor and legal adviser to the Crown and was involved in many of the great trials of the day. The contentious accession of James to the throne was the catalyst for all manner of plots and conspiracies, and Coke was kept busy with a caseload of treasons. He prosecuted Sir Walter Raleigh for treason in 1603, following the uncovering of his involvement in a plot to make Lady Arabella Stuart monarch in James's place. Coke's most notorious trial was of the surviving Gunpowder plotters in 1605. This was his last major trial before his elevation to the judiciary in 1606, when he became Chief Justice of the Common Pleas, a title he shares incongruously with a Wetherspoons in Keswick, Cumbria.

Coke was clearly a shrewd political operator, as he managed to keep head and neck together while proving a thorn in the side of parliament and the Crown after his judicial appointment. In 1616 James eventually ran out of patience and Coke was removed from his judicial post. This fall from grace proved no barrier to a subsequent political career for Coke, and in 1621 he became MP for Liskeard on the order of James. Coke retired from politics in 1629 and lived out a lengthy (in 17th-century terms) retirement at his Buckinghamshire estate. He died in 1634 at the grand old age of eighty-two, having fitted in two marriages, twelve children and an extensive corpus of legal writing alongside his career.

So what does the august Coke have to say on the subject of bloody murder and manslaughter?

Murder is where a man of sound memory, and in the age of discretion, unlawfully killeth within any county of the realm any reasonable creature in rerum natura under the King's peace, with malice aforethought, either expressed by the party or implied by law.

According to Coke, a killing was to be considered manslaughter when it took place 'upon a sudden occasion; and therefore is called chance-medley'. This was a historic term, a corruption of the French *chaude melle*, meaning literally 'hot fight', separating the premeditated 'cold-blooded' murder from the spontaneous 'hot-blooded' (but still intentional) attack, which was treated as chance-medley or manslaughter. Throughout its history, the legal dividing line between murder and manslaughter has been one of the most contentious issues in the canon of homicide law, and even following Coke's statement the positioning of the boundary between the two crimes would continue to tax the courts for the next two hundred years. But in the main, Coke's words were accepted as being the definitive statement of the law and have become something akin to the founding gospel of the English crime of murder.

*　　*　　*

In the four hundred years since Coke set out his definition it has not really been improved upon or superseded. A couple of centuries of case law have finessed its elements and introduced new aspects, but essentially this remains the legal definition of murder. Of course, Coke didn't create the offence – he was simply writing down the law as it was understood to be at that time. But his statement, chanted like an incantation by innumerable law students down the years, has been brought to life by successive generations of judges and lawyers applying it to the crimes that come before them and has long been applied as the definition of the crime of murder within English law. To get to the bottom of what murder truly means, we'll explore the crimes and cases that have been instrumental in shaping the conception and understanding of the law of murder, manslaughter and all things homicidal since Coke put pen to paper back in Jacobean times.

Under the umbrella term of 'homicide' sits a raft of crimes in descending order of heinousness, culpability and, consequently, notoriety. Top of this grisly pile is murder, defined by the presence of an intention to kill or cause serious harm to the victim concerned. All murders are homicides, but not all homicides are murders. Beneath murder sits manslaughter and, as we will see, 'of all crimes, manslaughter appears to afford the most difficulties of definition, for it concerns homicide in so many and varying circumstances'. Indeed, the spectrum of human tragedy covered by the offence of manslaughter ranges from the essentially murderous to the almost accidental. It encompasses those who kill deliberately in response to some antagonising action on the part of the deceased, right through to the careless or neglectful, who fail to heed the consequences of their actions.

The development of this concept of committing manslaughter by gross negligence has liberalised the idea of when and by whom manslaughter can be committed, incorporating deaths that occur in less traditionally murderous situations, such as healthcare settings and, for a while, out on the road. It also paved the way for the increasing criminalisation of companies in the 20th century, meaning that organisations and entities whose shoddy employment practices or disregard for public safety cause fatalities can be caught within the ambit of unlawful killings recognised by the law.

Finally, this 'pyramid of homicide' is supported by a broad base of other crimes relating to deaths in specific circumstances, where the legal requirements of murder and manslaughter are not met. These include the causing death by driving offences arising from fatal road traffic accidents, infanticide, and some offences under health and safety legislation. These offences are generally viewed as less serious; they are distinct from but are still descended from and related to the law of murder, its second cousins once removed, perhaps.

The offence of murder that Coke defined consists of two elements. Then, as now, a jury must be satisfied of both beyond reasonable doubt in order to convict someone of murder. The first is the killing of another person – in legal terms, this is known as the *actus reus* or prohibited act. The second element of the crime is the mental element, or *mens rea*. Literally, this translates as 'guilty mind' and is essentially the mental intention to commit an offence, which creates the concept of criminal 'fault'. To be guilty of murder, it is not enough to simply kill someone; you must have done it intentionally, as, by and large, you should only be criminalised for things you did on purpose. In Coke's parlance, it is that the killing was done 'with malice aforethought, either expressed by the party or implied by law'.

The phrase 'malice aforethought' has entered the lexicon and inspired the title of many a potboiler down the years. But it has also given rise to the most common misconception about the law of murder, which still informs much debate and discussion about the crime today. The modern interpretation of Coke's 'malice aforethought' is the intention to kill or commit serious physical harm. In popular culture, this has translated into a preoccupation with premeditation. While this can be strong evidence of intention, it is not a requirement of the definition. You don't need to have purchased the ice pick or dug the shallow grave in just the right spot for the jogger or dog walker to stumble over it in advance of the killing. The only thing that matters is what you intended at the time of the fatal act. It is irrelevant that this intention may have only crystallised in the seconds before you pulled the trigger or that it dissipated in the following instant, when the enormity of taking a human life hit you. At her trial for the murder of her lover David Blakely in 1955, Ruth Ellis, to whom we will return, was asked by the prosecution what she intended to do at the time that she shot him. Her reply is probably the most precise and succinct statement of the *mens rea* of murder ever uttered in a courtroom, and it probably signed her death warrant – 'It's obvious. When I shot him, I intended to kill him.'

*   *   *

In the intervening centuries, the law of homicide has undergone a remarkable transformation from the parameters first set down by Sir Edward Coke to the crimes that come before our courts today. To understand this, we must delve into the cases that make the headlines but also into plenty that don't, to explore the crimes and the characters who have been so instrumental in shaping the law over time, what it means for all of us today and the journey it has been on to get here.

The number of ways and means of ending a human life may have mushroomed over the years, but the fundamental reasons for doing so are enduringly constant. Greed, lust, rage and gain are the archetypal triggers for taking a life, and this is as true today as it has ever been. But in the century or so following Coke's bold statement of what murder was, the most important issue for the law was determining what it was *not*. The reasons for which it was excusable or even permissible to take a life would be born out of some of the most dramatic cases to ever trouble a courtroom.

While these stories reveal much about the time and place in which they occurred, they continue to resonate with us today. The circumstances in which we criminalise those who kill have revolved and evolved countless times since the law of murder was last defined half a millennium ago, changing and shifting to reflect the fears and obsessions of each successive generation. The law itself has been shaped by a cast of thousands over several centuries, more often than not being moulded by the unfortunate, ill-judged and misguided, rather than the truly wicked. In large part the history of the law of homicide is a tale of everyday human interactions gone slightly awry, with terrifying consequences for all concerned.

CHAPTER ONE

THE FIELD OF HONOUR

*'... from the rising of the sun until the
stars appeared ...'*

On a warm summer's evening early in June of 1707 as the sun
went down over the Thames, a small procession of Yeoman
Warders marched across the yards of the Tower of London
towards the outer wall. They clanged the gates of the castle
closed, marched back to the Tower Constable's rooms and
solemnly placed the keys into a safe, to be locked away until
the gates were opened again at sunrise the following day. As
the Warders trooped back to their barracks, a lone figure
slipped across the cobbles and up the stairs to the Tower's
Guard Room. The figure was John Mawgridge, one of the
Guard's drummers who was paying a visit to his close friend
Lieutenant William Cope. The pair had planned an evening of
carousing to celebrate Mawgridge's forthcoming commission
into the army. In the Guard Room the candlelight glinted on

the wine bottles that were laid out on the rough wooden table, ready for Mawgridge's arrival.

Cope had taken the liberty of inviting a 'certain woman of [his] acquaintance' to join the party, and as the evening wore on and the wine bottles were drained the atmosphere became increasingly ribald. But Mawgridge took the jokes a little too far. When he slurringly insulted Cope's lady friend, the lieutenant sprung to his feet and shouted at him to watch his mouth. Enraged, Mawgridge seized one of the bottles and lobbed it at Cope. The soldier retaliated, and, ducking to avoid the bottle flying towards his head, Mawgridge launched himself at his friend. One of Cope's soldiers, alarmed by the sound of breaking glass, rushed into the Guard Room to investigate. He found Mawgridge standing over the prone figure of Cope and still clutching the handle of the sword that was protruding from Cope's chest. The woman, whose honour Cope had given his life to defend, was crouched in a corner of the room. The stone floor was stained red with a mixture of wine and blood.

Mawgridge stood trial for the murder of Lieutenant Cope at the Guildhall, which served as a courthouse for the City of London at the time. He suggested that his attack on his friend was a justifiable response to Cope throwing a wine bottle at his head and, as such, he could only be guilty of manslaughter. In considering his case, the judges at the Guildhall mulled over the types of behaviour that the law recognised as sufficient provocation to justify taking the life of another. The rules that they set down would be a turning point in the demarcation between murder and manslaughter.

The court was clear that insults alone would never be enough and the provocation must have arisen from a direct action on the part of the victim: 'no words or reproach or infamy are sufficient to provoke another to such a degree of anger'. A physical assault on the killer, 'either by pulling him by the nose or filliping him upon the forehead', would suffice, as would catching another man *in flagrante* with your wife. Provocation could also arise where a defendant had fought back against an unjust deprivation of liberty or had apprehended a robber. In the light of this, the judges did not look favourably on Mawgridge's actions:

> But this case bears no proportion with those cases that have been adjudged to be only manslaughter and therefore the Court being so advised doth determine that Mawgridge is guilty of Murder.

In a case not short in dramatic twists, Mawgridge then made a daring escape from the court before sentence could be passed. He managed to get across the English Channel to Flanders, where he was able to lie low for several months. His fluency in French and Spanish meant that he could easily assume a new identity; but drink was once again to prove his undoing. A large reward had been offered for his capture and news of this reached the Continent. When Mawgridge was in his cups one night in a tavern in the city of Ghent, the locals became suspicious of his command of English. They turned him in and he was swiftly identified as the fugitive murderer of William Cope. Mawgridge was brought back to

England to answer for his deed and was executed in April 1708.

The trial of John Mawgridge was an early attempt by the English courts to lay down clear distinctions between the crimes of murder and manslaughter, but the boundaries between these most infamous categories of homicide never remain settled for long. The rules set out at his trial had expressly included the repelling of a physical assault by another as grounds for provocation. But in the years following Mawgridge's case, the law would go further and recognise that killing in self-preservation was a complete defence to a charge of both murder and manslaughter. This concept would come to the fore in one of the most notorious murder trials of Georgian London, which pitted pimps and prostitutes against some of the brightest stars in the capital's artistic firmament.

* * *

Down in the mid-Georgian archive of the National Portrait Gallery is a copy of an obscure portrait by the artist Sir Joshua Reynolds, painted in the 1770s. The subject is a gentleman in established middle age, heavy-set, with dark eyebrows, in a coat the same shade of brown as his hair, holding a small book close to his eyes with an air of intense concentration. This unassuming and scholarly gentleman was Giuseppe Baretti, an Italian émigré who had arrived in London in 1751 and swiftly established himself in the city's most influential literary circles.

Born in Turin in 1719, Baretti was a prominent writer and literary critic in his native Italy, his books including an Italian–

English dictionary. Following his arrival in London he made the acquaintance of England's foremost lexicographer Dr Samuel Johnson, and the two men of letters became fast friends. When Baretti returned to Italy in 1760 he kept up a regular correspondence with the good doctor, and in his *Life of Samuel Johnson*, Johnson's friend and later biographer James Boswell includes lengthy extracts from Johnson's warm and gossipy letters to Baretti:

> *I have risen and lain down, talked and mused, while you have roved over a considerable part of Europe; yet I have not envied my Baretti any of his pleasures, though perhaps I have envied others his company; and I am glad to have other nations made acquainted with the character of the English, by a traveller who has so nicely inspected our manners and so successfully studied our literature.*

Boswell adjudged the letters to be among the best Johnson ever wrote. After an extended sojourn on the Continent, Baretti returned to England in 1766 and resumed his position among London's literary elite. As well as Johnson, he counted Joshua Reynolds and the actor David Garrick among his close friends.

On the evening of 6 October 1769 Baretti was walking along the Haymarket en route to a meeting at the Royal Academy. The Academy had been formed just a year earlier under the presidency of Reynolds, and he had given his friend Baretti an honorary appointment as the Academy's Secretary for Foreign Correspondence. Somewhere near to where the Theatre Royal stands today, Baretti strolled past a lady of the night, leering out of a doorway. Although much of the city's sex trade centred on Covent Garden, it was by no means London's only red-light district and in fact much of what we now call the West End was well known for its after-dark offerings. The Haymarket itself was known colloquially as 'Hell Corner' and was particularly favoured by streetwalking prostitutes, as opposed to those who operated from the *bagnios* of Soho or the upmarket brothels of Mayfair. In *London: The Wicked City*, Fergus Linnane described the scene in the late 18th and early 19th centuries, which corresponds almost exactly with Baretti's encounter a few years before:

> *Whores paraded in the most fashionable parts of the city, particularly inside and outside the main theatres, calling out, plucking at the coatsleeves of passing men and making lewd gestures and suggestions. Covent Garden, the Haymarket, Regent Street, Cremorne Gardens, Fleet Street, the front of Somerset House and St James' were bazaars of sexual opportunity.*

According to Baretti, the woman 'clapped her hands with such violence about my private parts, that it gave me great pain. This I instantly resented by giving her a blow on the hand, with a few angry words.' After Baretti had fended off his amorous assailant, the woman's cries alerted her pimp, Evan Morgan, who came running to her aid with a couple of friends. Baretti fled round the corner into Panton Street, one of the narrow rat-runs between the Haymarket and Leicester Square, but he only got a few yards before Morgan and his gang caught up with him. In the ensuing fight, Baretti pulled out his pocket knife and stabbed Morgan, then stumbled into Oxendon Street, where he sought refuge in a grocer's shop. The magistrates were summoned by the shop owner and Baretti was arrested. When Morgan died the following day, the charge became one of murder.

On trial at the Old Bailey, Baretti argued that the attack had put him in fear for his life. The accounts of the killing were varied; the extent of the threat that Baretti faced from Morgan is unclear and there was no suggestion in any of the testimony that Morgan himself was armed. Before he died, Morgan had given his version of events to his fellow patients in the Middlesex Hospital. He was adamant that Baretti had attacked first, stabbing at one of his friends and then wounding Morgan twice when he grappled with him. He alleged that Baretti then turned and stabbed him a third time, inflicting a mortal wound in his stomach. Morgan's friends backed up his account in court, claiming that they had simply come to the aid of a woman in distress and that the defendant was the only aggressor. Baretti's own recollection of the fight was confused, but on one point he was clear: 'I am certainly sorry for the man, but he owed his death to his own daring impetuosity.'

Other witnesses testified to the dangers of walking along the Haymarket and its environs in the evening; a Major Alderton described being set upon by a gang of men and women on the corner of Panton Street in very similar circumstances just the previous year. But Baretti's defence largely came down to a question of character. Lined up against Morgan's insalubrious colleagues in the witness box were some of the great public figures of the day to vouch for Baretti. His illustrious friends Johnson, Reynolds and Garrick were among the witnesses who attested to his quiet, sober and gentle character. This starry defence line-up impressed the jury, who acquitted Baretti on the grounds of self-defence.

High brows and low lives mingled to a remarkable degree in Georgian London. The account of Baretti's trial in the *Newgate Calendar* makes clear that the real villains of the piece were not Baretti and his knife, but the after-dark denizens of the West End who had accosted him: 'The number of abandoned women, who infest the streets of the metropolis every evening, are in some measure to be pitied; but, when they add insult to indecent application, they ought to be punished with the utmost severity.'

Baretti's friends may have hesitated to agree with this statement. Sir Joshua Reynolds had a roster of courtesans who modelled for him; and Johnson and Boswell's circle also included the poet and writer Samuel Derrick, who had taken Boswell under his wing upon his arrival in London. Boswell noted rather peevishly in *The Life* that Derrick had not fulfilled his early promise to arrange the meeting with Johnson that Boswell so desired but acknowledged that Derrick was his 'first tutor in the ways of London and shewed me the town in all its variety of departments, both literary and sportive'. Given Boswell's predilections and Derrick's background, this description is somewhat coy.

Fleeing his destiny as heir to a Scottish lairdship, Boswell first visited London in 1760 at the age of twenty and wasted no time in acquainting himself with London's 'sportive departments'. He had kept a diary from the age of sixteen, and his comprehensive journals are peppered with references to his sexual encounters, often with prostitutes. Derrick was not in the same literary league as his friends, but he had had one notable – and notorious – success in print. In 1757 he ghost-wrote and published *Harris's List of Covent Garden Ladies*, a gazetteer of West End prostitutes based on a handwritten list apparently kept by Jack Harris, a local pimp and acquaintance of Derrick. Inspired by his more poetic efforts, Derrick enlivened Harris's original list of names and addresses, adding flowery descriptions of the women in question and extolling their particular specialisms. This roughest of guides remained in print continuously for thirty-eight years and it is inconceivable that Boswell didn't possess a copy.

The trial made little dent in Baretti's standing within his highbrow circle and the whiff of scandal attached even to his acquittal did no harm to his prospects. Johnson secured him a job with his friends, the wealthy Thrale family of Streatham Park, and he became a tutor to the children, teaching them Italian and Spanish. But others were not so amenable. While he remains studiously neutral on the subject of Baretti and his trial in *The Life*, Boswell's own journals tell a different story. He detested Baretti and the feeling was apparently mutual. Visiting Baretti's employers the Thrales, Boswell describes an awkward encounter on the doorstep, with a pointed nod to the Italian's brush with the law:

Just as the servant opened [the door], Baretti appeared. I coldly asked him how he did. Methought there was a shade of murderous blood upon his pale face. I soon made a transition from this disagreeable object to the parlour, where Mrs Thrale and Dr Johnson were at breakfast.

It was during Baretti's time in Streatham that the Reynolds portrait was commissioned; but things soured, and in a letter of December 1776 Johnson reported to Boswell that Baretti had left the Thrales 'in some whimsical fit of disgust, or ill-nature'. Baretti died in London, his adopted home, a couple of weeks after his seventieth birthday in 1789.

* * *

Boswell's animus to Baretti doubtless coloured his view of his acquittal, which was not entirely without controversy. Discussing it with friends a couple of years after the event, he noted that he himself considered the killing to be cold-blooded murder; one man argued that it was a clear case of self-defence, and another believed it to be manslaughter. This diversity of opinion is not surprising, as the extent to which the law of homicide permits the defence of one's self, one's honour and even one's innocence has a long and muddled history. Defending yourself against physical attack, even if it results in death, has always provided a complete defence to the crime of murder. In many US jurisdictions, this concept of self-defence has evolved to encompass defence of property with lethal force, often known as the 'castle doctrine'. As the law currently stands in several states, householders are permitted to kill those entering their property without permission, even if they are not under any direct threat themselves.

English law has resisted such a broad interpretation of the idea of self-defence, instead focusing on the concept of a man's right to defend his own honour by force, which can trace its ancestry back to the ancient Kingdom of Burgundy, which covered a tranche of central Europe from around the 4th century AD. Gundobad, King of the Burgundians, was credited with creating the concept of trial by battle or combat, which he proceeded to export to most of Europe. The idea arrived on British shores with the Normans and was an important element of criminal law enforcement until the Middle Ages, when a more formalised system of courts, which included the popularisation of jury trial, was ushered in by Henry II. Gundobad's invention rested on the logic of divine intervention, an assumption that providence would intervene and secure victory for an innocent party in a fight.

The battle itself had to be conducted with certain pomp and circumstance. A field of combat, sixty feet square, was chosen and the fight was to be observed by the judges and the combatants' lawyers. The parties were each armed with a staff and the battle itself commenced at sunrise. The defendant started proceedings by declaring his plea of not guilty and throwing down the archetypal gauntlet, which was then taken up by the opponent. The fighting continued until the stars appeared in the evening sky. If, by this time, the defendant was still standing – or had killed his opponent – then he was deemed victorious and acquitted. But if the defendant gave up the fight before the stars rose, he was to be executed without the possibility of a reprieve.

As English law developed a more sophisticated system of court trials through the 13th and 14th centuries, the practice of trying a criminal through combat faded into history. But the legitimacy of defending one's good name by physical force was resurrected by private citizens in Renaissance Italy, which hankered after all things chivalric and medieval. As in Gundobad's time, the idea once again spread across Europe and arrived in England in the 16th century. It boomed in popularity among the gentry and nobility, who were drawn to its ostensibly civilised (albeit lethal) approach to the settlement of disputes between gentlemen. The custom of duelling prevailed all over Western Europe and the Americas throughout the 17th to 19th centuries. In England, the practice reached its apex during the Georgian era, partly down to the increased profile of the military during the Napoleonic Wars. Duelling had found an enthusiastic home in the armed forces, where it was an offence for an officer to fail to defend their own honour or that of their regiment when challenged.

These quasi-military and aristocratic associations lent duelling an air of legitimacy that was not entirely warranted. Throughout its history, the practice had occupied a murky legal hinterland where it was officially prohibited but unofficially tolerated, and even encouraged. Both Oliver Cromwell and his successor Charles II were opposed to the English habit of the duel and passed laws to outlaw the issue of a challenge or the participation in a fight, which would itself always be subject to the other laws that apply to its outcomes; ranging from charges of homicide when the outcome was fatal, to offences of affray or assault if neither participant was mortally wounded.

But in practice, when a duel resulted in death, the surviving party usually managed to avoid the stigma of being labelled a murderer. Juries were generally reluctant to convict participants of murder and, if they did, often saw their verdict nullified by the issue of a pardon. Over time, the scarcity of murder convictions created an unwritten law that duellists could escape a murder conviction, but only provided that they had fought a clean fight and adhered to the accepted rules of battle, which were many and varied.

Each country had its own code for duelling, with varying degrees of formality and chivalry. Common to all was the requirement for the issue and acceptance of a formal challenge and the nomination of each party's 'second'. Described as an 'amalgam of umpire, cornerman and mediator', the appointment of the second was a throwback to the role of the squire in the age of medieval chivalry; in effect, the Sancho Panza to the duellist's Don Quixote. The seconds would have conduct of the arrangements for the entire process, including the date and time of the fight and the provision of the agreed weapons. As far as possible, they were also to attempt to reconcile the parties before the duel took place.

When Abraham Lincoln was challenged to a duel by the Illinois state auditor over the collapse of the state bank in 1842, it was their seconds that averted the fight, due to take place on an island in the Mississippi so as to avoid Illinois' anti-duelling laws. The large crowd that had gathered eagerly on the riverbank to watch the contest dispersed without satisfaction.

The question was as much one of class as law. Duels were almost exclusively fought by gentlemen and members of the nobility – those of lower status engaged in mere brawls. From the Middle Ages, peers had been allowed to claim the archaic rite of 'benefit of clergy' when facing execution for manslaughter and thus avoid the death penalty. This odd practice offered a reprieve for certain capital offences to members of the Church and was subsequently extended to the aristocracy and anyone who was able to read a prescribed oath in court, literacy being prima facie evidence of some form of religious calling.

Juries therefore did all that they could to reduce the conviction to manslaughter and so permit defendants from the upper echelons of society to plead benefit of clergy and save their necks. The lengths to which juries went to avoid convicting a duellist of murder played a key role in the development of legal dividing lines between murder and manslaughter. As was the case at John Mawgridge's trial in 1707, the behaviour of the killer was no longer the only thing under scrutiny in the courtroom. The jury's gaze would also turn to the actions of the deceased in the run-up to the fight to see whether they could find any basis to excuse their opponent's conduct. And more often than not, they did.

Hyde Park was a popular spot and it was here that Winston Graham's hero Ross Poldark fights a duel with louche MP Monk Adderley in the novel *The Angry Tide*, set towards the end of the 18th century. Adderley and Poldark argue in the House of Commons, ostensibly over a pair of gloves but in fact over the affections of Poldark's wife Demelza. The following morning, Adderley writes to Ross to challenge him to a duel in

Hyde Park. Ross kills Adderley but flees the scene as they had agreed in advance. His responsibility for Adderley's death is an open secret among his fellow MPs and wider London society; and his intractable enemy George Warleggan tries but fails to whip up any official interest in the shooting. Sir John Mitford, the real attorney general of the time, makes a cameo appearance in the novel and is remarkably dismissive of the whole affair.

This fictional parliamentary duel was probably inspired by a real case involving a duel that was fought one spring morning on the dewy grass of Tothill Fields by Richard Thornhill and Sir Cholmeley Dering MP. The pair were friends but had fallen into a drunken quarrel over dinner one evening at the Toy Inn at Hampton Court. A scuffle ensued in which Sir Cholmeley got the upper hand and beat Thornhill severely. They crashed into the wainscotting and Thornhill lost several teeth. After a couple of days of recuperation and brooding, Thornhill wrote to his erstwhile friend in combative terms:

April 8th, 1711
Sir,
I shall be able to go abroad tomorrow morning, and desire you will give me a meeting with your sword and pistols, which I insist on. The worthy gentleman who brings you this, will concert with you the time and place. I think Tothill Fields will do well; Hyde Park will not, at this time of year, being full of company.
I am,
Your humble servant,
RICHARD THORNHILL

Tothill Fields was an area of open land near to the River Thames in Westminster, its boundaries corresponding approximately with present-day Regency Street and Tachbrook Street. The land is now mostly occupied by the Cathedral and Westminster School's playing fields. In the early 18th century it was on the very edge of the metropolis, safely away from prying eyes. The only people likely to hear any gunfire were the inmates of Tothill Fields Bridewell, the same prison in which Giuseppe Baretti would be incarcerated while awaiting his trial for the murder of Evan Morgan a few decades later. Although Sir Cholmeley had had the advantage in the hand-to-hand combat at the inn, Thornhill was the better shot and he fatally wounded his opponent with his first bullet.

Tothill turned out to be less deserted than they had hoped and Thornhill was apprehended immediately by a passer-by who had heard the gunshots. He was arrested, tried for murder and convicted of manslaughter. The jury were sympathetic to Thornhill's tale of the beating he had received at the hands of the honourable member for Kent, and Sir Cholmeley himself even came to his former friend's aid from beyond the grave. He had given a deathbed statement to the effect that the entire affair was his fault and that all was forgiven. The MP's friends, however, were not so magnanimous, and Thornhill's liberty and life were to be short-lived. In August of the same year he was set upon by two men in Turnham Green and beaten to death, his attackers allegedly shouting that he must pay for Sir Cholmeley's death as they rained their blows and kicks down on him.

Despite its high-class practitioners, duelling and the law's lax treatment of it were not immune from opprobrium. The editors of the *Newgate Calendar* were unimpressed at Thornhill's acquittal of murder, proclaiming:

Horrid practice! Disgraceful to our country, and equally contrary to all Divine and human institutions! It is to be hoped that the time will come when the legislature shall decree that every man who is base enough to send a challenge shall be doomed to suffer death as a murderer.

This plea to parliament to outlaw the practice was always likely to fall on deaf ears, and Sir Cholmeley was far from the only MP to become caught up in a challenge. As well as US presidents, no fewer than four British prime ministers are known to have fought in duels, including Pitt the Younger and the Duke of Wellington, who both took up their pistols while actually serving PMs. As the 19th century progressed, however, attitudes were beginning to harden as public fascination with duelling began to wane. The courts took a more stringent approach in applying the law of homicide to such cases. Charles Mirfin, a twenty-five-year-old former draper, was killed by a Mr Eliot in a duel on Wimbledon Common in August 1838. Eliot himself had absconded but his friends and 'seconds' in the contest, Messrs Young and Webber, were apprehended and tried for murder. The court was clear:

Where, upon a previous arrangements and after there has been time for the blood to cool, two persons meet with deadly weapons, and one of them is killed, the party who occasions the death is guilty of murder; and the seconds also are equally guilty.

Duelling had first come to prominence in England at around the same time that Sir Edward Coke was preparing his treatise on the state of the law of the land as he saw it, and he covered the subject in his discussion of all things homicidal. Unlike some of his successors, Coke was clear on the law as he understood it. A duel fought in 'hot blood', where the participants immediately take up weapons upon whatever slight has been given or taken and one proceeds to kill the other, cannot be murder. There is no malice aforethought as the whole transaction has been one continuous course of conduct. But where arrangements are made to fight at a subsequent hour or day, when the blood has had time to cool, then that premeditation must make it murder. This distinction eventually lent its name to that most chilling of phrases, 'cold-blooded murder'.

The concept of manslaughter as a separate category of homicide from murder was only beginning to emerge at the time that Coke was writing, coinciding almost exactly with the popularisation of the duel itself. Certainly some members of the judiciary were supportive of the rights of the duellist and even participated themselves. When the concept of provocation emerged in the early 18th century, it provided a layer of validity for juries who wanted to acquit gentlemen duellers. The willingness to put one's life so directly in the firing line in defence of one's honour was seen to elevate the duel above the street fight or the tavern brawl. Writing in the late 1880s, prominent lawyer and legal historian Sir James Stephens repeated Coke's general statement of the law of homicide as it applied to duelling, but he noted that murder convictions relating to duels had been rare throughout its history.

The same class prejudices that fuelled the acceptability of duelling made themselves felt in all aspects of the Georgian justice system. Even in death the nobility received special treatment; aristocrats who were sentenced to death were beheaded, which was seen as a more dignified method of execution than hanging. In 1760 Earl Ferrers had the distinction of bringing this long tradition to an end. Ferrers had a history of odd behaviour towards his family and staff at the family seat at Staunton Harold Hall in Leicestershire. He habitually horsewhipped the servants for no reason, and on one memorable occasion he burst into his brother and sister-in-law's bedroom waving a pistol, forcing the couple to flee the house in their nightclothes at two o'clock in the morning.

One afternoon, Ferrers summoned his steward Mr Johnson to the house. When Johnson entered his employer's chamber, Ferrers ordered him to kneel on the floor and then shot him in the chest. A surgeon was called to Johnson's deathbed, and, aghast at the earl's actions, rounded up a posse of locals to seize the wayward peer and bring him before the law. When he saw them approaching the hall, Ferrers decided to evade capture in the nooks and crannies of the house, and so the gang had to chase him round the passageways and through the drawing rooms for some time before apprehending him.

As a nobleman, Ferrers was to be tried by his fellow peers in the House of Lords and he was taken to the Tower of London to await his trial. The verdict was in little doubt and he was sentenced to death by hanging. Ferrers was affronted and petitioned the king to allow him to be beheaded at the Tower, as befitted his noble status. But the king refused and on 5 May 1760 a huge crowd gathered to watch the procession through London carrying the earl from the Tower to his fate at Tyburn Gallows. When the minister accompanying Ferrers on his final journey commented on the size of the crowds, the Earl glumly replied, 'I suppose it is because they never saw a lord hanged before.' Of course, had Ferrers killed Johnson in a duel, he would most likely have walked free from court without a stain on his character, but instead he was doomed to go down in history as the first aristocrat in England to swing from a gibbet.

*   *   *

Duelling had come a long way from its origins in the 'trial by combat' of the Norman ages and by the 19th century these had almost been forgotten. But just as the practice of duelling was approaching its high point in England during the reign of George III, a provincial murder trial in the rural Midlands would hark back to the duel's historic roots in the concept of trial by combat, with dramatic effect. 'Bucolic' and 'Birmingham' do not often occur in the same sentence, but in the early 1800s the landscape around the second city was very different. Erdington, Tyburn and Langley have all now been subsumed into the suburbs to the north of the city, a run of dual carriageways, post-war semis and industrial estates. But two hundred years ago they were scattered villages in a still rural part of north Warwickshire, to the south of the town of Sutton Coldfield and a morning's walk from the centre of Birmingham itself.

Mary Ashford was aged twenty, and worked as a servant and housekeeper on her uncle's farm near the village of Langley. Contemporary engravings show Mary with the delicate features and flowing ringlets of any number of Jane Austen heroines. On Whit Monday of 1817 Mary and her friend Hannah Cox had taken themselves to a dance at the Tyburn House inn. At the dance Mary met Abraham Thornton, a local builder. In contrast to the depictions of Mary's limpid loveliness, sketches of Thornton from the time show a squat young man, with narrow eyes and beetle-brows underneath a mop of dark hair, more akin to Heathcliff than Mr Darcy. Thornton took a shine to Mary at the dance and apparently told a friend that he would have his way with her, one way or another. The couple left the dance together late in the evening. At around four o'clock the next morning Mary turned up at Hannah's house to collect the clothes she had left there the night before. Hannah was the last person to see Mary alive.

Not long after dawn, a couple of local labourers on their way to work found a blood-stained and bundled-up dress and pair of shoes next to a small pond a couple of miles to the north-east of Hannah's house in Erdington. They dredged the pond and pulled out Mary's body. Her face was pale and streaked with mud, some mulched oak leaves clinging to her hair. Close by, observers found blood and signs of a struggle in the grass. Two sets of footsteps in the mud led up to the patch but, ominously, there was only one set leading from the patch to the edge of the pond. A crude post-mortem was carried out by the local surgeon on a table in the kitchen of a nearby farmhouse. This examination confirmed that Mary had been raped before drowning in the muddy water of the pond. Plenty of people had seen her leave the dance with Thornton, and he was swiftly arrested. He admitted to having had sex with Mary but claimed it was consensual and that she was alive when he left her somewhere in the fields. He was charged with murder and rape, and tried at Warwick Assizes in August 1817.

Public opinion was firmly against Thornton at the time of his trial. His claim that Mary had consented to sex seemed an unlikely one. The prosecutor described Mary as 'a young girl of the most fascinating manners, of lovely person, in the bloom and prime of life' who had been subjected to 'a barbarous transaction'. One contemporary account of the case, written in the most floral of prose by a local vicar, likened Mary to 'the British Vestal' and asked 'what were the resistance of a Lamb within the grasp of a Lion?' An easy conviction was anticipated.

But Thornton's detractors reckoned without the problem of time-keeping. In rural England in the early 19th century very few people wore a watch, largely going by the light and the chimes of the church clock, whose timing varied enormously from parish to parish. One witness at the trial stated that he kept to Birmingham time, which was some forty minutes ahead of the locals in Erdington, less than five miles away. This meant it was impossible to pin down a time that Mary was attacked, and Thornton produced eleven witnesses in court, who all

42

confirmed that at the approximate time of the killing they had seen him out on the road a few miles away. Summing up to the jury, His Honour George Holroyd concluded that:

> From this it would appear, after making the necessary allowance for the variation in the clocks, the prisoner must have perpetrated the horrid deed and walked nearly three miles and a half in the short space of ten minutes.

This stretched the jurors' credulity, and Thornton was swiftly acquitted of both the murder and the rape of Mary.

The court of public opinion was not so easily persuaded. The *Lichfield Paper* reported that further steps were afoot by the local populace, as 'the acquittal of Thornton in this atrocious rape and murder has excited the most undisguised feelings of disappointment in all classes of people, from one end of the country to another'. Indeed, Mary's family and neighbours were not content to let the matter rest there. An enterprising lawyer pushed Mary's brother William to pursue another prosecution of Thornton, under an archaic piece of law that had been largely forgotten about for almost a hundred years. William Ashford had unwittingly resurrected the ancient doctrine of 'appeal of murder'. Dating back to Norman times, the appeal permitted the next of kin of a murder victim to bring a second prosecution against an accused who had been acquitted at a first trial.

Lawyers in the case were able to track down just two previous occasions where this had been used successfully: James Cuff had been executed in 1729 at the second time of asking for the murder of his fellow servant Mary Green at the Green Lettuce Inn in Holborn, and in 1709 the aptly named Christopher Slaughterford had been hanged at Guildford after an appeal of murder by the family of his girlfriend and victim Jane Young. But the appeal had disappeared from view for over a century and was generally considered defunct, until it was raised by William Ashford in the Thornton case. Such was the rarity of the procedure that the local court in Warwick was not up to the task of dealing with it. The case was transferred to the Court of King's Bench in London, where it would be presided over by the Lord Chief Justice of the day, Lord Ellenborough.

Whatever the outcry had been at Thornton's acquittal, he was not entirely without support and there was some public discomfort at the attempt to circumvent the jury's verdict by such antique means. It does, after all, fly in the face of the long-held principle of double jeopardy, which prevents a prisoner for being tried twice for the same crime. Even today, the modern Court of Appeal operates almost exclusively for appeals by defendants; either against their conviction or the length of their sentence. Prosecutors are only allowed to appeal against specific elements of a court's judgment and are not able to bring an appeal against the acquittal of a defendant.

A pamphlet, written and published in support of Thornton by 'A Friend to Justice', railed against the use of the appeal in the case:

Humane and enlightened people have been disgusted at the rancorous zeal with which this unhappy man has been pursued. They have seen a set of individuals, dissatisfied with one trial and striving to procure a second – contrary to the express spirit and most sacred principles of the laws of England – although conformable to an ancient black lettered barbarism, which the good sense of modern times had rejected, until it became almost forgotten even by the technical professor, and scarcely to be explored through the thick stratum of Norman French and bastard Latin with which it is incrusted.

In the face of this, Thornton played Ashford at his own game. He recruited lawyer Nicholas Conyngham Tindal to his legal team, a noted expert in medieval law and statutes. In court to answer Ashford's charge, Thornton staged his own piece of historical legal theatre. In a clear voice and with an appropriate sense of occasion he announced, 'Not guilty, and I am ready to defend the same with my body.' From the seat in front of him in the courtroom, his lawyer passed a pair of gloves to Thornton, one of which he drew onto his upraised hand. The other he threw down in front of him for Ashford to pick up.

Thornton's dramatic proclamation had caught the entire courtroom off guard. He had invoked another long-forgotten piece of legal history in his aid and exercised the ancient right to opt to be tried by 'wager of battle' – or trial by combat. After the creation of the nascent court system in the Middle Ages the practice had largely died out, and prior to Thornton's challenge the last recorded instance of such a trial dated from the reign of Charles I. Ashford's panicked lawyers, seemingly unconscious of the irony of their argument, claimed that 'wager of battle' was obsolete law and could not be invoked by Thornton. They pointed out the absurdity that Thornton should be permitted to acquit himself of killing Mary by also murdering her brother. Lord Ellenborough sharply rejoined that 'It is the law of England ... we must not call it murder.' And so, having upheld Ashford's right to the appeal, the court had little option but follow their own logic and accede to Thornton's request, in the process declaring that after several hundred years of obscurity, a right to trial by physical combat was indeed still the law of the land.

William Ashford was a scrawny teenager in less than robust health; he would stand little chance in a fight against his bull-necked and well-built challenger. Finding himself outwitted by Thornton and his lawyers, Ashford was permitted to withdraw his appeal, and there ended the legal wrangling over the death of Mary. In the wake of Thornton's acquittal, parliament moved swiftly to rectify the historical oversight. The Appeal of Murder, etc. Act 1819 abolished both the appeal of murder and trial by battle, thus formally ending eight hundred years of legal history.

But speculation over the case was not so easily quashed. Rumours continued to dog Thornton and there were reports that he had confessed to killing Mary to various people while being held in jail before his trials. One inmate claimed that Thornton had told him that he had raped Mary violently, she had died 'under him' during the struggle and so he had thrown her into the pit. Yet another witness suggested that Thornton had claimed that he had not murdered Mary but was 'the occasion of her death', implying that the shame of having had sex with him, whether consensually or otherwise, compelled her to commit suicide by drowning herself in the pit. But, regardless of these stories, as he had successfully defended the appeal, Thornton could not face a further trial for Mary's murder.

No longer welcome in Tyburn and the surrounding villages, Thornton emigrated to America at the first opportunity. He sailed from Liverpool in 1818 under an assumed name, having been kicked off other vessels for being an ill omen when the crew had discovered his identity. It is unclear what became of him. One report had it that he settled in Baltimore and made his fortune from a fishing fleet on the eastern seaboard, while another suggested that he moved on from America to Australia and became a man of property there. He reportedly died in around 1860.

In the Birmingham area the story has lived much longer in the memory, leaving some unsettling codas to the case. Balladeers and hack writers at the time rushed out songs and plays, sold on the streets for a couple of shillings. One such composition, a drama in three acts entitled *The Murdered Maid; or The Clock Struck Four!!!*, relocated the action to the more glamorous setting of a chateau in Normandy but retained the key events of Mary's tragic story. A local exhibition on Mary's death in the 1980s prompted Thornton's solicitors, still in business in Sutton Coldfield over a century after his trials, to write to the local paper to protest at the strong suggestion that their former client had got away with murder.

As recently as 1973 Mary's ghost was apparently sighted one evening, wandering the cul-de-sac that had been built on the fields where she had died. The area had changed beyond all recognition since the last time that Mary had last seen it. The meadows and fields have been replaced with housing estates and retail parks, and Erdington and Tyburn could no longer be described as villages. The country lanes and cartways are buried beneath the M6, which ties itself into knots at Spaghetti Junction just to the west.

Perhaps Mary's spectral visit was in fact a warning from the other side, as just a year after the ghost sighting was reported the area was shocked by another horrible murder case with some uncanny parallels to Mary's death. The only surviving remnant of the countryside where Mary strolled on her last night on Earth is Pype Hayes Park. Away from the modern playground and car park, there are still knots of old oak trees and gently sloping valleys that have remained unchanged through the intervening years. At the centre of the park sits Pype Hayes Hall, a manor house constructed on the eve of the Civil War for the aristocratic Bagot family. Birmingham City Council purchased the house in the early decades of the 20th century and used it as a children's home from the 1950s onwards.

In 1974 twenty-year-old Barbara Forrest was working at the home. After failing to return home from a night out in Birmingham over the Whitsun Bank Holiday, her body was found on the edge of the park just a mile away from where Mary had been discovered almost 160 years before. She had been raped and strangled. The local CID officers investigating Barbara's murder were apparently sufficiently spooked by the coincidences between the two cases that they raided the police archives to consult the papers relating to Mary's murder. The chief suspect was one of her colleagues at the children's home, named Richard Thornton. Like his namesake Abraham, he was acquitted of the killing following a trial. As in Mary's murder, no alternative suspect was ever identified and the case remains unsolved.

* * *

Murder in the 18th and early 19th centuries was entering its own age of enlightenment. It wasn't all sordid brawls in barracks or narrow side streets. It could be stylised, formalised and even civilised, even if inconsistently criminalised. Its exalted criminal status within the Bible was not always reflected in the law's treatment of it, particularly during times when so many other, lesser crimes merited the same fatal sanction. But as the number of capital crimes shrank, murder began to rise above the field. The development of the concept of manslaughter demanded a more nuanced approach.

The first attempt to do this, at the trial of John Mawgridge, laid the foundations for what is still a controversial element of the law of homicide – provocation. As other killers like Richard Thornhill had success in arguing that the injury, insult or affront they had suffered from their victim was sufficient to reduce their culpability for the killing, the law began to look at the reasons that make someone kill, not simply the methods that they employ.

Gradually this concept of provoking behaviour justifying a lethal response would come to be applied to homicides in all kinds of circumstances. One of the challenges facing the law of murder, particularly from the 20th century onwards, was how these concepts should apply to those who killed in such differing scenarios. This remains the case today, with the use and application of the defence of provocation itself being one of the most provocative aspects of the law of murder. But even while the seeds of our modern law of homicide were germinating, murder's more primeval roots were still making their presence felt. The pomp and circumstance associated with the medieval practice of trial by combat made a brief resurgence before being snuffed out for ever in the wake of Abraham Thornton's trial.

At the heart of the murder trials of people like John Mawgridge and Richard Thornhill were questions as to whether their victims had somehow brought their murder upon themselves through their own behaviour. Even the blameless Mary Ashford had to be painted by lawyers as an almost superhuman paragon of virtue, lest jurors concluded that she was at fault for consorting with Thornton in the first place. Juries must never speak of the reasons behind their verdict, and so it is impossible to know if their acquittal of Thornton owed as much to victim-blaming as to the discrepancies over time-keeping. These difficulties have recurred in troubling cases throughout the long history of murder in the courts.

But as the 18th century gave way to the 19th, there was a shift in focus from the victim's behaviour to that of the killer. We are all equal before the law, but whether this law should be applied equally to all is another matter. A dawning interest in the complexities of the mind was to be a bellwether for change in how the courts treated those who came before them, particularly those whose actions and personalities did not conform to society's expectations. The law of murder would have to grapple with the question of how to deal with people who were driven to kill not by the riling behaviour of their victim, but from some unknowable struggle within themselves.

CHAPTER TWO

THE MADNESS OF BADNESS

'He spoke of being troubled by the blue devils'

Perhaps uniquely among mass transit systems around the world, the London Underground has a particularly rich seam of ghost stories stretching back to its earliest days. At Bethnal Green station the screams of the people crushed to death while seeking shelter during a Second World War air raid still echo around the platforms from time to time. A ghostly passenger is said to ride trains on the Bakerloo line regularly, only visible in the reflections in the carriage windows. And on quiet nights at Liverpool Street station the anguished cries of the departed can still be heard. This is maybe to be expected, for the station was built on the former site of one of medieval London's most notorious institutions, the Royal Bethlehem Hospital, better known by its infamous nickname, Bedlam.

The Bethlehem (or 'Bethlem') was established in 1247 as a priory, on a site in Bishopsgate that is now covered by the concourse of the station. During the Middle Ages religious institutions often provided sanctuary for the sick and unfortunate, becoming in effect the earliest hospitals. By the mid-1300s Bethlem had begun to take in those suffering with mental illness (described in its ledgers from the time as 'six men whose minds have been seized'); by the Reformation it was the only institute within London offering care for such patients. At the same time, Henry VIII bestowed his regal seal upon the hospital and so it became known as the 'Royal' Bethlem Hospital.

By the time it moved to its new site in Moorfields in 1676 the nickname of 'Bedlam', a cockney contraction of 'Bethlehem', was in wide usage. The entrance to this 'New Bethlem' was through a gateway topped by two gargantuan male figures carved from Portland stone. Lying supine on either side of the gate's arch, they represented respectively 'Mania' and 'Melancholia', the two broad classifications of mental disorder recognised by medicine at the time. 'Mania' was depicted raging and writhing against the chains binding his hands and feet – in contrast, 'Melancholia' lay calmly, with a peaceful but vacant expression on his face. Locals took to calling the statues the 'Brainless Brothers'.

Over the course of the 18th and into the 19th century, Bethlem Royal Hospital and institutions like it would play host to some of the most notorious killers of the age, who had taken another's life in often extraordinary circumstances. How far a killer's mental disorder or affliction could and should relieve them from criminal liability for their actions would give rise to some of the most intriguing cases of the era, as political conflict, mental illness and personal accountability fused together in the courtroom. Some thirty years before the multiple Burke and Hare killings made Edinburgh infamous in the annals of murder, an odd little trial took place that rattled the upper echelons of Edinburgh society but also heralded the tentative beginnings of a revolution in the way that the criminal law treated those suffering from mental illness.

*   *   *

Archibald Gordon Kinloch was born in around 1749, the middle son of Sir David Kinloch, the 5th Baronet of Gilmerton. The ancestral seat of Gilmerton House, twenty miles east of Edinburgh, is still in the Kinloch family. A handsome and mellow Georgian mansion, it has had a new lease of life as an upscale wedding and function venue. But away from the marquees and the Rolls-Royces, there is a darker element to the house's history.

In February 1795 Sir David passed away at Gilmerton, in the bosom of his family. The baronetcy automatically passed to his eldest surviving son Francis. Archibald received a legacy of £1,300 but was unhappy about the amount that he received from his father's will. His resentment was stoked when he found out that Francis had burned a large number of his late father's papers, believing that they were rubbish. But Archibald became convinced that the documents contained details of other gifts to him that had been withheld. Francis was sufficiently concerned by his brother's accusations to consult a lawyer in Edinburgh, who opined that the will was safe from challenge. Aside from this, the brothers' relationship was good, and friends remarked on Francis's affection and tolerance for his brother's whims, which in the months after their father's death took a decidedly strange turn.

By April 1795 the family were sufficiently concerned about Archibald's behaviour that they decided to stage what might now be termed an 'intervention'. With some difficulty, they persuaded him to come back to Gilmerton, where they had arranged for a local doctor and nurse to attend on him in the coming days, equipped with a straitjacket. Perhaps sensing that something was amiss, Archibald reached some sort of crisis on his arrival back home. He strode around the house wielding a blunderbuss and wandered from room to room, throwing himself onto the floor and wailing. Francis was sufficiently unnerved by his brother's behaviour to lock his door when he went to bed. This was an unnecessary precaution, as Archibald had taken to spending the night roaming around the woods near to Gilmerton.

On the evening of 14 April Francis had dinner guests at Gilmerton, but Archibald kept his station above stairs. Francis's friends recollected that he frequently left the table to check on his brother and seemed to be the only member of the household capable of calming him during his apparent fits of mania. At about three o'clock in the morning, Archibald came downstairs armed with two loaded pistols concealed in the pockets of his breeches. The party was still in progress and the port was being passed around the dining table. Francis ushered his brother back to bed, but as they were climbing the stairs Archibald pulled a pistol from his pocket and pushed it against Francis's chest.

Hearing a noise, the dinner guests ran out of the room just in time to see a pistol flash as Francis fell down, shouting that he was 'done for'. They carried him to his room, while the servants wrestled Archibald to the floor and strapped him into the straitjacket. Despite medical attention, the unfortunate baronet was not long for this world and he died from his injuries on 16 April. In what must have been a day of mixed emotions for Archibald, his ascension to the baronetcy upon his older brother's death was almost immediately followed by arrest for his murder.

His trial commenced at the Edinburgh High Court on 30 June 1795. When asked to enter his plea, Archibald invoked that most infamous of defences to a murder charge – not guilty by reason of insanity. While Archibald was not the first to raise his sanity as a defence, the transcript of his trial is one of the earliest and most complete records of an insanity plea in a murder case. Family members, friends and servants gave evidence of Archibald's fluctuating mental state to the court. This seemed to have its roots in his youthful service in the army; as one of the family's traditional 'spares', Archibald had entered the military and bounced around the world for a number of years, serving in Cork, Nova Scotia and the West Indies. While stationed in St Lucia in around 1780, he was taken ill with a severe fever. As the sickness raged, he had to be pinned down in his bed by two soldiers and did not recognise fellow officers when they came to visit him. He was despatched to Barbados to recuperate, and on the sea journey his servant contracted the same fever and threw himself overboard while in the grip of its fits.

Archibald did make a full recovery from his illness, physically at least, but his friends and colleagues were perturbed.

The man that they knew, renowned for his generosity and kindness towards the men under his command and respected throughout his regiment for his good conduct and smart military appearance, was gone. When a long-time acquaintance bumped into Archibald in the Strand a few years after he had left the army, he almost didn't recognise the slovenly dressed, mumbling gentleman in front of him. Most startlingly of all, he noticed that Archibald's formerly brown hair had turned completely white. But the changes in Archibald went far deeper than hair colour.

Six years before he shot his brother, Archibald had tried to slit his wrist in a lodging house in Edinburgh's Grassmarket. He had also told friends of being plagued by visions of figures he called the 'blue devils'. Lieutenant Colonel Samuel Twentyman, an army friend of Archibald who had served with him in St Lucia and seen him during and after his illness, was emphatic:

> *In my own mind, I never had the smallest doubt, that Sir Archibald's intellects were deranged in consequence of that fever, and that he had periodical attacks, that rendered him insane, and consequently not master of his own actions.*

The particulars of Archibald's periods of derangement left him between two stools in legal terms. English (and Scottish) law had long recognised that a person found to be insane could not be guilty of a crime. Insanity afforded them a complete defence, as those not in their right mind could not be capable of forming the necessary mental intent that constituted *mens rea*, an essential element of a criminal conviction. For several hundred years until the late 18th century, those adjudged to be insane by a criminal court were acquitted and released back into the care of their family or society at large. Especially dangerous 'lunatics' could be further dealt with by the courts after their release under the laws relating to vagrancy, but this was rare.

The state took no role in providing any sort of facility or treatment for those with mental illness, and private asylums proliferated. For those able to afford them, these provided families with a convenient means of confining troublesome members from public view and, for those patients who suffered from the double affliction of eccentricity and wealth, even a route for less scrupulous relatives to take over their property once they had been admitted.

But in Archibald's case there was a suggestion that his periods of incapacity were intermittent, rather than altogether chronic. The prosecutor seized on this, combining it with the details of Archibald's disappointment at his inheritance to make the case that the shooting of Francis was not the action of a madman, but rather a calculated revenge killing of the favoured sibling. The law did not recognise any concept of partial insanity; it was all or nothing. In the case against Archibald, the risk was that he was not quite mad enough. According to the prosecutor:

> that degree of melancholy and depression of spirits, which, though it may border on insanity, is nevertheless accompanied with a sufficient share of judgement to discern good from evil, and moral right from wrong; which never has and

never can be sustained as a bar to trial, or a defence against
punishment for a crime so atrocious as murder.

The jury found Archibald guilty of killing his brother but also declared him to have been insane at the time of the act. The effect of this conclusion was, while he was guilty of the killing, he was not culpable for the crime of murder. However, the judges in court were concerned at the risk that Archibald posed to both himself and the public at large if he were to go free by virtue of the verdict. In an unusual order, he was sentenced to life imprisonment but with a proviso that he could be released to house arrest upon a payment of £10,000.

Dr William Farquharson, the Edinburgh medic who had attended Archibald after his suicide attempt in the Grassmarket and had given evidence in his defence in court, stepped forward with the required security and Archibald was discharged from the city's Tolbooth prison into the doctor's care. The pair lived at Farquarson's home in World's End Close, just off the Royal Mile, but Archibald died just five years after his trial at the age of around fifty. Whether his death was related to his illness is not recorded.

*   *   *

Although they may not have realised it, the judges at Archibald's trial had presided over a turning point in the law's treatment of mental illness and crime. The next fifty years would bring a raft of sensational murder trials that changed and shaped the law and society's understanding of mental illness in revolutionary ways.

Archibald's conviction represented a key divergence between English and Scottish law; in declaring him insane, the Scottish courts had effectively recognised a new category of partial insanity, and the English law of homicide wouldn't catch up with this until the creation of the defence of diminished responsibility over 150 years later. His unusual sentence was also a precursor to more immediate and fundamental changes in how the law treated those found not responsible for their own lethal actions. The final trigger for this would be pulled shortly after Archibald's sad case, with an attempt on the life of no less a personage than the king himself.

Mental turmoil and illness have no respect for rank. Opening the case for the defence at the Kinloch trial, Archibald's lawyer pointed out that insanity was 'one of those high and dreadful visitations of Providence, to which we all, the wisest and the best of us, are equally liable, and from which even thrones are not exempt'. He was referring of course to the reigning monarch King George III, who was himself plagued by episodes of delusions and mania throughout his reign.

In 1800, five years after Archibald's trial and while George was enjoying a period of good health, the king was taking his seat in the royal box at Drury Lane's Theatre Royal when his evening was interrupted by a pistol shot whistling past his ear. The gunman was James Hadfield, who believed that he could bring about the second coming of Christ by getting himself executed for killing the monarch. Hadfield was also a former soldier and had suffered serious head wounds in action, which left him brain damaged. Just two days before he shot at the king, he had tried to kill his infant son. As his assassination attempt was unsuccessful, Hadfield was put on trial for treason rather than murder.

He was acquitted on the basis of his obvious insanity, and his lawyers were among the first to deploy medical experts in his defence at trial. But that of course left the king's would-be killer at large. Parliament hastily rushed through the Criminal Lunatics Act, which required that those acquitted on the grounds of insanity were to be detained at His Majesty's Pleasure. 'His Majesty's Pleasure' refers to a custodial sentence of indeterminate length and is used for the most serious offenders. This so-called 'special verdict' was an acquittal in name only. In *Crime and Insanity in England* (vol. I) criminologist Nigel Walker observed that:

> *a criminal lunatic might be as morally innocent as a man who had done harm by accident or in self-defence, but the danger of treating him as innocent was too great. The solution was to pay lip service to his innocence but use the law to make sure he remained in custody.*

In furtherance of this, Hadfield was ordered to be detained indefinitely at the only institution in the country able to house him. He passed beneath the Brainless Brothers and through the crumbling gates of Bethlem Royal Hospital. The Moorfields building had fallen into a state of considerable disrepair, and by the time that Hadfield arrived it was quietly sinking into the London mud.

The legislation passed in the wake of the Hadfield case had dealt with the problem of ensuring that those acquitted of serious criminal offences due to their lack of mental capacity could not pose a further risk to society. But *how* the courts were to determine whether or not someone was judged to be insane in legal – as opposed to clinical – terms was still left remarkably vague. This was until the establishment was rocked by another political grievance played out on the public stage, this time with deadly consequences.

*   *   *

The concept of political assassination is often seen as an American invention, but it was alarmingly prevalent in Georgian and Victorian England as well. The word 'assassin' can trace its ancestry back to the Hashshashin, a secret cabal of Muslim soldiers who specialised in carrying out clandestine killings of enemy personnel during the Crusades. The concept of an 'assassination' has retained this original sense and is generally used to distinguish the planned killings of high-profile victims – such as political or religious figures – usually for mercenary or abstract motivation, from the more emotional (and emotive) 'murder'. Hadfield was in fact the second person to be incarcerated in Bethlem Royal Hospital for an attempt on the life of George III; in 1786 Margaret Nicholson had tried to stab the king outside St James's Palace and was confined to the hospital for life.

In 1812 Prime Minister Spencer Perceval was walking through the lobby of the House of Commons late one afternoon when he was felled by a bullet fired from behind one of the doors. The stricken Perceval collapsed with a cry of 'Murder!' and was carried into the Speaker's Office, where he expired almost immediately. Perceval's assassin was John Bellingham, an insurance broker from Liverpool with a rather chequered past. As a young man he had gone out to Russia and worked for a merchant in the city of Archangelsk on the White Sea in Russia's far north. But Bellingham fell out with his employer in a dispute over finances and ended up in a Russian debtors' prison when he lost a legal case against the merchant. During his time in jail he brooded on the ineffectual assistance he had received from the British embassy in his hour of need.

By the time that Bellingham finally returned to England on his release from prison, his grudge had expanded to encompass the entire British government, whom he believed had abandoned one of its citizens to the mercy of foreign powers. He wrote to the Treasury and to Perceval personally several times to demand compensation for his troubles.* After a final rebuff, when a minister dismissed his claim and told him that the government would see him in court, Bellingham took this as a 'carte blanche to take justice into his own hands and he accordingly determined to take such measures as he madly supposed would effectually secure that ... consideration for his case, which he deemed it had not received'. Speaking eloquently in his own defence in court, Bellingham insisted that his attack on Perceval had not been motivated by personal animosity, but was rather the culmination of his years of suffering in Russia and his frustration at the government's indifference towards him. Friends testified that he had been in a state of derangement ever since returning to England.

* Perceval was serving as both Prime Minister and Chancellor at the time.

Lord Chief Justice Mansfield explained to the jury how they must approach the question of whether Bellingham was in fact insane:

It must, in fact, be proved beyond all doubt that, at the time he committed the atrocious act with which he stood charged, he did not consider that murder was a crime against the laws of God and of Nature.

The jury deliberated for less than fifteen minutes before rejecting the insanity plea and convicting Bellingham of murder. His own speech to the court had lambasted the government at length for the illegal injustices that he believed that they had inflicted upon him and left little room to conclude that he did not comprehend the workings of the law himself. But thirty years later, another Westminster assassin would play a pivotal role in reshaping the law on insanity that had sent Bellingham to the gallows.

*   *   *

Daniel M'Naghten was a woodturner living a quiet and industrious life in Scotland in the first half of the 19th century. Accounts of his personality are varied. A printer with whom he shared a room in a Glasgow tenement recalled his habit of pacing up and down in the middle of the night, muttering darkly under his breath. He was said to have a gloomy and unsociable disposition, but other acquaintances disputed this, saying he took pleasure from feeding the birds and watching children play. Whatever the truth of M'Naghten's mental state, he was a hard worker and his carpentry business thrived. Although he had received little formal education, he was equally assiduous in his leisure time, studying Shakespeare, reading about philosophy and teaching himself French.

But at the age of around thirty he became plagued by intrusive and paranoid thoughts, mostly involving authority figures such as the police or Church officials. These thoughts developed into a fixation on the ruling Tory party, which manifested in a belief that he had been singled out by them for persecution. In the days before secret ballots, he deduced that they had got it in for him after he voted against their candidate in an election. He went as far as reporting his fears to his local constabulary but they took no action, which gave further weight to his beliefs that the powers that be were in league against him.

In late 1842 he travelled to the capital and took a room in Poplar, East London. By Christmas he had formed a plan. He spent the next three weeks loitering around Westminster and Whitehall, watching and waiting. But he himself was under observation as well. While walking his beat around parliament, Metropolitan Police Constable Silver filed a report on a 'seedy looking person, height about five feet six who frequents the Houses of Parliament to solicit Conservative members, he is stout and ... wears a broad brimmed hat'. Soldier Richard Jones had also noticed M'Naghten's presence and become suspicious. He accosted him, and on the pretext of persuading him to join his regiment, took the surly Scotsman for a drink in a nearby tavern. But under Jones's persistent questioning as to why he was loitering in the area, M'Naghten stubbornly repeated that he was merely waiting for someone and refused to elaborate. When he left the pub, Jones reported his encounter to the first police officer that he could find. The police did not intervene, however, and M'Naghten continued to maintain his vigil.

On the afternoon of 20 January 1843 M'Naghten stalked a lone figure walking along Whitehall towards Downing Street. The target in his sights was Edward Drummond, the private secretary to Prime Minister Robert Peel. M'Naghten caught up with him near Horse Guards and shot him at point-blank range in the back, in the mistaken belief that he had in fact assassinated the prime minister. M'Naghten made no effort to escape and was arrested at the scene of the shooting. At first Drummond seemed to have escaped serious injury and he was able to walk to his home to receive medical attention. The pistol ball was removed from his body and the prognosis was good. However, complications set in and he deteriorated, passing away five days after being shot.

The statement that M'Naghten gave to the police upon his arrest gives some insight into his tortured mental state:

The Tories in my native city have compelled me to do this. They follow and persecute me wherever I go, and have entirely destroyed my peace of mind. They followed me to France, into Scotland and all over England; in fact they follow me wherever I go. I cannot sleep nor get no rest from them ... I believe they have driven me into a consumption. I am sure I shall never be the man I was. I used to have good health and strength, but I have not now. They have accused me of crimes of which I am not guilty; in fact they

*wish to murder me. It can be proved by evidence. That's all
I have to say.*

At his trial at the Old Bailey M'Naghten pleaded insanity.
The prosecution had to concede that he was mentally ill, as
evidenced by his delusions of persecution. Otherwise, the
Crown would have been placed in the unenviable position of
asserting that M'Naghten's belief that the government was
conspiring against him was at best plausible and at worst
probable. The point of contention was therefore the nature
and extent of M'Naghten's affliction. The prosecution maintained that his delusions were not, of themselves, sufficient to
demonstrate that he was totally insane and therefore secure
an acquittal. The effect of them on his mind must have been
such that it had eradicated his ability to tell right from wrong.

In his defence, M'Naghten's lawyers effectively argued that
the law should recognise partial insanity as a defence to
murder. The soundness of his mind in other aspects of his life
was irrelevant; if he had been acting under the force of his
delusions at the time of the killing, then he must be considered
insane. In support of this they cited his behaviour in the act of
the killing itself. He had shot Drummond in broad daylight in
front of witnesses on one of London's busiest streets, then
stood by and awaited arrest. Hardly the modus operandi of a
calculated killer, who surely would have picked a more discreet
location and time.

The doctors who had examined M'Naghten characterised
his behaviour as a form of monomania, an insane fixation upon
a particular issue, subject or person. A sufferer could be rational

and coherent, sane to all intents and purposes, on any subject other than their specific fixation, over which they had little to no control. Such was the weight of testimony from M'Naghten's doctors that the prosecutor, under direction from the judge, agreed to withdraw the case. The jury were given no option but to deliver a verdict of not guilty on the ground of insanity.

M'Naghten was ordered to be held indefinitely at Bethlem Royal Hospital, which had moved location again in 1815 to a site south of the Thames in Southwark, at St George's Fields.* His acquittal was greeted with uproar from all sectors of society. If M'Naghten, a man who was capable of running a successful business and had the wherewithal to plan and execute a killing at the highest level of government, could successfully claim to be insane, then where would the defence end?

Such was the concern that the case was debated in the House of Lords for further consideration of the legal aspects that it raised. This was not any sort of appeal against the judgment, which was not possible at the time. But so great was the controversy and the confusion over how the court at M'Naghten's trial had been persuaded that he was in fact insane, the government decided to ask the Law Lords to give further clarity on the law and set out the legal test for judging whether or not a prisoner was sane.

On the face of it, M'Naghten could not be said to be entirely out of his mind. He had sufficient lucid periods in which to build up a prosperous business and had never been treated or

---

* Part of the original hospital building now houses the Imperial War Museum.

institutionalised prior to his killing of Drummond. With no recognition of temporary or partial insanity in English law, was it correct that he should still be considered insane and therefore not guilty of murder? The House of Lords were satisfied that it was, provided that the accused met a very particular threshold. The 'rules' on insanity that they set out have gone down in history as the 'M'Naghten rules' and are still applied today in English courts as well as in Commonwealth countries and other international jurisdictions, such as the US.

The Lords were clear that the starting point must be a presumption that every defendant is sane; but this presumption can be rebutted if the defendant can provide sufficient evidence of their insanity. In order to do this, they must satisfy the following test:

> To establish a defence on the ground of insanity, it must be clearly proved that, at the time of the committing of the act, the party accused was labouring under such a defect of reason, from disease of the mind, as not to know the nature and quality of the act he was doing; or if he did know it, that he did not know he was doing what was wrong.

So the 'M'Naghten rules' is really a rather grandiose title for what boils down to four essential points that a defendant must prove in order to satisfy the court that they are not responsible for the consequences of their actions on the grounds of insanity. First, the defendant must establish an underlying medical condition ('disease of the mind') and, second, prove that this condition has caused an impact on their mental processes and understanding ('defect of reason'). If the court are satisfied of both of these, that leaves two further hurdles to clear to succeed with an insanity plea. Either the defendant did not understand what they were doing at the time of the criminal act ('nature and quality of the act'), or if they were aware of what they were physically doing, they did not realise that this act was prohibited ('doing what was wrong').

These new rules built on the definition of insanity applied in John Bellingham's case back in 1812, which was only concerned with whether Bellingham knew that his murder of Perceval was a crime and contained no reference to any mental illness. One of the quirks of the case was that M'Naghten was never actually judged against the rules that bear his name. They were created by the judges in a vacuum, several months after he had been committed to an asylum for the rest of his natural life. Had the rules been applied to M'Naghten himself, he would probably have been convicted.

In 1864 he was transferred from Bethlem Royal Hospital and became one of the earliest patients of the newly opened state asylum in the rolling Berkshire countryside, the now infamous Broadmoor. Broadmoor's creation came out of the work of the parliamentary-appointed Lunacy Commissioners, who by the mid-19th century were recommending the construction of a publicly run specialist institution for 'criminal lunatics', i.e. those detained under (by now) *Her* Majesty's Pleasure following an insanity acquittal at a criminal trial. When Bethlem moved to its new home in Southwark in 1815, the hospital building included two wings that had been funded by the government to house criminal lunatics. However, there was no other dedicated facility for such inmates anywhere else in the country and many more were housed alongside regular patients at smaller county asylums across the country.

Broadmoor was the first specialist institution for the criminally insane to be opened, and following the transfer there of patients like Daniel M'Naghten, Bethlem's criminal wings were closed and demolished. Broadmoor was followed by Rampton in Nottinghamshire in 1912. Another, at Moss Side in Liverpool, was slated to open shortly afterwards but was commandeered by the army as a hospital for shell-shocked soldiers on the outbreak of the First World War. This would eventually become Ashworth, England's third high-security psychiatric institution.

All three facilities operate outside of but alongside the criminal justice system and are hospitals, not prisons. Moors Murderer Ian Brady was held in Ashworth for more than thirty years, and Soham killer Ian Huntley was detained in Rampton before being adjudged sane and fit to stand trial. Broadmoor has generally specialised in the most dangerous patients, mostly those of above average intelligence suffering from psychopathy or schizophrenia. Gangster Ronnie Kray was transferred to Broadmoor after a diagnosis of paranoid schizophrenia partway through serving his life sentence for the 1966 murder of George Cornell at the Blind Beggar in Whitechapel. Peter Sutcliffe, the Yorkshire Ripper, spent thirty years in the hospital before being moved to a regular prison in 2016 when a tribunal found that there were no longer any clinical grounds to keep him at Broadmoor. Like Kray, he had been diagnosed with paranoid schizophrenia while in prison, serving twenty life sentences following his conviction for the murders of thirteen

Moran raised the possibility that the verdict may have owed as much to political expediency as mental illness:

> The M'Naghten case demonstrates the ease with which psychological descriptions can serve to discredit political offenders. By interpreting his act as the product of a diseased mind, the insanity verdict dishonoured Daniel M'Naghten and denounced the political ideas that he represented ... His allegations of persecution came to be regarded as symptoms of his mental illness; his political opinions as the disease itself ... Thus what was probably a purposeful act of political criminality became transformed into a meaningless act of criminal lunacy.

But the story cannot be verified and, if M'Naghten's madness were indeed an act, it was one that he managed to keep up, despite being under close supervision for over twenty years. His patient notes from Bethlem Royal Hospital record that he was 'an incurable' and showed no signs of clinical improvement during his confinement.

*   *   *

The defence of insanity applies to all criminal offences. But in the wake of M'Naghten's acquittal, the most celebrated and sensational cases involving his eponymous rules were murder trials. After all, the more outrageous the act, the more inclined a jury was to accept that someone was out of their right mind when they did it. In 1861 the Offences Against the Person Act came into force, which restricted the use of the death penalty to murder only. This brought to an end the indiscriminate application of capital punishment to a host of non-fatal offences and ensured the sovereignty of murder above all other crimes. From then on, in the absence of a good argument for manslaughter, a successful insanity defence could therefore be a matter of life and death for those on trial for murder.

In particularly shocking or violent killings, there was a fear that the defence could be abused to give rise to a kind of post hoc fallacy – if a killing was so brutal, then surely only a madman could have committed it. Sceptics of the insanity defence were therefore concerned that it could be exploited by those who were simply bad, rather than mad, to escape the gallows. In an era not short on shocking murders, one particularly heinous crime would typify these concerns, but the case would go down in history for entirely different reasons.

Early in the evening of Saturday 24 August 1867 labourer Thomas Gates was making his way home from work, ambling through the hop fields surrounding the town of Alton in Hampshire, bathed in the warm evening light that follows a hot summer's day. He nearly lost his footing over a couple of hop poles that had been laid out on the ground near a hedge that bordered the field. When he looked down to check his step, his eye was caught by a dark shape resting between the poles. It was a severed head of a young girl, no more than seven or eight years old. Summoning his considerable presence of mind, Gates picked up the head and ran down the hill with it towards a row of cottages where he could see several people gathered outside in animated conversation.

A child from one of the cottages had been playing in the hop field that afternoon but had failed to return home with her friends and people were starting to worry. They glanced up the lane to see Gates galloping towards them carrying his grim burden. He was directed to one of the cottages and knocked on the door. It was opened by Mrs Harriet Adams, who had returned home after a fruitless afternoon's searching, only to be presented with the horrific sight of Gates clutching the decapitated head of her eldest daughter, Fanny.

The account given by Fanny's friends was every parent's worst nightmare. As the girls were playing in the fields just up the lane from the cottages, a man had approached them. He was later identified as Frederick Baker, a clerk at a local firm of solicitors. He offered Fanny a halfpenny to accompany him on a walk into the field and sent her friends away with money to buy sweets. As her friends toddled off down the track, they turned and saw Baker leading a tearful Fanny by the hand up the lane. This was to be the last sighting of Fanny alive. Following the discovery of her body a short while later, the police wasted no time in heading straight round to the offices of Messrs Clements, solicitors at law.

Baker strenuously denied any involvement in Fanny's death but it was soon apparent to the local police superintendent that this was implausible. His colleagues in the office confirmed that he had been absent from work for long periods during the afternoon, on closer inspection his clothing was found to be heavily bloodstained, and when the police searched his desk they found their metaphorical smoking gun: Baker's diary, in which he had recorded an entry for the day that was chilling in its banality – 'Killed a young girl. It was fine and hot.' Pressed to explain the comment, he claimed that he had omitted a comma after the word 'Killed' and that he had simply been recording the report of the murder in his diary. By the time the constables took Baker from his office to the police station, an angry crowd had gathered in the high street.

Baker was well known in the town. He had been born in Guildford but had moved to Alton about a year before the murder of Fanny, ostensibly to make a fresh start after a broken engagement to a local girl. The heartbreak apparently sent him into a spiral of drink and depression, but the press reports contain hints of something darker. His fiancée and her family were apparently scared off by an anonymous letter about Baker, and his father reportedly had a breakdown when told of his son's past indiscretions – but no further details were made public. He considered himself to be a reformed character following his move to Alton, forswearing drink and becoming a conscientious churchgoer.

The inquest into Fanny's death opened a couple of days later. At the time, coroners and the inquest process played a much more active role in criminal investigations relating to unexpected deaths. An inquest was in effect a mini-trial, and coroners were able to conclude proceedings with a verdict of murder or manslaughter against a named individual, after which they would be committed for a full criminal trial. This power to name and find against an individual in a coroner's verdict was eventually abolished in the 1970s, when the Criminal Law Act 1977 came into force. While a coroner can still make a finding of unlawful killing (either murder or manslaughter), this is now entirely separate from any criminal proceedings and usually follows, rather than precipitates, a murder trial.

In Baker's case, the inquest was almost a foregone conclusion. After two days, according to the *Police News* account:

> the Coroner then summed up, and the jury returned a verdict of 'Wilful murder against Frederick Baker, for killing and slaying Fanny Adams.' The warrant was then made out for the committal of the prisoner to Winchester Gaol, to await his trial on the charge of murder.

Baker pleaded insanity, but the Victorians had their image of a madman and Baker did not match it. Madmen did not hold down respectable jobs and go to church, while participating in local societies and paying court to local girls. Baker, moreover, was short and slight, with a countenance that was pale and unprepossessing – the stuff of penny dreadfuls, the deranged child-killer walking among them undetected. Nevertheless, in court Baker spun a tale of a family history punctuated by episodes of apparently hereditary mental disorders. His maternal uncle was confined in the county asylum and had previously been in Bethlem Royal Hospital. His father had been prone to violent rages and threatened to kill Baker and his siblings, one of whom, a sister, had later died from some unspecified 'brain fever'.

As a child, Baker had suffered from nose bleeds and pains in the head which were so debilitating that he had not gone to school until the age of twelve. The doctors called to give evidence at the trial testified that he suffered from 'homicidal mania', a diagnosable mental condition that was:

generally shown by the destruction of some loved object. The person need not be generally melancholy or gloomy. He might usually be kind and still subject to homicidal mania ... insanity may be transmitted by descent and that where a person's relatives ... have shown traces of insanity, the presumption is that the person would be affected in the same way.

The jury was not persuaded. The only insanity he could be said to have suffered from was what one contemporary reporter termed 'the madness of badness, when vile and frightful passions, by long encouragement, win the upper hand and sweep sense, self-government, and wit away together, in a torrent of Satanic impulse'. Baker was very bad, but under English law the jury decided that he was not mad. He was executed at Winchester early on the morning of Christmas Eve 1867, with a crowd of several thousand gathering to watch.

In the accounts of her murder, Fanny exists largely in the abstract. Her childish innocence is stressed, to contrast with Baker's murderous depravity, but of Fanny herself there is little. The reporting of the case continued what Baker had started in the field – the dehumanisation of the little girl. The press coverage of the murder lingered over every detail of Fanny's fate with a degree of relish that would make most modern tabloid editors blush. The general public were no better, and the day after the killing the papers reported that 'On Sunday, the greatest excitement prevailed in the town and thousands of persons visited the site of the harrowing tragedy where pools of the life-blood of the innocent child were pain-fully visible.'

Nevertheless, Fanny herself did leave one lasting legacy. In a display of linguistic gymnastics as inventive as it was tasteless, the British Navy of the time appropriated the term 'Sweet Fanny Adams' to describe substandard meat rations, compar-ing them unfavourably with poor Fanny's dismembered remains. The term eventually was applied to anything deemed worthless or pointless, and often abbreviated as 'Sweet F.A.', particularly in American English, which incorporated its own translation of the phrase. But however it is written and what-ever it is said to stand for, the term owes its entry into the English language from the brutal death of a small girl on a sunny afternoon in the hop fields of rural Hampshire.

*   *   *

The exploration of Baker's mental state and history at his trial was somewhat cursory, but this approach was about to change. The growth of clinical interest in the diagnosis and treatment of mental illness in the latter half of the 19th century meant that medical experts would play an increasingly prominent role in court, providing expert testimony on the psychiatric state of a defendant claiming to be insane. The doctors were fast taking centre stage in the most sensational courtroom dramas.

Shortly after seven o'clock on the evening of 16 December 1897 a hansom cab pulled up on the corner of Maiden Lane and Bedford Street in London's Covent Garden. Out stepped William Terriss, the doyen of the West End, who was starring in the play *Secret Service* at the Adelphi Theatre just around the corner on the Strand. Terriss was accompanied by his friend Harry Graves. The pair dismissed the cab and strolled along Maiden Lane to a private back door of the theatre. Terriss had his own key and preferred to avoid the crowds that gathered at the main stage door. According to Graves, as Terriss fumbled with his keys and Graves looked on:

> *somebody rushed from across the road and struck him two blows most rapidly on the back. I thought at first they were given in good fellowship and it occurred to me how exceedingly rough the act of friendship was. Terriss turned around instantly, and the man then struck a third blow in Mr Terriss' chest. Mr Terriss said, 'My God, I am stabbed.'*

Terriss was carried into the theatre, where he died a short while later. He had suffered two stab wounds in the back and a third, fatal, blow to the chest, which penetrated his heart. His attacker made no attempt to flee and was arrested at the scene. His name was Richard Archer* and he gave his occupation as actor.

The evidence given at Archer's trial at the Old Bailey in January of the following year could have sprung from the script of a melodrama played out on the stage of the Adelphi. A native of Dundee, Archer had been a jobbing actor in both

---

* Archer seems to have had several aliases. He is sometimes listed as Richard Archer Prince, the transcript of his trial calls him Richard Arthur Prince, and other sources suggest he was also known as William Flint. It is possible that some of these names were adopted for the stage.

Scotland and England, and his sporadic appearances on the stage had to be supplemented with stints labouring in the shipyards and foundries of Dundee. When not at work, he had a habit of walking the streets of the Scottish city in extravagant costumes more suited to his appearances on stage, earning him the nickname 'Mad Archer'. In London he had worked with Terriss in minor parts in a couple of productions.

But Archer had a somewhat overinflated sense of his own talents and harboured a grudge against the theatrical establishment, particularly in London, whom he believed were deliberately overlooking him for the plum roles he thought he deserved. His lack of professional success had become so chronic that he was forced to apply to the Actors' Benevolent Fund for hardship payments, and Terriss had provided a reference in support. A couple of hours before he approached Terriss at the theatre door, Archer had visited the fund's office to be told that his most recent application had been unsuccessful. Perhaps it was this news that proved to be Archer's final tipping point.

In spite of Terriss's offers of assistance, Archer had become convinced that his fellow actor was behind all of his theatrical misfortunes. When he was arrested, he muttered darkly to the police that he had been the victim of blackmail and Terriss had got what was coming to him. But his family told a different story. Since his youth, Archer had been plagued by paranoid delusions. He accused his mother of trying to poison him and on another occasion informed her that she was the Virgin Mary, which of course made him Jesus Christ. More worryingly, he had launched an unprovoked attack on his brother with a poker. Mrs Archer traced his problems back to an episode of severe sunstroke he suffered as a baby when she had left him in a field on a sunny day. On his father's side there was a history of mental illness, and two of Archer's brothers had been similarly afflicted, although never formally diagnosed – his brother David was described as 'silly' and had been sent to live on a farm in the country.

Several medical experts testified in Archer's defence at his trial. They included one of the senior doctors at Bethlem, who rejoiced in the name Theophilus Bubbly Hislop. Dr Bubbly Hislop had examined Archer while he was on remand and was satisfied that his delusions were genuinely held, resulting from an unsoundness of mind. In his practice he had seen several cases of mental disorder resulting from episodes of sunstroke in infancy. Dr Hislop concluded his evidence with a particularly trenchant observation – 'He [Archer] fell in with one's usual experience in Bethlem; he was most indignant that there should be any question as to his mental condition.'

The evidence of the doctors was unanimous. Archer was suffering from a mental disorder and, while his attack on Terriss was obviously planned and premeditated, his condition was such that he had little to no control over his actions and could not be said to know whether the act was wrong or not. In short, he must be considered to be insane under the test of the M'Naghten rules. Despite the fact that the jury agreed with the medical experts, Archer would still be found guilty thanks to a change in the law that had taken place in the intervening period. The 'special verdict' of not guilty by reason of insanity that had been available to the court in M'Naghten's time had been abolished in 1883 by the Trial of Lunatics Act. This required juries in insanity cases to return a new special verdict to the effect that the accused was guilty of the crime charged but was insane at the time of the act. The effect of the verdict remained the same – indeterminate detention at Her Majesty's Pleasure.

Archer was sent to Broadmoor, where he died in 1937. His victim, however, made several encore appearances. William Terriss's ghost is reported to haunt the Adelphi Theatre and has also joined the cast of phantoms that haunt the London Underground. His favoured stage is Covent Garden station, which was built on the site of a bakery that he used to frequent between performances. A tall man, dressed in a Victorian frock coat and wearing Terriss's trademark white gloves, has been spotted in the station by Underground staff several times over the years before disappearing without a trace; the most recent reported sighting was in the 1970s.

*   *   *

Like the screaming spectres of Liverpool Street and William Terriss's posthumous performances on the Tube, all tales of murder are, in essence, ghost stories. In the telling of these cases and trials, the victim returns from beyond the grave to live again and see their death avenged. But the law is rarely so black and white. The extent to which justice was served by convicting and then executing those who killed under the influence of mental illness had always been debatable, but for a long time the prospect of spending an indefinite confinement in an institution like Bethlem Royal Hospital was a fate worse than death for many.

As late as the 1820s patients were routinely kept chained to the walls and members of the public could pay an entrance fee to visit the wards for a diverting day out. Frederick Baker's own lawyer strongly refuted the idea that an insanity plea represented an easy way out for his client, describing 'the awful punishment involved in the consigning of [Baker] to a living grave in a lunatic asylum, a punishment in itself more terrible than death'.

With the creation of the M'Naghten rules, the courts at last had something approaching a system to determine sanity and thus how far the law should excuse the behaviour of someone driven to kill by internal forces that they could not control. But external pressures and desperate circumstances can prove just as irresistible; whether they should also provide an excuse for murder had long attracted controversy. Twenty years after M'Naghten died, another extraordinary case that would cast an equally long shadow reached the courts. The English law of homicide would have to look over the seas and far away, to unpick a mass of maritime lore and moral relativism in order to answer a vexed question – is eating people always wrong?

CHAPTER THREE

OUT OF HER MAJESTY'S DOMINIONS

'As idle as a painted ship upon a painted ocean'

On a Saturday morning in early September 1884 the redoubtable Sergeant James Laverty of the Falmouth Harbour Police was patrolling his beat around the Cornish port's quayside. As one of the most important harbours on the south coast and the historic home of the speedy Falmouth Packet ships that delivered the Royal Mail around the world, the town had long been the first place in the country to hear all sorts of sensational stories from the high seas. News of the victory at Trafalgar first landed on British shores at Falmouth in 1805, before it was relayed by stagecoach to London.

Laverty's beat took him around the harbour wall of the town's Custom House Quay, from where he looked out onto the wide blue waters and green wooded slopes of the Carrick Roads estuary. As he turned back towards the dockside, his eye was caught by the party disembarking from a ship anchored at the side of the quay. The ship flew a German flag, but the voices drifting across the basin from the three scruffy sailors stumbling down the gangplank were English. His interest piqued, Laverty watched them walk up from the harbour and turn right onto Arwenack Street. At a discreet distance, he followed.

Reaching the white columns of the town's neo-classical Custom House, Laverty tripped smartly down a couple of steps and passed underneath the gaudy royal crest. He tracked his quarry into the Custom House's Long Room, where they stood before the desk of Mr Robert Cheeseman, Falmouth's Customs Officer and less than energetic Collector of Dues. On closer inspection, Laverty saw that the three sailors were emaciated and bedraggled, their skin leathery and hair unkempt. As the sergeant took a seat in the corner of the room, the sailors took turns to lean onto Cheeseman's desk and sign a sheaf of papers spread out before them. When this was done, one of them began to speak. He identified himself as Thomas Dudley, erstwhile captain of the yacht *Mignonette*. With his first mate Edwin Stephens and mate Edward Brooks standing beside him, Dudley proceeded to recount the tragic events that had brought them to Falmouth quayside. They had been hired to sail *Mignonette* from England to deliver it to its new owner in Australia, accompanied by one other crew member, Richard Parker, the cabin boy.

They had sailed from Southampton in May and the voyage was largely uneventful until they reached the mid-Atlantic, off the west coast of Africa, in early July. Struck by a storm, the yacht foundered somewhere between Tristan da Cunha and

Saint Helena. By the skin of their teeth, the four seamen escaped the wreck in the yacht's small lifeboat. After drifting at sea for thirty days, the *Mignonette*'s lifeboat was eventually sighted by the *Montezuma*, a German cargo vessel en route from South America to Germany. When the larger ship drew alongside the lifeboat to haul the occupants aboard, they found only Dudley, Stephens and Brooks in the boat. A large sun-bleached bone and some pieces of dried-out meat were lying in the keel. These comprised the only earthly remains of Richard Parker.

As conscientious sailors, the *Mignonette*'s crew had presented themselves promptly to the maritime authorities, embodied by the august figure of Mr Cheeseman, to provide their report of the wreck in sworn statements as required under the Merchant Shipping Act 1854, which regulated all aspects of shipping in British seas or otherwise out of Her Majesty's dominions around the world. They made no bones about the fate of Parker, whose life had been sacrificed to provide sustenance for his hungry colleagues. At the conclusion of Dudley's grisly tale, Sergeant Laverty swung into action. He had long been suspicious of Cheeseman's lax approach to the enforcement of excise laws and was concerned that the Customs Officer would take the view that cannibalism at sea fell outside of his remit. Laverty bustled out of the Customs House and went straight to the town clerk's office, where he prevailed upon the Mayor of Falmouth to sign an arrest warrant. The three sailors were apprehended and imprisoned in the town lock-up to await a court hearing.

Two days later they were marched through the town and up the hilly high street to the courthouse. A squat, grey building, the twin-arched windows betrayed its origins as a Congregational chapel of the early 18th century. After a stint as Falmouth's town hall, it now housed the magistrates court and had seen a succession of seafaring ne'er do-wells, who had strayed from the path of righteousness on arrival in the boisterous port. But it had never seen the likes of Dudley, Stephens and Brooks in its dock before. Rumours had quickly spread through the town about the German ship and the strange tale told by its passengers, and a large crowd was gathered in the narrow street outside the courthouse.

Mr Danckwerts, the government lawyer sent west to push for a murder charge, faced a dilemma. The only witnesses to Parker's killing were the prisoners themselves and, as the law stood at the end of the 19th century, they were not permitted to give any evidence in court, even in their own defence. The legal privilege that protected defendants from incriminating themselves was taken to its logical conclusion and they were prevented from testifying at their own trial other than to outline the reasons for a 'not guilty' plea. In order to proceed with a prosecution Danckwerts needed a star witness, and so, after weighing up the evidence against Brooks (whom Dudley and Stephens accepted had taken no part in the despatching of Parker), the Crown formulated a plan. The case against Brooks was dropped and he then turned Queen's evidence to testify against his shipmates, along with Sergeant Laverty, Mr Cheeseman and one of the sailors from the *Montezuma*. The magistrates charged Dudley and Stephens with murder and committed them for trial at Exeter Assizes that winter. A Falmouth businessman and local eccentric named John Burton stood bail for both prisoners and they left Falmouth on the evening train, bound for home to await their day of reckoning.

*   *   *

The trial of Dudley and Stephens was to be a murder trial unlike any other. As well as the comparatively prosaic law of homicide, the case was wrapped up in the semi-mythic traditions and superstitions of the sea. Dudley and Stephens's arrest and prosecution would seem almost inevitable following their detailed report to Mr Cheeseman and Sergeant Laverty, but they were taken completely by surprise by it. Their frankness was not perhaps as ill-advised as it first appeared. Aside from the natural human revulsion at eating one's fellow man, they had not given much thought to the consequence of their actions.

Cannibalism born out of desperation following a shipwreck was a long-held (but little acknowledged) 'custom of the sea'. Alongside other traditional edicts such as a captain going down with his ship, and women and children first, these customs form part of the unofficial protocol observed by mariners when at sea. They fall outside the formal body of maritime law that governs practices and offences on the ocean wave but are nonetheless considered to be binding on those who observe them. The crew of the *Mignonette* believed that they had simply done what any other seaman would have done in their horrific situation and, in accordance with the prevailing 'custom', their actions could not be considered to be murderous or even unlawful. They had reckoned without Sergeant Laverty's intervention in the matter.

The question of the legality of this 'custom' had long been a niche but troubling issue for the English authorities. In his 1984 book about the case, *Cannibalism and the Common Law*, legal academic A. W. B. Simpson identified a rich history of cannibalism among the maritime fraternity, largely coinciding with the rise in global exploration and sea travel from the 18th century onward. In the same year as the *Mignonette* tragedy, there were strong suspicions that a beleaguered US Army expedition team in the Canadian Arctic had resorted to cannibalism, although this was strongly denied by the survivors. Substantiated reports were rare, and criminal cases even rarer, but the acceptance of the practice among sailors and even the general public was fairly widespread.

Corroborating evidence was naturally difficult to obtain. Eating a body is an extremely effective way to dispose of incriminating evidence, and in such a perilous situation a missing survivor is not necessarily suspicious. When Cheeseman, under pressure from Laverty, reported the case to the Board of Trade, it was referred up to the Home Secretary Sir William Harcourt, who made the decision to prosecute. Harcourt saw the case as a golden opportunity to finally clarify the law and disabuse the maritime community of the notion that there was nothing inherently wrong with eating a cabin boy.

At the trial in Exeter the true horrors of the ordeal suffered by all on the voyage were revealed. The *Mignonette*'s journey had begun well. They had sailed from Southampton on Monday 19 May, the day carefully selected to avoid sailing on a Friday, which was believed to bring bad luck. The trip to Sydney was expected to take around 120 days, and Dudley had planned the route to include stops in Madeira, Cape Verde and Cape Town. He had also taken a calculated risk in sailing out in the mid-Atlantic, to keep the small yacht out of the way of the busy shipping routes closer in-shore. This decision would of course come back to haunt him.

On the afternoon of 5 July the *Mignonette* was struck by the storm somewhere between Tristan da Cunha and Saint Helena in the South Atlantic. The side of the yacht was smashed in by a huge wave, and with just minutes before the boat sank, Dudley retrieved the chronometer and sextant from the submerged cabin and jumped into the lifeboat with the other three sailors. They could only watch helplessly as the *Mignonette* slipped beneath the waves and left them to contemplate their fate, over a thousand miles from the nearest land in perilous seas. Dudley recalled that later on that first dreadful evening 'a great shark nearly as long as our boat came knocking his tail at our boat's bottom; the thought of a monster like him near us was not very agreeable … after a few hits on the head from our oar he left'. Like all sailors, they viewed a sighting of a shark as an omen of impending death on board.

Their survival rations consisted of some tinned turnips and a hapless turtle that they had managed to drag from the sea. Drinking water was harvested in sou'westers when the rains came or else they drank their own urine. The lifeboat was narrow and open, offering neither shade from the sun nor shelter from the winds. The chronometer and sextant enabled Dudley to find the boat's position but, having decided to sail well clear of the main shipping routes, he knew that the chances of a vessel passing were slight. One afternoon, he took a pocketknife and inscribed a message in the lid of the sextant box, in the hope that it would at least tell their tale if the boat were ever to be found:

> We, Thomas Dudley, Edwin Stephens, Edward Brooks and Richard Parker, the crew of the yacht Mignonette which foundered on Saturday the 5th of July, have been in our little dinghy fifteen days. We have neither food nor water and are greatly reduced. We suppose our latitude to be 25° South our longitude 28° W. May the Lord have mercy upon us, please forward this to Southampton.

With their meagre supplies exhausted, and with no sign of deliverance on the horizon, thoughts turned to self-preservation. Aged just seventeen and already ill from drinking seawater, Parker was the youngest and weakest of the four. Twenty days after they were wrecked and around ten days after they had last eaten, Dudley and Stephens passed the point of no return. As Parker lay prostrate in the keel of the boat, Stephens held him down while Dudley slit the boy's throat with his pocketknife. They drained his blood to drink and prepared to gorge themselves on Parker's flesh and organs. Brooks had refused to have any involvement in the killing of Parker and buried his head underneath his oilskins while the deed took place. But he overcame his scruples pretty quickly when presented with the remains of his former colleague. Stephens, however, lost his appetite and ate very little of Parker's remains.

In a remarkable turn of fortune, four days after the killing the three sighted a sail on the horizon, the Hamburg-bound

Montezuma. Summoning what strength they had – albeit comparatively fortified by their recent meal – the three rowed desperately towards it. The captain of the German vessel spotted the tiny craft and changed course to rescue the castaways. Five weeks later they arrived in Falmouth.

For a brief time Dudley and Stephens flirted with the possibility of an insanity plea. This was endorsed by the public and the press, who, while fully aware of the need to arrest them after such a shocking confession, believed that justice would be best served by an acquittal. The *Falmouth Packet and Cornwall Advertiser*, a provincial newspaper suddenly thrust onto the national stage by the notoriety of the case, was unequivocal in its push for an insanity verdict:

> *It is utterly impossible that man can endure the torture of nineteen days' starvation, the exquisite agony of a long continued thirst, the anguish of mind and the prospect of an excruciating death, and the nervous prostration caused by the continual dread of being capsized and drowned, without the mind becoming in a measure at least deranged; and without their becoming to the fullest extent, irresponsible for their actions.*

But such a strategy was not without risk. They had virtually no chance of satisfying the test for insanity under the M'Naghten rules, which required they prove that they did not understand what they had done or, if they did comprehend it, they failed to realise that it was wrong. Even if they earned the sympathy of the jury on the basis of an insanity argument, they would then face the bleak prospect of indefinite detention in an asylum. They decided instead to gamble on a not guilty plea, with the aim of complete exoneration, and, if this failed, the hope at least of clemency from the authorities.

So Dudley and Stephens ran a defence of necessity at the murder trial. They claimed that the killing of Parker was vital to ensure the survival of the rest of the crew and, accordingly, could not be unlawful. After hearing all of the evidence, while they were satisfied that Dudley and Stephens had indeed killed Parker, the jury were unable to come to a decision as to whether the killing was murder. In an unusual move, the court ruled that the jury could give a 'special verdict', which would record the facts of the case that had been revealed at the trial but without drawing a conclusion as to the prisoners' guilt. The case was then transferred to the Royal Courts of Justice in London, where a panel of five judges had to rule on whether, based on the facts of the case recorded by the jury in the special verdict, Dudley and Stephens were guilty of murder.

In Samuel Taylor Coleridge's epic *The Rime of the Ancient Mariner*, the eponymous sailor relates his misfortunes becalmed in the Southern Seas, including encounters with an almost mythical albatross and a ghostly ship of the damned. Almost a century after the poem's publication, Lord Chief Justice Coleridge's mind may well have drifted to his great-uncle's celebrated words as he took his seat on the judge's bench to preside over the second instalment of Dudley and Stephens's murder trial. The two sailors facing him may not have read the poem, but they certainly would have seen the echoes of their own ordeal in the Mariner's sad tale:

Day after day, day after day,
We stuck, nor breath nor motion,
As idle as a painted ship
Upon a painted ocean.

The desperate circumstances of the wreck had been covered at length in the court proceedings at Exeter and set down in the jury's verdict. The hearings in London were focused solely on the unappetising question of whether the natural human instinct for survival in the direst of situations could justify the taking of another's life. Could murder ever be considered to be a necessity? Dudley and Stephens's lawyers knew they faced an uphill battle to persuade the court to answer the question in the affirmative. The key to an acquittal, they believed, lay in another tale of nautical disaster that had taken place some forty years earlier in the icy North Atlantic.

*   *   *

The *William Brown* was a small American emigrant ship that plied its trade on the transatlantic routes in the first half of the 19th century. When it sailed from Liverpool in March 1841, bound for Philadelphia, its hold was full of cargo and its cabins packed with sixty-five Scottish and Irish passengers bound for a new life in Pennsylvania. Four weeks into the voyage, the ship came to grief a few hundred miles south of Newfoundland, in the same North Atlantic corridor where the RMS *Titanic* would sink in strikingly similar circumstances seventy-one years later, almost to the day.

On the evening of 19 April the *William Brown* struck an iceberg and began to go down by the bow. The ship only carried two lifeboats; the captain and half of the crew commandeered the first, the second was filled with the remainder of the seamen, together with some of the passengers. Thirty-one of the passengers were left on the decks of the ship when it went down. All of the crew escaped in the lifeboats, which were picked up by a passing French fishing vessel two days after the sinking. When some of the surviving passengers eventually reached Philadelphia, they made a complaint to the district attorney's office about what had happened on the lifeboat after the ship had sunk. Only one of the *William Brown*'s crew, an able seaman named Alexander Holmes, could be traced in the city. He was arrested and charged with an offence unique to US law – manslaughter on the high seas.

The tale told by the ship's surviving passengers was a horrific one. In the hours following the sinking, the conditions in their lifeboat had worsened. Most had fled from their beds in nightshirts and underclothes when the ship struck the iceberg, not ideal attire for sitting in an open boat in the icefields of the North Atlantic. Coupled with this, the wind had begun to rise and it started raining; worst of all, the boat had sprung a leak. By the following night the crew in the boat feared that it was at serious risk of capsizing. Holmes and his fellow seamen decided to take action and began to throw the male passengers overboard. Some begged for mercy, some pleaded for time to say their prayers, others struggled. But it was to no avail and by the time the crew had finished, they had emptied the lifeboat of fourteen male passengers. One, Frank Askin, had escaped from the sinking ship with his two sisters, and they now refused to be parted from him. When Holmes tossed Askin over the shallow sides of the lifeboat, his sisters threw themselves overboard after him.

The state's case against Holmes largely rested on the nature of the relationship between the ship's crew and its passengers. By virtue of his employment, a crewman has accepted the unavoidable element of risk in going to sea, and sacrificing passengers to preserve his own life flies in the face of this. This would have been news to the *William Brown*'s captain, who had prioritised himself and his crew for places in the lifeboats and then sailed away from the scene of the sinking. Holmes denied the manslaughter charge on the grounds of self-preservation, and his lawyers stressed to the jury that the only fair way to judge his actions was to place themselves in the same boat, figuratively at least:

This case should be tried in a long-boat, sunk down to its very gunwale with 41 half naked, starved and shivering wretches, the boat leaking from below, filling from above, a hundred leagues from land, at midnight, surrounded by ice, unmanageable from its load, and subject to certain destruction from the change of the most changeful of the elements, the winds and the waves.

Evidence was given that Holmes's actions throughout the catastrophe had not been entirely self-serving. As the ship was tilting for its final plunge, he had climbed back onto the decks from the lifeboat to rescue a young girl. The jury was clearly in two minds about the defendant before them. After much deliberation, they found Holmes guilty of manslaughter, but made a recommendation for mercy. The offence was not a capital one and so Holmes was sentenced to six months' hard labour in the state penitentiary and a fine of $20. Like his seafaring brethren Dudley and Stephens, he attracted considerable public sympathy but an appeal to US President John Tyler for a full pardon was refused.

Although Holmes was indeed convicted of manslaughter, one particular section of the US court's judgment in the case caught the eye of Dudley and Stephens's defence lawyers. There was no doubt that their case was unique; no one had been prosecuted for maritime cannibalism in the English courts before. So they had to cast their net widely to find some semblance of a precedent on which to hang a necessity defence. In summarising the law to the jury at Holmes's trial, Circuit Justice Baldwin commented at some length on the legal quandary posted by disasters at sea where the fate of the many could hinge on the sacrifice of the few. In such circumstances, including cases of survival cannibalism, the only possible justification for such action would be if the victims had been fairly selected by the drawing of lots or some other mechanism. This tied in with the tenets of the so-called 'custom of the sea' – from this, Dudley and Stephens extrapolated the argument that in Holmes's case, the court had effectively approved the defence of necessity, but found that the *William Brown*'s crew had not complied with it by indiscriminately throwing passengers overboard.

This reasoning got short shrift from Lord Justice Coleridge. He did not consider the American case to be a binding authority on the English courts, and, even on their own interpretation of the Holmes case, the crew of the *Mignonette* had themselves made no attempt to draw lots or otherwise impartially select one of their number to be consumed by the rest. They had picked on Parker because he was the youngest and weakest, the least able to physically resist his fate. Dudley and Stephens maintained that Parker was already so ill that it was only a matter of time before he died in any case, and, to some extent, the killing was as much an act of mercy to Parker as it was an act of salvation for them.

There is no doubt that allowing a defence of necessity to murder into English law would pose some awful moral dilemmas, which were highlighted by Justice Coleridge as he delivered the court's judgment in Dudley and Stephens's case. 'Who is to be the judge of this sort of necessity?' he asked. 'By what measure is the comparative value of lives to be measured? Is it to be strength, or intellect, or what?' Ultimately the court was more afraid of what might follow in Dudley and Stephens's wake if they were allowed to get away with murder. The panel of judges came to a unanimous conclusion:

It is therefore our duty to declare that the prisoners' act in this case was wilful murder, that the facts stated in the verdict are no legal justification of the homicide; and to say that in our unanimous conclusion the prisoners are ... guilty of murder.

The only sentence was, of course, death. But almost since they had come ashore at Falmouth, the weight of public opinion had swung behind the unfortunate sailors. The Mayor of Falmouth had received an anonymous letter threatening in 'filthy and disgusting language' that he would be shot in retaliation for signing their arrest warrant. Even Parker's family were largely supportive of them. His brother had travelled to Falmouth for the initial court hearing and had made a point of shaking Dudley's hand in court after the murder charge had been announced. As seafarers themselves, they recognised that the crew had only followed the same dreadful course that most sailors would have done in such an awful predicament. The Thames Yacht Agency had established a public subscription fund that met the costs of Dudley and Stephens's expensive legal team, with enough left over to make a bequest to Parker's sister.

The national newspapers were firmly on their side as well. On 22 September, the London *Evening Standard*'s letters page carried a missive from Dudley, probably the only time that the paper has ever published a letter from a self-confessed cannibal awaiting trial for murder:

SIR – May I, through the medium of your widely circulated paper, express my thanks for numerous favours of sympathy for myself and companions during our past terrible sufferings and privations on the ocean, and our present suspense under the ban of the law; being charged with an act which certainly was not accompanied by either malice or premeditation, as our consciences can affirm.

I am, Sir, your obedient servant, Thos. Dudley

There was also the political dimension to the case to be considered. Sir William Harcourt had got his legal clarity; the judges had given a decisive judgment that necessity was not and could never be a justification for taking a life. In return, when the sentence was referred to Queen Victoria with a plea for mercy, Harcourt was prepared to recommend that the capital sentence be commuted to a short spell in prison. Dudley and Stephens were sentenced to six months in prison and released on 20 May 1885, a year and a day after they had departed from Southampton on what was to be the *Mignonette*'s final voyage.

After his release, Dudley swiftly emigrated to Australia with his family, which had been his original plan after completing the voyage. He carved a living as a sailmaker known to his local community by the nickname 'Cannibal Tom'. He kept hold of the yacht's sextant as a grim souvenir, and in the 1970s it was discovered in a house clearance in Australia. Stephens, meanwhile, descended into alcoholism and poverty. Mate Edward Brooks, who had never actually faced trial with his shipmates because he had agreed to give evidence against them, was keen to trade on the fleeting fame brought by the case. He exhibited himself in the touring freakshows and circuses that abounded at the time, under the moniker 'The Cannibal of the High Seas'. He would gnaw on pieces of raw meat thrown into the showground by the audience.

Parker's remains were returned to England with his shipmates and he was buried in the churchyard of Jesus Chapel near his home in Itchen Ferry, Southampton, from where he had set off on what should have been the adventure of his young life. But he went on to enjoy his own form of immortality in literature, where the name Richard Parker crops up with uncanny regularity in connection with those in peril on the sea. The hero of Yann Martel's novel *Life of Pi* shares a lifeboat with a Bengal tiger named after Parker. Edgar Allan Poe's novel *The Narrative of Arthur Gordon Pym of Nantucket* features the cannibalistic killing of a sailor named Richard Parker by his starving crewmates following the wrecking of their ship. In an eerie twist of which Poe himself would have been proud, the novel was published in 1838, some fifty years *before* the real Parker met his maker at the hands of his hungry colleagues.

Just four years after their trial, Jack the Ripper went on his murderous rampage through East London and the cannibal sailors of the South Atlantic were largely relegated from the annals of infamous Victorian murderers, forgotten by all but law students and maritime historians. Dudley and Stephens were not mad, and certainly not bad enough to make them the truly terrifying bogeymen that we love. As a result they have never entered the public consciousness in the same way as other murderers of their era. Perhaps this is because, tragic and pitiable as Parker was, his killers were equally so.

There are no neat victims and villains in the *Mignonette* tragedy, and the story forces people to consider what they would have done in the same horrible circumstances. It is easy to distance oneself from the actions of a Dr Crippen or a Ripper. But it is difficult to be so certain that, placed in the same literal and metaphorical boat as Dudley and Stephens, you too wouldn't have killed and eaten Richard Parker.

*   *   *

Although the public's appetite for a grisly death remained undimmed, as the 20th century dawned and the Victorians passed into history, the country would be shaken by killing on an industrial scale that wholly eclipsed the terrors of Whitechapel and its like. But although the sheer magnitude of the slaughter on the Western Front might have been expected to render people immune to tales of individual human brutality, this was not to be. The First World War's most shocking killing occurred not on the frontline, however, but in a comfortable redbrick villa in Hampshire.

In early December 1915 the 9th Canadian Mounted Rifles arrived at Bramshott Camp in Hampshire. Five temporary camps were set up on Bramshott Common to house Canadian infantry troops awaiting deployment on the Western Front alongside the British Army, and the resident soldiers nicknamed the camps after the Great Lakes. Among the new arrivals was Sergeant Henry Ozanne, aged thirty-seven and a native of St Peter's Port on the island of Guernsey. He had lived and worked in London as a clerk for a number of years, before emigrating to Canada in 1911 to start a new life as a farmer. He joined up shortly before Christmas 1914, little suspecting that the biggest threat to his life came not from a German sniper but from one of his fellow officers.

The regiment's top brass were billeted in the village of Grayshott, a few miles from the camps. They lived in comparative luxury in the Victorian houses that lined the main road through the village. On the afternoon of 8 December Ozanne was summoned to see one of the officers at their quarters at Arundel House in the village, but when he failed to return to camp later that day the alarm was raised.

The following morning his body was found in the stable block at Arundel House wrapped in blankets. Local doctor Henry Williams was summoned to the stable and his findings were grim. Ozanne's face had been horribly disfigured by over forty separate knife wounds and his teeth had been knocked out. The doctor opined that these frenzied wounds might have been an attempt by his killer to disguise Ozanne's identity. His skull had been fractured by a heavy blow but this was not the cause of the soldier's death. Dr Williams noted that 'the neck was severed right down to the vertebra and all of the arteries and muscles were cut. This was done by a series of hacks, vicious hacks.'

Suspicion soon alighted on Lieutenant Georges Codere, the officer whom Ozanne had been due to meet at the house. Aged just twenty-two, he had joined the army on the outbreak of the war and his reputation had preceded him to England. His comrades nicknamed him *Le Fou Codere* ('Codere the Fool') on account of his erratic and abnormal behaviour, and his commanding officer Major Gaston Hughes had already decided that he would not be taking Codere to France as he considered him 'unable to handle men from the moral or mental point of view'. He had difficulty understanding orders and people found it almost impossible to conduct a conversation with him because his attention bounced from topic to topic without a coherent thread. He was wont to smash up furniture for no reason and had attacked a bystander who had stopped to watch his regiment out on parade back in Canada. There was no need for Codere to put his underpants on his head and stick pencils in his nostrils to get out of being sent to the front line; his colleagues and superiors were already convinced that he was quite mad enough. Hughes's plan was to have Codere declared medically unfit on account of his asthma and then ship him back to Canada as soon as possible.

A complicated story emerged about a plan by Codere to defraud the regimental coffers that Ozanne administered. The lieutenant had been living beyond his means since his arrival in England and had recently ordered a car from America, with no means to pay the outstanding balance on it. He offered to help Ozanne by exchanging some Canadian money into sterling in London but had decided to keep the cash for himself. To avoid his theft being detected, he then resolved that his only option was to kill Ozanne. Remarkably, Codere had discussed his intentions with some of the soldiers in his regiment, one of whom had even debated with him the comparative merits of poisoning versus beating Ozanne to death. The other soldiers later claimed that they were simply humouring Codere and had not expected him to carry out his plan, putting the talk down to his usual strangeness. On the afternoon of Ozanne's murder, he had summoned the sergeant to Arundel House on the pretext of discussing the money issue. He had first offered Ozanne a glass of whisky, laced with drugs. When this had no effect on his victim, he attacked him. With the gracious house's floorplan resembling a Cluedo board, it was undoubtedly Lieutenant Codere, in the smoking room, with the trench stick.

Codere then dragged Ozanne, who was unconscious but still breathing, along the hall passage to the top of a flight of steps leading down to the house's cellar. He threw Ozanne down the stairs into the cellar before following him down to slit his throat. Two servants, Lance Corporals Keller and Desjardins, were summoned by Codere to the smoking room and asked to clean up the blood on the floor from Ozanne's head wounds. Then Codere took them to the top of the cellar stairs to show them Ozanne's body, which he asked them to wrap in a blanket and hide in the stables. Desjardins immediately ran out of the house. Keller, too dumbstruck and perhaps in awe of his senior officer, meekly complied.

Later that evening, Major Hughes came into the kitchen and found Keller busying himself with preparing the officers' dinner. Sweat was dripping off the corporal's nose and he avoided eye contact with the major, keeping his focus on the bowl of potatoes that he was peeling. Baffled by Keller's odd behaviour, the major made a mental note to check the contents of the liquor cabinet. At dinner, Keller served the officers their meal, acutely aware of Codere's eyes following him around the room. He feared that Codere would slaughter them all if he breathed a word of what was lying in the stable block. To Desjardins, watching through the serving hatch, Codere appeared 'kind of queer, kind of white', but he was keeping up an animated conversation with the major and the colonel, who seemed entirely oblivious to the fact that anything was amiss. When Codere left Arundel House the following morning, Keller found his tongue and told the major what had happened to Ozanne. On his return, Codere was placed under arrest.

On trial for murder at Winchester Assizes, Codere pleaded insanity – at the same time, he maintained that he had not killed Ozanne. He wrote a letter to Keller in which he accused the lance corporal of the murder and urged him to confess. However, the witness evidence against Codere was overwhelming. The jury deliberated for half an hour before returning a verdict of guilty:

In answer to the Clerk (of the court) why sentence of death should not be passed upon him, the prisoner said – 'All I have got to say is that I am not the man who did it.'

Grayshott is just a dozen or so miles to the south-east of Alton, and Codere pleaded for his neck on the basis of insanity in the same Winchester courtroom where Frederick Baker had been sentenced to death for the murder of Fanny Adams, after a similarly unsuccessful insanity claim. But the Canadian soldier had a second bite of the cherry that was not available to Baker fifty years earlier. In 1907 the Criminal Appeal Court had been created, giving defendants the ability to appeal against a conviction or sentence handed down in a criminal case. The British legal community was surprisingly reluctant to adopt a formal appeals structure. After all, a judicial system that was the envy of the world was surely its own best protection against injustice. The flaws in this stance were becoming apparent by the late 19th century and a Court of Appeal for judgments given in civil cases was created in 1875.

But the criminal courts resisted such a reform for another twenty years. The reasons for this perhaps go to the heart of the criminal law and its role in society. Its most treasured and mythologised feature has always been the right to jury trial.

The fear was that an appeals court took the final decision away from the 'twelve good men and true', placing a defendant's ultimate fate in the hands of a judge. Reformers also faced the argument that the status quo worked well enough as it was, and the creation of an appeal process was disproportionate to the relatively small number of cases involving a serious miscarriage of justice, such as the execution of someone who was in fact innocent. This rather conveniently overlooked the prevalence of capital punishment at the time. After all, dead men tell no tales.

Codere appealed against the rejection of his insanity defence, and in doing so gave the youthful Court of Appeal an opportunity to sense-check the M'Naghten rules some seventy years after their inception and ensure that they were still fit for purpose. Codere's lawyers rehashed the limited medical evidence that they had presented at his original trial. Psychiatrist Dr Stoddart, called to give evidence for the defence, reported that Codere had told him that he had been under the 'hypnotic influence' of some unnamed man when he killed Ozanne. The doctor was also satisfied that there was an extensive history of mental illness on both sides of Codere's family; having noted the recurrence of a limited number of surnames in the family tree, Dr Stoddart speculated that the Codere gene pool might not be as deep as one would hope, which would exacerbate any genetic predisposition towards mental illness.

Codere's mother Eugenie gave a lengthy statement about his past problems. He had been a sickly child and had suffered from fits since he was a toddler, which she believed had affected his development. As a child he had been expelled from several schools and had a disturbing habit of trying to kill his pets. In adulthood his behaviour became more and more outlandish. He proposed to several girls and then married a young woman the day after meeting her. When he joined the army, Codere told his friends and neighbours that he had been appointed to the Canadian government as the Minister for Militia. Mme Codere had become convinced that some terrible disaster would befall her son in England.

But the sticking point was Codere's understanding of his actions, as indicated by his careful and open planning of the killing of Ozanne, followed by his subsequent attempts to frame Keller for the murder. His lawyers argued that the M'Naghten rules had not been applied correctly in previous cases and that their correct interpretation was that a murderer must understand that the act of killing was morally wrong, not simply prohibited by law. This was in effect a claim that insanity should be determined according to a subjective assessment by the defendant as to the wrongness of their own actions in killing. Unsurprisingly, this was roundly rejected by the Appeal judges, who were adamant that the act must be judged by the standards of a hypothetical 'reasonable man', to mitigate the dangers of judging a criminal's action by their individual moral compass, which may be aberrantly calibrated.

Codere was declared sane, his conviction upheld and his capital sentence affirmed. His parents travelled from Canada to see him in his final days in Winchester Gaol. The Canadian government lobbied the home secretary hard for a reprieve and the citizens of his home town of Sherbrooke in Quebec sent a deluge of letters of support across the Atlantic. Mindful of the risk to Anglo-Canadian relations, the British government had to tread carefully. A week before Codere's scheduled execution on 15 March, the home secretary reached a decision:

> *In view of the doubt as to the prisoner's mental capacity and the fact that it would be impolitic for the administration of justice in England to come into conflict with Canadian public opinion on the case of a Canadian officer stationed here on account of war service, it is submitted that the clemency of the Crown may properly be executed in this case. The sentence of death has therefore been respited with a view to its commutation to one of penal servitude for life. The prisoner will be removed to Parkhurst convict prison where careful observation will be kept on his mental condition.*

Codere's prison records reveal that, while he suffered no resurgence of the mania that fuelled his savage attack on Ozanne, his time in Parkhurst was not entirely without incident. There were attempts at self-harm, and on one occasion he was caught with a contraband razor blade and a letter to a fellow inmate, written on the prison's thin and shiny latrine paper, which contained 'very suggestive and improper remarks'. His family did not rest and continued to petition the English authorities on his behalf, requesting that he be released and sent back to Canada before his mental state deteriorated further.

By 1930 Codere had served over fourteen years in prison and, although the Parkhurst governor and doctors considered him to be still potentially dangerous, the Home Office finally consented to his release. A Canadian government agent named

Dr Verge was despatched to escort him home, and on 21 February 1930 Codere walked out of the prison gates to be met by the doctor. The pair boarded the passenger liner *Ansonia* at Southampton, bound for Halifax in Nova Scotia. Ozanne never made it home and was buried with full military honours at Guildford Cemetery. As it passed through Grayshott the funeral cortege halted on the road outside Arundel House, where the regimental trumpeter played the 'Last Post'.

*   *   *

Georges Codere, Thomas Dudley and Edwin Stephens may seem to have sprung from the pages of a melodrama or a historical novel, but they were real people whose very real crimes continue to have an impact on the law today. In the century or so since Dudley and Stephens disembarked at Falmouth there have been periodic attempts to continue their line of argument and introduce a defence of necessity into English law. All have failed; no matter how many guns are held to your head, it does not entitle you to put one to someone else's. In the latter half of the 20th century the question has most commonly arisen in medical cases, where the courts have had to navigate a minefield of law, science and ethics in order to answer questions of life and death. As recently as twenty years ago the fate of Richard Parker was debated by the courts once again as they wrestled with the legal constructs that have grown up around the sanctity of life.

In 2000 the Court of Appeal heard the heartrending case concerning the fate of one-month-old conjoined twin girls, whose names were pseudonymised to Jodie and Mary. The case made headlines around the world. Doctors treating the twins wanted to perform surgery to separate them. If the operation was not carried out, their prognosis was bleak and both girls would die within a matter of months. But the surgery itself would result in its own awful outcome as well. The configuration of the babies' blood supply and internal organs meant that only Jodie, the stronger of the two, would survive after the operation. Mary would die shortly after being separated from her sister, who was keeping her alive.

There were no good conclusions for the family, only a less dreadful one for Jodie. The girls' parents believed that their condition was an act of God and that it was not for them to decide that one of their children should die to save the other. They therefore refused to give their consent to the hospital to perform the operation. The hospital then applied to the court for a ruling that the surgery could go ahead without the family's agreement and that it would not be unlawful in such circumstances.

Nobody was on trial for any crime in Mary and Jodie's case. Nevertheless, in order to grant the order sought by the medical team to confirm that the operation was lawful, the judges had to consider whether there were any circumstances in which it could be deemed to be *unlawful*. No court of law can authorise an illegal act. The performance of the surgery would undoubtedly bring about the death of Mary. The court therefore had to consider the possibility that this could make the surgeons guilty of murder and, in doing so, address whether a theoretical defence of necessity could apply to obviate the potential illegality of the operation.

The fundamental problems with the concept had not altered since it was considered in the context of Richard Parker's death in 1884, as Lord Justice Brooke observed in the twins' case:

> We do regard the right to life as almost a supreme value, and it is very unlikely that anyone would be held to be justified in killing for any purpose except the saving of other life, or perhaps the saving of great pain or distress. Our revulsion against a deliberate killing is so strong that we are loth to consider utilitarian reasons for it.

The influence of Dudley and Stephens's case was debated by the judges, but ultimately they decided that the conviction of the sailors for murder could not be applied in Mary and Jodie's case to make the surgery illegal. The balancing of the girls' interests meant that it would be lawful to act to save Jodie's life even at the expense of Mary's. The operation lasted almost a day and was carried out shortly after the court gave its ruling. Mary died a short while after the surgery was completed. Jodie has gone on to live a healthy life with her family.

*   *   *

The medical techniques which made the surgery to separate Jodie and Mary possible would have been inconceivable in Dudley and Stephens's day. Well into the 20th century, medical procedures that are taken for granted today could pose a real risk to life and limb. In the days before the use of analgesics, anaesthetics and antibiotics was widespread, and with universal access to healthcare via the NHS still several decades away, there was nothing inherently suspicious about a fatal outcome to even seemingly routine medical complaints.

This is to cast no aspersions on the medical professionals themselves, who were often working in comparatively prehistoric conditions to the best of their ability, with the odds stacked against them and their patients. In 1925 the mortality rate for women dying in childbirth was around 400 out of every 100,000 births; by 1980 this had dropped to approximately 10 deaths in every 100,000 cases. But women giving birth in the inter-war years still faced about the same risk of death as expectant mothers in the early Victorian era, almost a century earlier. These considerable uncertainties gave a certain latitude to those doctors who were perhaps not as wedded to the tenets of the Hippocratic oath as one would hope.

One particularly grisly case would set the stage for an overhaul of homicide law and a revolutionary new approach to the categorisation and criminalisation of those killings that, while not apparently intentional, were still sufficiently reprehensible to warrant a criminal conviction. The boundaries between the law of murder and manslaughter, which would go on to fluctuate almost continuously throughout the rest of the 20th century, would trace their first dramatic shift back to an expectant mother lying in bed in the attic room of a Deptford tenement in the mid-1920s.

CHAPTER FOUR

TRUST ME,
I'M NOT A DOCTOR

'One golden thread is always to be seen ...'

It began, as it so often does, with a woman's body on a mortuary slab. Her name was Mary Ann Harding and she was thirty-three years old. She had been brought into south London's Deptford Infirmary on 28 July 1924, with severe internal injuries. In no state to withstand surgery and with little else that could be done for her, she declined steadily and passed away two days after she was admitted. Unfortunate, but not unusual in the days before antibiotics, ultrasound or effective anaesthesia. Nevertheless, the circumstances of her admission to the infirmary and the injuries she had suffered aroused suspicion among the medical staff, and so a post-mortem was ordered. Deep in the tiled bowels of the infirmary's mortuary, the pathologist laid out his instruments before carefully selecting a scalpel.

Checking the letter provided by her doctor when she arrived at the hospital, the pathologist noted that Mrs Harding had been admitted due to 'complications arising after childbirth'. The letter gave no further details. As the examination progressed, he observed the rupturing of the bladder, the crushing of the colon against the base of the pelvis and the tears to the intestines. These injuries were unusually severe but they were not entirely inconsistent with a difficult delivery, involving manual intervention by a doctor. But he was unable to account for what he found – or rather did not find – next. The pathologist set down his instrument and stared into the open cavity in Mrs Harding's abdomen, baffled as to how complicated a birth would have to be for the uterus to vanish into thin air.

*   *   *

Like many victims, Mrs Harding knew her killer. He was a local man, well known and even respected by the residents of the cramped streets of terraced houses where she lived. She had invited him into her home and trusted him entirely. As was often the case, it was her desperate circumstances that placed her in his path. The Royal Dockyards, which had brought prosperity to Deptford in the 18th and 19th centuries, had closed in the 1860s, hastening the area's economic decline.

The Harding family's situation was typical of many in the area. They lived in two attic rooms on the fourth floor of a terraced house on Brookmill Road in Deptford's New Town. The area had been developed in the mid-19th century as Deptford boomed, with the coming of the railways and continued industrial expansion. Between 1801 and 1901, the population had increased tenfold to 100,000; and 10,000 of these souls were crammed into the streets of the New Town. Mary Ann's husband George, like many of their neighbours, was a labourer, but employment prospects in the area had declined significantly, and by the end of the First World War Deptford had become a byword for post-Victorian metropolitan poverty.

Squeezed into their meagre accommodation were Mary Ann, George and their four children, ranging in age between thirteen and four. Just over a week before she died, the Hardings were awaiting the birth of their fifth child. Home birth was a necessity rather than an option for most, and the costs of calling out a doctor meant that the vast majority of women relied on a local midwife to attend them. Mary Ann's previous births had been uncomplicated, and when she went into labour she had no reason to suspect this one would be any different. But as soon as she arrived, the midwife was concerned that the labour was failing to progress as it should. She feared the baby had become stuck and so, late on the night of 23 July, decided to call for the local doctor.

Dr Percy Bateman was roused from his bed by the ringing telephone. A local man in his mid-thirties, he had worked in the area for several years. He was under no illusions as to the nobility of his work – his was a 'slum practice'. He knew what to expect from the call. A doubtless well-meaning but unqualified midwife would have spent hours trying to help with the birth, probably in squalid conditions, only giving in and calling a doctor at the eleventh hour. He would be expected to step in to salvage a more or less hopeless situation. If things went well, the mother or the baby might survive, but probably not both.

He packed his medical bag and walked the mile or so from his home in a yellow-bricked Georgian terrace on the main New Cross Road to the Hardings' tenement. When he examined Mrs Harding, he confirmed the midwife's fears. The baby was stuck and a natural delivery would be impossible. For two hours, with the smell of blood, sweat and chloroform mingling in the stuffy air of the garret room, Dr Bateman tried to deliver the baby, first with forceps and then with his bare hands. At midnight the baby was born, dead.

While the midwife attempted to console George with the reassurance that at least his wife had survived the birth, Dr Bateman remained with Mary Ann in the bedroom. After the horror of the stillbirth, he now had to turn to the removal of the placenta. With Mary Ann exhausted and heavily sedated by the chloroform, he again had to perform this manually. When the placenta proved unusually resistant, he applied further force and continued to pull. Eventually something gave and Mary Ann began to bleed heavily. Dr Bateman packed away his instruments into his Gladstone bag. Almost as an afterthought, he quickly wrapped the organ he had removed in some cloth and placed it in the bag, before summoning the midwife. He promised to return the following day to check on his patient and, with that, he left.

In the days following the birth, Mary Ann lay in bed, drifting in and out of consciousness. True to his word, Dr Bateman returned to visit her twice daily. As her condition worsened, George pleaded with Dr Bateman to admit her to the local infirmary but he steadfastly refused. Although he did not confess as much to George, it was clear to him that there was little point in taking her to hospital; it would only prolong the inevitable. However, on the fifth day, he relented. Mary Ann was finally taken to the local infirmary on 28 July. On admission, Dr Bateman provided the hospital doctors with only scant details of the difficulties with the birth. The doctors at the hospital concluded that Mary Ann was simply not strong enough to withstand any surgery and nothing more could be done for her.

But the pathologist's findings at the post-mortem raised some disturbing questions. And so, to his consternation and that of the entire medical profession, six months after the post-mortem had been completed, Dr Bateman found himself in the dock of the Old Bailey on trial for manslaughter.

*   *   *

Doctors do not often find themselves on trial for homicide. How, then, had it come about that Bateman, who claimed to have been simply going about his job to the best of his ability, could be prosecuted for such a horrendous crime? From its inception, the offence of manslaughter has always existed in the liminal spaces between moral and legal culpability. For centuries the courts have struggled with giving meaning to an offence that has to cover such a wide variety of lethal acts. These range from at best merely accidental, to at worst recklessly stupid; or perhaps stupidly reckless. The extent to which foolishness, carelessness and even incompetence should be criminalised when they cause a death is an eternal and ongoing struggle for the criminal law. Defining manslaughter has always required a degree of fault on the part of the defendant – fault that has led to the death. They must have done something objectively wrong, even though they did not intend to kill, to be convicted.

There is, of course, nothing criminal in a doctor treating a patient. Sometimes that treatment will, inevitably, be unsuccessful. Such is life, and indeed death. But this fails to account for cases where a patient has died apparently as a result of, rather than in spite of, a doctor's ministrations. However scathing the assessment of Dr Bateman's care towards Mrs Harding, there was no evidence that he had actually intended to kill her, such as would be required for a murder conviction. This left manslaughter as the only option for the police and the Crown to pursue in respect of Mrs Harding's death. Could the offence of manslaughter extend to such a case?

At the beginning of the 20th century the answer was almost certainly no. Historically the courts had been reluctant to criminalise accidents or mistakes, particularly as manslaughter remained a capital offence until the 1860s, when the death penalty was restricted almost exclusively to murderers. To build its case against Dr Bateman, the Crown would have to persuade the court that his treatment of Mary Ann fell so far below that expected of a reasonably capable doctor and showed such utter disregard for his patient as to amount to a crime. This was new territory for the law of homicide.

There were three specific allegations of negligence made against Dr Bateman, namely the causing of Mrs Harding's internal injuries during the delivery; the complete removal of her uterus, which he had pulled out while trying to remove the placenta; and his delay in sending her to the infirmary. Dr Bateman denied them all. Giving evidence in his defence, he said that the position of Mrs Harding's baby was the most difficult he had ever seen. He suggested that it would have been virtually impossible for any doctor to have saved the baby or to have delivered it without causing injury to Mrs Harding. He also belatedly explained the absence of Mrs Harding's uterus, a *mea culpa* that was not for the faint of heart or stomach. When attempting to remove the placenta, he had in fact taken hold of a tear in the wall of the womb by mistake. This was why it had been so resistant to removal. By sheer brute force, he had wrested the wrong organ from Mrs Harding's body.

Bateman was unable to explain why he had seen fit to take the uterus with him, away from the prying eyes of Mr Harding and the midwife. This supported the prosecution's theory that Dr Bateman realised very quickly that he had got things horribly wrong. He had hidden the removed womb and refused to take Mrs Harding to the infirmary to cover up his actions, knowing that as soon as she was examined at the infirmary, questions would be asked about what he had done. His desire to disguise his error and so preserve his professional reputation had overwhelmed any considerations he may have had for helping Mrs Harding.

As far as the prosecuting counsel was concerned, this was the killer blow. The jury may well have felt unable to pass a judgment on his medical expertise, even after hearing the testimony of expert surgical witnesses. But the wickedness of a calculated cover-up of his mistakes by Dr Bateman was simple enough to grasp. This was a callous and deliberate act of self-preservation that had hastened Mrs Harding's death. In the parlance of the court, it was 'grave, wicked neglect and culpable neglect of duty in not taking some steps to remedy what had been done by his own fault ... but he did not do anything because he wished to save his reputation'.

The prosecution was right. The jury found Dr Bateman guilty of manslaughter and he was sentenced to a suspended sentence of six months in prison. His conviction provoked an immediate outcry from doctors up and down the country, who were aghast that Dr Bateman had even been charged and were apoplectic that he had been convicted.

*   *   *

The medical profession of Dr Bateman's time was in a state of flux. Although the advent of fully socialised healthcare for the entire population was still a couple of decades away, there had been moves in that direction for a number of years. Up until the turn of the 20th century, most medical care was provided on a privately paying basis. Some of the big industrial employers funded healthcare provision for their workers, and local organisations, such as friendly societies, sometimes ran medical subscription clubs for people living in their area. Families could also take out their own 'contracts' with a doctor directly. Those doctors who worked in affluent areas could be sure of a steady stream of income from wealthy patients with the means to pay. But in working-class or rural areas it could be difficult to make a decent living from a medical practice.

In 1913 the so-called 'panel' system of healthcare came into being under the National Insurance Act. This legislation provided a form of state health insurance for working-age people, subject to an income threshold. Doctors would work on an insurance panel to serve the patients covered, with the state meeting their fees. GPs like Dr Bateman, who were based in densely populated industrial areas such as Deptford, could establish a sizeable practice from the local populace. By the mid-1930s around nineteen million people were insured under the scheme. As a working man, George Harding would have been covered by the panel arrangements for his healthcare needs, but the insurance did not extend to his wife and children. Dr Bateman's fee for attending on Mary Ann was therefore met by the local council, who usually stepped in to cover the gaps in provision. His fee was two guineas – around £120 in today's money.

For medics, the panel scheme provided a guaranteed level of income that could still be supplemented by more lucrative private work. The arrangements between the British Medical Association and the Ministry of Health expressly provided for doctors to earn half of their net income from panel patients, while only requiring them to spend 30 per cent of their time on the work. This incentivised a speedy turnaround of panel appointments to free up time for the better-paying private jobs.

A review of the panel arrangements published in the 1980s commented:

> The insurance system institutionalised an existing conflict between the interest of patient – and society – in an improved quality of medicine, and the interest of the majority of the medical profession in higher incomes. It was this conflict which contributed to the replacement of the panel system by the National Health Service.

By the 1920s and 1930s there was unease that the panel arrangement had contributed to a two-tier standard of care; obstetrics and maternal deaths were particular areas of concern. This was, to some extent, nothing new. Certainly by the mid-19th century, as a result of the risks of childbirth and sky-high infant mortality rates, the beginning of a new life was fraught with danger for both mother and child. The increasing enthusiasm of doctors for the use of chloroform in childbirth has been blamed for a threefold increase in maternal deaths in the latter half of the 19th century (the practice was still common in the early 20th century – Dr Bateman had administered chloroform to Mary Ann).

On top of these perils, late Victorian England was gripped by what came to be known as the 'infanticide panic'. Lurid accounts from social reformers such as William Burke Ryan, who published a book about the subject in 1862, suggested that it was virtually impossible to walk down a street, along a canal or through the woods, even to sit in a railway carriage, without finding the body of an infant who had either been abandoned to die, or worse, been murdered by its mother.

While doubtless somewhat of an exaggeration, infanticide was more than an urban myth at the time. For working-class women in particular, the combination of a lack of available contraception coupled with the stigma and financial hardship of raising an illegitimate child alone left them with an unenviable dilemma if they were to fall pregnant. Some of the more enlightened campaigners were uneasy that mothers, who may have been driven to kill their child in desperate circumstances (and may even have believed that they were saving the baby from a life of poverty and deprivation), were being convicted and executed as murderers.

From the 1870s onwards there was a push to mitigate the severity of the punishment meted out to mothers who killed their infants. But its difficult progress through parliament meant that significant legislative change was stalled on several occasions, and it wasn't until 1922 that the Infanticide Act finally became law – by which point the issue had largely receded from the popular imagination. To address the perceived reluctance of juries to convict women of murder in such cases, the Act created a new homicide offence of infanticide, applicable only to a woman who had killed her newly born child while the balance of her mind was disturbed from the effects of pregnancy or birth, or what we might now classify as post-natal depression. A conviction for infanticide carried a custodial sentence rather than a capital one.

Although Mary Ann Harding's case didn't involve infanticide, it was part of the same nagging public-health concern that pregnancy, childbirth and infancy were perilous times for both mothers and babies. Maternal deaths and stillbirths remained at almost Victorian levels, and there was a belief within the medical profession that this was at least in part down to the inbuilt inequalities of the care from doctors under the panel system, combined with the shortcomings in support provided by local midwives to pick up the slack in antenatal care, particularly for poorer women. Dr Bateman's case provided a timely opportunity to make an example.

The *British Medical Journal* was then, as now, the main mouthpiece of the profession and its letters page carried an impassioned running commentary on the prosecution. As the profession saw it, Dr Bateman had been placed in an impossible position by the unfortunate circumstances of the case. The real culprits were the unqualified midwives, who proliferated in what were euphemistically described as 'industrial areas'. One correspondent, a Dr Broadhurst, a practitioner from the north-east, proposed direct action in response to the court's handling of the case:

> If [the conviction] is not quashed on appeal I suggest that doctors should in future cease to attend midwives' cases at the patients' own homes but send them all into hospital. I do not believe the results would be any better ... but we should at least escape the possibility of a fate like Dr Bateman's.

All were agreed that the case had set a dangerous precedent. If doctors were to be criminalised when treatment went wrong, they would be reluctant to treat at all, especially in difficult cases. Dr Bateman's wife was sufficiently moved by the support shown towards her husband by his professional brethren that she wrote to the *BMJ* to express her gratitude:

> Permit me ... through your columns to thank those loyal gentlemen who so ably defended my husband in court, also in your valuable journal. My husband got out of his bed to do all in his power to help this poor woman, and his reward is to be branded in a court of justice as a criminal.

Mrs Bateman's robust defence of her husband was slightly disingenuous, in that it omitted one important qualification – the manslaughter conviction was not the first entry on Dr Bateman's criminal record. He had three prior convictions for being drunk and disorderly. The most recent of these was from September 1924, while he was awaiting trial for Mrs Harding's death. He had returned from the pub and tried to kick down his neighbour's front door. Dr Bateman claimed that his behaviour was the result of his 'frightful and unbearable worries' over his upcoming prosecution, but he was still fined forty shillings by the Greenwich Magistrates.

Nevertheless, buoyed by the support of his professional brethren, Dr Bateman appealed against his conviction for manslaughter. Before three Court of Appeal judges over a hearing lasting several days in February 1925, Dr Bateman's lawyers argued his case again. The *BMJ* reported breathlessly on each day's proceedings. The rapidity with which his appeal had come to court augured well for Dr Bateman and suggested that the judiciary were sufficiently alarmed by the calamitous predictions of the medical establishment to want to re-examine the case quickly. Dr Bateman reasserted that he had done all he could in very difficult circumstances. Mrs Harding's injuries and even the removal of her womb were, in effect, to be expected due to the complications with the birth. At most he was guilty of making a mistake, and this was not sufficient to make him criminally liable for manslaughter.

The Court of Appeal was persuaded. They decided that Dr Bateman's treatment of Mrs Harding did not meet the high threshold of criminal negligence that would be required to make him guilty of manslaughter. But in overturning the conviction, the court simultaneously set out the standard that a prosecution must prove in order to rely on negligence as a foundation for a manslaughter charge. In the words of Lord Chief Justice Hewart, delivering the verdict of the Court of Appeal:

> The prosecution must satisfy the jury that the negligence went beyond a mere matter of compensation and showed such disregard for the life and safety of others as to amount to a crime against the state and conduct deserving punishment.

The setting-out of this test effectively created a new category of manslaughter – manslaughter by gross negligence – and although it was not met in Dr Bateman's case, it could form the basis for other prosecutions in the future. While the trial broke new ground and in effect gave birth to the modern law of manslaughter, a decade later the courts would be forced to go back to the very basics of homicide. A world away from the slums of south London, the villages of the West Country would be shocked by a domestic drama that shook the criminal law to perhaps its most fundamental foundation.

* * *

On the morning of 10 December 1934, in the small Somerset village of Milborne Port, Mrs Daisy Brine was in her backyard, hanging out the washing. The snug row of cottages where she lived was something of a family enclave. Next door to Mrs

Brine lived her sister Mrs Lily Smith, who was widowed. Next door to Mrs Smith lived their other sister Mrs Rosalind (known, appropriately enough, as Rose) Budd, with her husband Bert and their two children. The three sisters and their families were close. Daisy knew that all was not well in the adjacent cottage. Lily's daughter Violet Woolmington, who lived with her husband Reg and their baby son in the nearby village of Castleton, had recently moved back to her mother's home after a fight with Reg. The couple had only been married for three months but the newly wedded bliss had worn off quickly.

Through her billowing sheets, Mrs Brine spotted Reg's bike leaning up against the wall of the cottage next door and then heard the raised voices of the young couple from inside. While Violet's mother was out, Reg had obviously come round to persuade his wife to return to him. As she eavesdropped on the couple's row from over the yard wall, she heard a sharp report from inside the cottage, followed by Reg storming out of the front door. Daisy shouted to him, but he put his head down, scrambled onto his bike and pedalled off furiously. Mrs Brine let herself into the neighbouring cottage, expecting to find Violet in tears after the latest fight, perhaps with something smashed on the flagstones to explain the loud noise. Instead, she found her niece lying dead on the rug in the small front parlour, with a gunshot wound in her chest. The baby was lying in his pram, a few yards from his mother's body.

Reg and Violet had been 'courting' for around two years when the inevitable happened and a wedding had to be hastily arranged in August 1934. Their son was born in October and was named after his father. Violet was just seventeen, while Reg was a few years older and worked as a farm labourer in the villages around the town of Sherborne. Shortly after the marriage, they had moved into a cottage on his employer's farm and initially things had gone well. But after the arrival of the baby, their relationship soured.

Dark-haired and lantern-jawed, Reg was well known as an amateur boxer in the area and it seems he was not averse to using his fists on Violet on occasion. Mrs Smith grew increasingly concerned and, when baby Reginald was just a few weeks old, she persuaded Violet to leave her husband and come to stay with her. With time to think, Violet decided that she was not going back. Before her marriage she had worked in the domestic staff for a draper's firm near Bath and she planned to resume a career in service. When Reg turned up at her mother's cottage that morning to make another plea for her return, she told him of her decision.

In the aftermath of the shooting, Reg cycled straight home. He bumped into his mother and his employer Mr Cheeseman, who owned the farm that he worked on. To both of them he explained that he had shot Violet. The police were called to the farm cottage, where they found Reg sitting at the kitchen table waiting for them. When he was arrested, they found a note in his pocket, which indicated that he planned to commit suicide after killing Violet. The scribbled message read:

Good bye all. It is agonies [sic] to carry on any longer. I have kept true hoping she would return this is the only way out. They ruined me and I'll have my revenge. May God forgive me for doing this but it is the Best thing ... Her mother is no good on this earth but have no more cartridges only one for her and one for me. I am of sound mind now ... I love Violet with all my heart. Reg.

His initial statement to the police tallied with his note and indicated that he accepted full responsibility for Violet's death, which he attributed to his rage at her mother's interference in the couple's relationship. He had also found out that Violet had recently gone to the pictures in Sherborne with another man. The note indicated that he planned the shooting as his revenge. A shotgun belonging to Mr Cheeseman, with the barrel sawn off, was identified as the murder weapon. It seemed to be a straightforward case of murder. But Reg would swiftly change his tune.

On trial at Taunton Assizes in January 1935, Reg put a very different spin on the events of that December morning. He claimed that his intention when visiting Violet was to frighten her into returning to him. He had gone to the cottage with the gun hidden under his coat in a makeshift shoulder holster and planned to threaten to shoot himself in front of her if she did not agree to come home. Under cross-examination in court, he explained what had happened when Violet told him of her decision to make the separation final and return to work:

REG: I unbuttoned my overcoat and pulled up the gun and as I did so it went off.

JUDGE: Why did you have to hold it up?

REG: *I wanted to show her that as a last resort I would shoot myself.*

JUDGE: *And you pointed it at your wife?*

REG: *I don't know. I was not looking at where it was pointing.*

DEFENCE COUNSEL: *As far as you know did your finger touch the trigger?*

REG: *No, sir. It was a shock to me when it went off.*

The coldly planned execution by a jealous husband had now become a desperate show of devotion culminating in a tragic accident. The timing of the writing of Reg's 'suicide' note became crucial. The prosecution believed it had been written *before* he had gone to visit Violet and thus was clear evidence that the shooting was premeditated. Reg claimed that he had written the note on his return to the farm cottage *after* he had killed Violet in a garbled attempt to explain what he had done. He had not yet mustered the wherewithal to shoot himself by the time the police arrived to arrest him. The jury at Taunton were left somewhat befuddled by Reg's tale, to the extent that they were unable to agree on a verdict. The case was relisted for a second trial at the Police Courts in Bristol where, on Valentine's Day 1935, Reginald Woolmington was convicted of the murder of his wife and sentenced to death.

Reg appealed against the conviction straightaway, arguing that the verdict was wrong in law. While the Court of Appeal did not entirely dismiss this argument, it was not sufficient to sway them. Even if there had been some question over the law as it was applied in the Woolmington case, the Court of Appeal remained satisfied that no substantial miscarriage of justice had occurred. In other words, an issue with the means did not negate the end. The conviction and the capital sentence stood. But the case was about to take a further dramatic twist, which would ensure its place in legal history.

Although the Court of Appeal itself was not prepared to reverse the jury's decision, it did have some concerns about the conduct of the Bristol trial, particularly the presiding judge's interpretation of the law of murder. It is the judge's role to explain the law to the jury; the jury must then decide whether the facts of the case fit the law as it stands. The Court of Appeal therefore ordered that the case should be examined by the House of Lords. From the late 19th century until the creation of the Supreme Court in 2009, the House of Lords also operated as the ultimate appeal court in the country, in addition to its constitutional functions. From among its noble benches, several peers would be selected to sit as Law Lords in the role of judges presiding over appeals from the lower courts in all manner of cases.

Reg Woolmington's lawyers had seized on one particular statement made by the judge in his summing-up of the law to the jury. Elaborating on the law of murder to the jury, Justice Swift had outlined the law as follows:

The killing of a human being is homicide, however he may be killed, and all homicide is presumed to be malicious and murder … Once it is shown to a jury that somebody died through the act of another, that is presumed to be murder, unless the person who has been guilty of the act which causes the death can satisfy a jury that what happened was something less, something which might be alleviated, something which might be reduced to a charge of manslaughter, or was something which was accidental, or was something which could be justified.

The effect of this statement, according to Reg's defence team, was to completely misstate the law of murder to the jury and tear down one of the cornerstones of the English legal system – the presumption that someone is innocent until proven guilty. In setting out the law as he had, the judge had effectively told the jury that the onus was on Reg to show that the killing was accidental, when it was in fact for the prosecution to prove that the killing was deliberate.

As they considered the case, the House of Lords trawled through the history of homicide, going all the way back to the ancient laws of *mord* and *murdrum*, via the writings of Sir Edward Coke and his contemporaries, right up to the 20th century. What they found was that, while the parameters of the law of murder and the conventions of the evidence required by the courts may have shifted over the centuries (they quoted one Victorian lawyer who had dismissed Coke's writings as 'loose, rambling gossip'), there was one fundamental point that remained constant:

Throughout the web of the English Criminal Law one golden thread is always to be seen, that it is the duty of the prosecution to prove the prisoner's guilt ... and no attempt to whittle it down can be entertained.

The House of Lords had the same ability as the Court of Appeal to reject an appeal if they considered that there had been no overall miscarriage of justice. But they preferred to err on the side of caution in a capital case such as Woolmington's. The Law Lords considered that, had they been given the correct explanation of the law, the jury could well have reached a different verdict. While they could have substituted the murder conviction for one of manslaughter, the House of Lords chose to quash the verdict entirely. Reg Woolmington was a free man. As the decision was read out to him in the courtroom, he 'stood still as if stupefied and unaware of the meaning of what was being said'.

Back in Sherborne, Reg's parents had collected over 14,000 signatures on a petition demanding a reprieve if the conviction was upheld, but this was not required. He journeyed home to Somerset in triumph and received a welcome more befitting a returning war hero than a self-confessed killer. Mr and Mrs Woolmington held a celebratory tea party round their kitchen table, and in villages across the county the bunting was put out. In Milborne Port, Mrs Smith could only look on in horror at the festivities accompanying the release of her daughter's killer. Reginald Junior was removed from her care to be brought up in a children's home, leaving her bereft of both her daughter and her grandson. As for the baby's father, he left

Dorset shortly after his release and started a new life in Jersey under an assumed name. His son was later adopted and didn't learn of the tragic story of his birth parents until he was in middle age.

The little row of cottages was to be the scene of a further, eerily familiar, tragedy for Mrs Smith and Mrs Brine just a few years after Violet's death. In September 1942 they were summoned to the third cottage in the terrace to see their sister Mrs Budd. She was languishing in bed and told them that she had become unwell after a fall, but soon admitted the truth. Her husband Bert, who was in the Home Guard, had been cleaning his bayonet when he had accidentally stabbed Rose in the groin. Her sisters persuaded her to go to hospital, where she was found to have a perforation of the lower abdomen. Peritonitis had set in and she did not survive surgery to repair the wound.

The day after his wife died, Bert Budd's body was found in a barn, with his gun in one hand and a family photograph clutched in the other. The coroner at the inquest into the couple's deaths was sceptical that the stab wound could have been inflicted accidentally and there were local rumours that Bert had been jealous of his wife talking to soldiers stationed in the area. But the inquest closed with a verdict of accidental death for Rose, and suicide 'while the balance of [his] mind was disturbed owing to the distress caused by [her] accident' in respect of Bert.

The deaths of Rose and Bert Budd attracted little comment beyond the immediate area and even the local press didn't make the family link with the earlier murder of Violet in the adjacent cottage. But the Woolmington case would go down in history as the first time that the House of Lords had over-turned a capital sentence. The Lords' description of the 'golden thread' running through the English justice system is the defin-itive modern statement of the principle of the presumption of innocence that underpins the criminal law. In among all of the high-flown legal argument and the academic interest that the case attracted, however, there was one troubling detail that was apparently overlooked as the case progressed through the appeals process.

Woolmington's own testimony at trial was that the gun had gone off accidentally as he swung it *upwards* from underneath his coat to wave it at Violet as he threatened to shoot himself. Buried in the reports of the original trial at Taunton was the evidence of pathologist Dr Godfrey Carter. Dr Carter was adamant that the bullet had been fired into Violet's chest from a distance of about a yard, on a clear *downward* trajectory, which clearly undermined Reg's description of the accidental shooting. But the significance of this point apparently bypassed the House of Lords and the truth, it seems, has been consigned to history.

* * *

The House of Lords' decision to overturn Reg Woolmington's conviction attracted huge publicity and was front-page news up and down the country. Such cases come along but rarely and this was the highest-profile judgment by the Law Lords since they had set out the M'Naghten rules almost a century earlier. But within just two years of the Woolmington case, the highest court in the land would once again be called upon to determine the future direction of the law of homicide.

The new category of gross negligence manslaughter set out in Dr Bateman's case could be applied to a wide variety of situations where death had resulted from a serious lapse in care or judgement, rather than from a discrete criminal act. A finding of negligence requires the establishment of a duty of care owed by the killer to the victim, the breach of which has resulted in death. The duty of care intrinsic to the doctor–patient relationship made it the natural starting point for the development of a law of manslaughter based on negligence. But the next, and perhaps more important, stage was to take it beyond the obvious scenarios and see whether it could stand on its own two feet in the real world. And in the first half of the 20th century, the real world was in thrall to what is quite possibly the most accessible deadly weapon in the history of mankind – the motor car.

The first fatal car accident in England occurred on the afternoon of Monday 17 August 1896. On a visit to London's Crystal Palace to attend the Catholic League of the Cross's annual temperance fete, forty-four-year-old Bridget Driscoll was knocked down by one of the new exhibition motor cars that were ferrying excited passengers around the Palace grounds. Mrs Driscoll's daughter and her friend looked on in horror as the car zig-zagged across the track before it ploughed into her, at a speed compared to a galloping horse by one incredulous eye witness. The car drove straight over Bridget's prostrate body and crushed her skull. Mercifully, a doctor who rushed to the scene concluded that she had died almost instantly.

Testifying at the coroner's inquest the following day, Arthur Edsell, the driver of the car, confirmed that he had only been driving it for three weeks. He believed his speed at the time of the collision was around four miles per hour and he claimed that he had shouted to Mrs Driscoll to get out of the way, but she seemed 'bewildered' at the sight of the vehicle. This was disputed by other witnesses, who said that they had heard no warning from the car, nor had they seen the 'Beware of Horseless Carriages' signage apparently displayed throughout the grounds. Although it denied any responsibility for the accident, the Crystal Palace Company did offer to pay for Mrs Driscoll's funeral.

The verdict of the inquest jury was that Bridget's death had been accidental and there had been no negligence on the part of Mr Edsell as the driver. Indeed, most of the early fatalities on the road were classified as accidents and there simply weren't enough drivers or cars on the roads to make the risk that they posed a pressing concern. But the number of drivers in Britain boomed during the inter-war years, from one million in 1921 to three million by 1939. This explosion meant that road safety became an increasingly hot topic and by the early 1930s the government had enacted the first in a venerable line of Road Traffic Acts, to regulate all aspects of life on the roads, including standards of driving.

The law was now set on a collision course with bad drivers, such as the rather unpleasant Wilfred Andrews. On a June evening in 1936 Andrews was on a night shift as a driver for the Leeds Corporation transport department. At about 10.30 p.m. he was called out to assist a broken-down bus and set off in a works van. Andrews' route took him west out of the city, along the main Tong Road through the suburb of Armley. Growing impatient with the driver in front of him, Andrews accelerated and overtook the other vehicle. A short distance ahead, William Craven stepped out to cross the road on his way home to Grasmere Street, one of Armley's backstreets.

Andrews was still travelling in excess of the urban speed limit of 30 miles per hour (which had been introduced a year before) and had no chance of stopping in time. But nor did he attempt to avoid the pedestrian who had stepped into his path. The van struck Mr Craven at a speed of about 35 miles per hour and he was carried on the bonnet for a short distance before he slid off into the path of the vehicle. Andrews drove straight over him, narrowly avoided hitting a passing cyclist, and carried on into the night. Fifty-five-year-old Mr Craven was taken to Leeds General Infirmary but died of his injuries later that evening.

Meanwhile, Andrews did his best to cover his tracks as quickly as possible. He lied to colleagues when he returned to the Corporation garage, saying he had returned early from the call because he was unable to find the bus. He lied to the police when they caught up with him a couple of days later, denying being on the road in question at the time when Mr Craven was killed. He lied to the court when on trial for manslaughter, testifying that he had no recollection of the journey at all.

Nevertheless, the jury was happy to convict. Andrews was sentenced to fifteen months in prison and banned from holding a licence for life, effectively ending his career as a driver. He immediately appealed on the basis that his driving had not been grossly negligent. As this category of manslaughter was only just over a decade old and the law around motoring offences even younger, the government of the day was concerned that there be no scope for misunderstanding. The attorney general referred the appeal up to the House of Lords on the basis of its exceptional public interest.

Andrews was one of the first drivers to be prosecuted for killing someone on the roads. The case was also the first significant test of the new law of gross negligence manslaughter established in Dr Bateman's case. Causing death by dangerous or careless driving was not yet a criminal offence, and so manslaughter was the only option for prosecuting those who killed from behind the wheel. But before Dr Bateman had ushered in the concept of gross negligence manslaughter, such a prosecution was tricky. Manslaughter had historically depended on establishing an element of unlawful behaviour that led to the death. This was difficult to prove in cases that were more often than not viewed as accidents. Once gross negligence manslaughter was enshrined in the law, prosecuting the truly bad driver was much more feasible.

The idea that drivers owe a duty of care to pedestrians to avoid crashing into them was not controversial. Andrews' situation presented an ideal test case for applying the new concept for manslaughter. In reviewing Andrews' conviction, the Law Lords acknowledged the almost infinite shades of grey in the law of manslaughter. As Lord Atkin, the leading judge in Andrews' appeal case in the House of Lords, put it:

Of all crimes manslaughter appears to afford most difficulties of definition, for it concerns homicide in so many and so varying conditions.

The Lords, however, were unanimous. The principles set out in the Bateman case should apply to deaths caused by bad driving as well as any other cases involving any form of negligence that resulted in a fatality. To be convicted of manslaughter, a defendant must have been driving in a way that showed disregard for the life and safety of others. The House of Lords was satisfied that in hitting and killing Mr Craven, Andrews met this threshold. His conviction was upheld and gross negligence manslaughter was firmly embedded in English law.

In the decades after Andrews was convicted, car ownership grew exponentially, as did the number of fatalities on the road, but manslaughter convictions in driving cases remained stagnant. By the 1950s parliament was concerned that the courts were not up to dealing with drivers who killed behind the wheel. Juries were failing to grasp the legal complexities of negligence and often declined to convict drivers of manslaughter on that basis. But lesser offences, such as driving dangerously, did not adequately reflect the seriousness of cases where someone was killed by bad driving.

The government's proposed solution was to create an entirely new offence of causing death by reckless or dangerous driving, which was incorporated into the new Road Traffic Act when it became law in 1960. Although the conviction of Wilfred Andrews had set a precedent that manslaughter could and should apply when a death resulted from bad driving, juries were often reluctant to convict. Manslaughter remains an extremely serious offence, and a conviction carries a stigma that is second only to murder.

The low number of guilty verdicts in Andrews' wake was the result of twin difficulties facing juries in these cases. There were often conceptual difficulties in applying the test of gross negligence to driving cases where, after all, there is no objective standard. The jury itself will be made up of good and bad drivers who will all have a different subconscious barometer against which to judge someone else's driving. Coupled with this was a nagging doubt that, certainly in some cases, being a bad driver did not necessarily warrant a conviction for an offence as serious as manslaughter.

The introduction into English law of the new offence solved these problems. Causing death by dangerous driving did not require proof of negligence and carried a maximum sentence of only five years. Over the seventy years since its inception, the death by driving offence has remained on the statute books, augmented by more modern offences relating to deaths caused by drink or drug driving. These have largely supplanted the use of manslaughter in all but the most serious cases. A murder charge in relation to a fatal car accident remains a possibility in situations where a vehicle itself is used as the lethal weapon, for example when it is driven deliberately into pedestrians with a clear intent to kill.

*   *   *

In the space of just over a decade between the world wars, the landscape around homicide law changed dramatically, thanks in large part to some expansive interventions by the courts. While the Bateman case had created a brand new category of manslaughter, Reginald Woolmington had sought to defend himself with a version of events that was almost quaint in its conformity to the 'traditional' view of the offence; that of the deadly weapon or force, unintentionally deployed in the heat of the moment.

Negligence as a basis for a manslaughter conviction was now firmly established in law and would go on to be applied by the courts in ever-widening circumstances as the century wore on. After the end of the Victorian era, the time was ripe for such a change. In the aftermath of the Industrial Revolution, in many respects daily life had become more dangerous. But the criminal law had not kept pace with the dangers of modern life in the 20th century. A reappraisal of the law of manslaughter was long overdue.

The avalanche of medical manslaughter prosecutions predicted by the *British Medical Journal* at the time of Dr Bateman's original conviction never really came to pass. In a 2005 paper for the Medico-Legal Society, doctor and barrister Michael Powers QC found only two successful prosecutions of doctors between 1925 and 1969; it wasn't until the 1990s that such cases increased in any notable fashion, and by the early 21st century approximately a dozen doctors a year were facing manslaughter charges. Alongside this individual accountability, the past fifty years have also seen a swing towards institutional liability for deaths in a healthcare or other professional environment. This began with the health and safety legislation of the 1970s and culminated with the creation of a standalone offence of corporate manslaughter in 2007, which has placed hospital trusts in the dock alongside, or sometimes in place of, the doctors they employ.

From its beginnings in Deptford in the 1920s, gross negligence manslaughter has swelled to encompass a wide variety of professional, then personal, mistakes. The Crown Prosecution Service's current guidance on the offence recognises that it can arise in circumstances which 'are almost infinitely variable', albeit it is most frequently encountered in healthcare, custodial or workplace settings. The existence and subsequent breach of a duty of care owed by the defendant to the victim is an essential component of the negligence that must be established in order to secure a conviction. Such duties are most easily found in professional or fiduciary relationships, such as those between a doctor or patient, or an employer and employee.

But the offence has proved itself to be surprisingly adaptable to the dangers and hazardous temptations of modern life. In December 2015 Charlotte Brown was tragically killed in a speedboat crash on the River Thames in central London. She had been taken out on the river by the boat's owner Jack Shepherd. Shepherd was drunk while driving the boat at high speed; he had given Brown the wheel just before it crashed, even though she had never driven a boat before. Shepherd had also failed to pack any lifejackets. All of this was sufficient to persuade a jury that he had been grossly negligent. He skipped the country just before his trial and was convicted in his absence. He eventually returned to the UK in 2019 and was handed a six-year prison sentence for Brown's manslaughter.

As its ancestry shows, the law of homicide isn't changed by the sensational cases, the shadowy stalkers or the under-the-patio buriers. It's the mediocre GPs or the dodgy van drivers whose mistakes and misadventures really affect the way the law is made. People who happen to find themselves in horrible situations and whose reactions, while often all too human, are found wanting. The widening of the boundaries of manslaughter to include gross negligence had set homicide law on a path of review that would continue into the second half of the 20th century.

The willingness of the House of Lords to completely exonerate Reginald Woolmington when, just two years later, they upheld the conviction of Wilfred Andrews for something that would have been viewed as accidental only a couple of decades earlier pointed to another growing area of disquiet. Woolmington would have been executed had his murder conviction stood, whereas Andrews faced only a relatively short spell of incarceration and the inconvenience of being unable to drive. The Lords were not prepared to send a man to the gallows on the word of a judge who had fundamentally misunderstood one of the main tenets of the English legal system. And the wider concern that the death penalty itself was too far from infallible would continue to gnaw away. In the years after the Second World War, England would be rocked by a clutch of troubling cases that wracked the country's collective conscience and led to the most dramatic overhaul of the law of murder in its long and controversial history.

CHAPTER FIVE

DIMINISHING RETURNS AND CAPITAL GAINS

'This was the thing I thought would never come'

The Magdala Tavern stands on a curve in the rise of South Hill Park in Hampstead, along the side of Hampstead Heath Overground station. The high-rising Royal Free Hospital dominates the scene but it's still a quiet spot on a tree-lined avenue, backing onto the southern edge of the heath and over-looking yet standing back from the bustle of the South End Green parade of shops. Its name commemorates the British victory in the battle of Magdala, in what is now Ethiopia, in the 1860s. The pub itself is slightly battle-scarred by a couple of small holes in its frontage underneath a window, but the pub's role in one of the most notorious murder cases of the 20th century has secured its immortality.

On the evening of Easter Sunday 1955 Ruth Ellis gunned down her lover David Blakely on the pavement outside the Magdala and stepped into history as the last woman to be hanged in England. Her murder trial, which came on the heels of two other highly contentious cases, proved to be a catalyst for the most significant reforms to the law of murder in its history. The courts, the government and society would be forced to ask existential questions about how we categorise, criminalise and penalise those who kill.

*   *   *

Ruth Ellis's story has inspired films, books, plays and countless documentaries. She was born in Wales in 1926 but was living in London by the early 1950s. She worked as a hostess and manager in the upmarket drinking clubs that blossomed in the West End in the post-war years as the privations of war and rationing eased. In 1953 she began a relationship with David Blakely, a regular at the club that she ran. Blakely was a couple of years younger than Ellis and a few rungs higher up on the social ladder. He had been privately educated at Shrewsbury School and spent most of his time on the periphery of the motor racing scene, wealthy enough for it to be more than a hobby but not quite good enough to make it into a full-time career. A stint as a management apprentice at a hotel in Knightsbridge was short-lived, and he was largely bankrolled by his wealthy stepfather and then by Ellis's earnings from her work in the club.

Blakely was chronically feckless and faithless; during his relationship with Ellis he announced and subsequently broke off an engagement to a young woman from a wealthy Yorkshire family and carried on affairs with several women in London. But Ellis remained besotted and their tumultuous relationship endured, after a fashion, for the next two years. When Blakely failed to return home on Good Friday of 1955, Ellis's suspicions were aroused. She ran him to ground at his friends' flat in Hampstead and spent so long watching the property from the street that a neighbour invited her in for tea. Later that evening, David's friends called the police when they found Ellis trying to damage his car, which was parked on the road outside their flat. Ellis returned to her own rented room in Knightsbridge, seething.

On Easter Sunday she came back to Hampstead, this time armed with a .38 Smith & Wesson, and waited for Blakely outside the Magdala. Drinkers in the wood-panelled bar recalled seeing a bespectacled blonde, peering in through the dimpled glass of the window. When Blakely emerged from the pub with a friend, Ellis slid out of a nearby doorway and called out to him. Upon seeing her, Blakely quickly turned away and went to get into his car. To Ellis it was the final insult. She pulled out the gun and shot him four times on the pavement outside the pub. She was detained on the spot by an off-duty policeman and stood trial at the Old Bailey in June 1955. The trial lasted just two days and she was convicted of Blakely's murder on 21 June. Three weeks later she was hanged.

As can probably be guessed from its duration, the trial itself was straightforward. Ellis pleaded not guilty to murder on the basis of provocation. It was for the judge to first decide whether there was sufficient evidence of provocation for the defence to be put to the jury to consider. In Ellis's case he decided that there was not. The jury therefore only had to consider whether or not she was guilty of murder – there was no option to render the lesser verdict of manslaughter. And on the murder charge there was little room for doubt, reasonable or otherwise. There was no dispute that she had shot Blakely. In response to the prosecution's question as to what she had meant to do at the time that she fired the gun, Ellis simply stated, 'It's obvious. When I shot him, I intended to kill him.'

The venerable defence of provocation was not designed to help the likes of Ruth Ellis. Since its heyday in the Georgian era, the concept of provocation had been progressively narrowed by the courts. The law as it stood in 1955 favoured the hot-tempered who acted before thinking but also required some form of positive action by the deceased that had precipitated the killing. The provocation defence had last come before the courts five years before Ellis's shooting of Blakely, in a case that had some unsettling parallels with her own.

Nineteen-year-old Renee Duffy lived with her husband George and their baby son in the Cheetham district of Manchester. The couple had been married for eighteen months and were sharing their flat with Renee's grandmother, which undoubtedly put a strain on marital relations. On the evening of 7 December 1948 George and his wife argued violently when she told him that she wanted to leave. He grabbed Renee's arm and twisted it up behind her back; she managed to break free and ran out of the room. A short while later, Renee's grandmother heard the front door of the flat slam shut. She went into the couple's bedroom and found George lying unconscious on the bed. His head was covered in gaping wounds and a hatchet lay on top of the eiderdown next to him. Blood was splashed up the walls. Despite the best attempts of doctors at the local hospital, George died of his injuries the following day.

On trial for his murder, Renee claimed that George was frequently violent towards her, and this story was supported by her sister, who testified that she had witnessed her bruises and black eyes on several occasions. But the jury rejected Renee's defence of provocation and convicted her of murder, albeit with a strong recommendation to mercy. Sentencing her to death, the judge acknowledged that she had been the victim of a 'long system of cruelty and beastliness', but his hands were tied. Renee was remanded at Strangeways prison to await her fate.

The image of the teenage wife and mother, doomed to die after being pushed to the edge by her violent husband, struck a chord with the public. While she languished in jail, Renee garnered offers of support from some unexpected quarters. The *Aberdeen Press* ran a story about George Bouche, a 'thin and lonely thirty-three-year-old Paris factory worker' who had heard of Mrs Duffy's plight and was petitioning the British embassy in Paris for a reprieve, so that he could marry Renee upon her release. And in a proposal as patronisingly bizarre as it was chivalrous, a British soldier offered to take her place on the gallows. Warrant Officer Reed-Thomson proclaimed to newspapers that he had a 'tremendous admiration for the women of this country [and] whenever I have heard a word against our women I have always been the first to take up arms in their defence'. Reed-Thomson considered that the best way to show his gratitude to all of womankind was to take Renee Duffy's punishment himself. The reaction of his wife – to whom he had been married for a decade – to his offer was not recorded.

A bid to overturn the murder conviction at the Court of Appeal was unsuccessful. The judges placed considerable weight on Renee's actions in leaving the room, finding the hatchet and attacking George as he was lying down, all of which ran counter to the usual concept of provocation. But all was not lost. The day after the Court of Appeal upheld the murder conviction, Home Secretary James Chuter Ede announced a reprieve. The death sentence was commuted and Renee was sent to Aylesbury Prison.

In November 1951, after serving just over two and a half years, she was released. The sentence was an astonishingly light one, given the savagery of George's death, and was a reflection of the enormous amount of public sympathy for Renee. But the tragedy of the Duffys typified the inherent contradictions in cases involving allegations of provocation. In the aftermath of Renee's reprieve, George's father wrote to the *Manchester Evening News* to dispute the portrayal of his son in the papers and in court as a violent wife-beater. His politely furious letter made the point that every story has two sides, and in his son's case only one side lived to tell the tale.

* * *

The test that the court had applied in the Duffy case was endorsed by the Court of Appeal as a 'classic' definition of provocation, and so this remained the legal threshold that Ruth Ellis had to reach in order to avoid a murder conviction five years later:

Provocation is some act, or series of acts, done by the dead man to the accused, which would cause in any reasonable person, and actually causes in the accused, a sudden and temporary loss of self-control, rendering the accused so subject to passion as to make him or her for the moment not master of his mind.

It was difficult to show what this could have been on the part of Blakely. Indeed, what had irked Ellis was the very fact that he had entirely absented himself for the two days prior to the killing and had avoided even speaking to her when she telephoned his friends' house. The judge at her trial was clear; while Ellis may well have lost self-control, there was nothing sudden or temporary about it. In her own evidence she had described her increasingly frantic sorties to Hampstead over the Easter weekend as the actions of 'a typical jealous woman', and the law has always been resistant to any suggestion that jealousy could amount to a defence to murder.

Part of the problem that Ellis faced was that there was not one instance of provocative behaviour from Blakely; there were many. Almost from the outset the relationship had been fraught, passionate and problematic in equal measure. Both parties were prone to jealous rages, but Blakely's became increasingly violent as time wore on. Friends had often seen Ellis covered in bruises and some had witnessed Blakely beating her at first hand.

About a month before she shot him, Ellis discovered she was pregnant. She had already aborted one pregnancy earlier in the relationship, and ten days before the killing Blakely had punched her in the stomach so hard that she miscarried. She was bedridden for a week but appeared to have forgiven him. This was why she had taken his disappearing act over the Easter weekend so hard. But the court was unmoved. However reprehensible Blakely's conduct had been over the course of their affair, in the eyes of the law he had not provoked Ellis into killing him. The verdict was one of murder and the only sentence was death. Like Renee Duffy, the behaviour of Ellis's victim was not considered sufficient to reduce her crime to manslaughter; unlike Renee, the jury in Ellis's case made no recommendation of clemency.

On paper, it is difficult to argue with the legal basis of Ruth Ellis's conviction. Her shooting of Blakely was brutal – a post-mortem revealed that all of the shots had been fired into his back and at least two of the bullets struck him while he was already prostrate on the pavement. Her own statement at the trial that she had shot to kill effectively signed her death warrant. But the case was a missed opportunity. Over the two hundred or so years since the provocation defence had emerged in the 1700s, its scope had grown progressively narrower and more exacting. The threshold that Ruth Ellis had to satisfy was almost insurmountable compared with the wide categories pronounced by the court at Mawgridge's trial at the beginning of the 18th century. As Thomas Grant QC observed in his book *Court Number One*:

> *It would take much longer before the law of provocation adapted itself, albeit imperfectly, to the special position of women who, having been abused over a protracted period,*

*kill their partner. Over all these changes, the ghost of Ruth
Ellis seems to hover.*

Fifty thousand people signed a petition appealing for her death
sentence to be commuted to life imprisonment and the *Daily
Mirror* ran a spirited campaign in support of clemency. All of
this was in vain, and on 13 July 1955 Ruth Ellis was hanged
by executioner Albert Pierrepoint at Holloway Prison while
several hundred people held a vigil outside. The legal implications of her case are often overshadowed by contemporary
fascination with the world that she inhabited.

Ellis and Blakely's tragic story took place against a backdrop
of saloon bars and mansion flats, in a world where it was never
too early for a drink and serious domestic abuse was brushed
off as 'knocking her about'. By ignoring the role that Blakely's
behaviour had played in the relationship and the build-up to
their fateful encounter outside the Magdala, the court gave rise
to one particularly sad irony that is often overlooked in
accounts of the case. Imagine for a moment that the roles had
been reversed; that Blakely had stepped out of the pub, flown
into a rage when he saw Ellis waiting for him and had fatally
attacked her. It is certainly possible that, in the light of her
actions over the weekend – stalking him round Hampstead,
smashing his car, harassing his friends – a 1950s jury would
have acquitted Blakely of murder on the grounds of Ellis's
provocation.

* * *

Two years before he sent Ruth Ellis down into the long drop, Pierrepoint also presided over the execution of nineteen-year-old Derek Bentley, amid a similar groundswell of public unease. On 2 November 1952 Bentley had gone out for the evening with his friend Christopher Craig. Craig was three years Bentley's junior and believed to be a bad influence by Bentley's family. The pair were walking along Tamworth Road in Croydon looking for somewhere to burgle when they came across Barlow and Parker's confectionery warehouse. They scaled its fence and shinned up a drainpipe onto the warehouse roof to try to find a way in. But the lads' shifty behaviour caught the attention of a resident who lived opposite, and he went to the nearest phone box to call the police.

On arrival, one police officer, DC Frederick Fairfax, scaled the roof while others surveyed from the street. Having cornered them on the roof, DC Fairfax managed to grab hold of Bentley, but Craig backed off and pulled a gun from his coat pocket. He fired at Fairfax, wounding him in the shoulder. PC Sidney Miles had arrived on the scene a short while earlier. He was aged forty-two and was well known in the local area. He had received medals for long service and good conduct, and doubtless also deserved one for gallantry. Miles and a group of other officers were waiting at the top of the stairwell to come to the aid of DC Fairfax. With an apparent lull in the shooting from Craig, the officers decided to make a move and PC Miles led their charge.

As he stepped out of the stairwell door onto the roof, Craig fired again. PC Miles was hit straight between the eyes and died instantly. In the aftermath, Bentley remained with Fairfax but Craig jumped from the roof, breaking his back when he landed. The accounts of the events on the rooftop given by the other police officers on the scene varied in several respects, but in one they were remarkably consistent. Immediately before Craig had started shooting at Fairfax, each of the officers reported hearing Bentley shout, 'Let him have it, Chris.'

At sixteen, Craig was old enough to be criminally responsible for the killing but too young to face the death penalty. And although he had not fired the fatal shot or even laid a finger on the murder weapon, under the law of joint enterprise Bentley found himself on trial for murder alongside his friend – but he was old enough to be hanged if convicted. The two faced different legal hurdles, which, in combination, would prove fatal for only one of them. Craig denied murder and claimed that he fired the gun indiscriminately to scare the police into backing off, with no intention to kill. This seemed a stretch, given his vituperative comment to the officers when he was arrested, that he 'wished [he'd] killed the fucking lot'.

The prosecution's case against Craig was grounded in the legal doctrine of constructive malice. This held that a defendant who intends to commit one crime (here, burglary of the warehouse) and then kills in the course of committing that crime is in effect automatically guilty of murder for the killing. The malicious intention for the theft is transferred across to the killing, to make it murder. The guilt of one crime is constructed out of the intention to commit the other. The prosecution did not need to prove that Craig intended to kill PC Miles, only that he had intended to commit the robbery that resulted in the fatal shooting. Craig's defence was a non-starter and this would ultimately seal his friend's fate as well.

Bentley's responsibility for the killing rested on a different, but no less controversial, aspect of the criminal law, that of joint enterprise. For centuries, the law has treated those who aid, abet, counsel or procure the commission of a criminal offence by another in exactly the same manner as the principal offender. At Bentley's trial the prosecution sought to prove that Bentley and Craig had gone out that evening with an agreed plan to both break into the warehouse and defend themselves with violence, including gunfire from the weapon carried by Craig, against anyone who tried to stop them. If Bentley had signed up to the entire escapade, in the eyes of the law he was as guilty as Craig for its eventual bloody outcome. Craig's conviction for murder was pivotal to this. If he were only found guilty of manslaughter on the basis that the killing was accidental, then there could have been no joint plan made in advance to which Bentley was a party.

Bentley's participation in the scheme was, in the prosecution's case, clearly demonstrated by his shout to Craig to 'let him have it'. The Crown's case against Bentley was based almost entirely on two hotly disputed points: what he meant when he said 'let him have it' and at what point he knew that Craig was armed. Bentley claimed he did not know that Craig was carrying the gun until he pulled it on DC Fairfax on the roof. If he was unaware of the gun until that point, he could not have agreed to a joint enterprise on the terms claimed by the prosecution.

As to the now infamous five-word phrase, its meaning has been debated ever since Bentley stood in the dock. Did it signal his withdrawal from the joint enterprise, an acceptance that the game was up and an instruction to Craig to drop the weapon? Or was it an incitement to his accomplice to pursue their plan to its ultimate conclusion and shoot the police officers? For his part, Bentley denied even uttering the phrase, and Craig backed him up in the witness box.

In an odd coincidence, the phrase and the circumstances of the case as a whole bore several uncanny resemblances to a trial that had taken place just over a decade earlier. A pair of burglars, William Appleby and Vincent Ostler, had been caught by police trying to break into a local Co-operative store in the village of Coxhoe, County Durham. Appleby allegedly shouted, 'Let him have it' just before Ostler proceeded to shoot and kill PC William Shiell. Both were convicted of murder and executed at Durham Prison in July 1940. Bentley's lawyers were loath to risk losing the sympathy of the jury by impugning the credibility of the police officers in court, but after the trial there was no shortage of theorising that the use of the phrase in the officers' statements was more than coincidental and was deployed as a tested method to secure a double conviction.

After a trial lasting two days, on 11 December 1952 both Craig and Bentley were convicted of murder. The jury made a recommendation of mercy for Bentley but this fell on deaf ears. He appealed unsuccessfully and a plea to the home secretary for a reprieve from the hangman was rejected. He was executed at Wandsworth Prison on 28 January 1953, amid similar scenes to those that accompanied Ruth Ellis's hanging two years later.

There were serious and uncomfortable questions over Bentley's ability to mentally process and understand what had happened to him. He had bounced around a succession of approved schools following some petty offending as an adolescent and had seen a barrage of educational psychologists over his formative years. At the time of the killing, he suffered from epilepsy, was unable to read or write, had an IQ of 77, and a mental age assessed as being between eleven and twelve. Regardless, he was found fit to stand trial and the medical evidence carried little weight either in court or when the sentence was referred to the home secretary to consider whether a reprieve should be granted. Unfortunately for Bentley, the debate around the entire question of the death penalty was raging and the issue of a reprieve arose at a crossroads where the political and the legal collided head on.

*　　*　　*

The public disquiet about the executions of Bentley and Ellis did not die down. At the start of the decade, confidence in the efficacy and accuracy of capital punishment had been shaken by the hanging of Timothy Evans, another of Pierrepoint's jobs. Evans was executed in March 1950 for the murder of his infant daughter at his home at 10 Rillington Place, west London. Evans was posthumously exonerated when three years later his neighbour John Christie confessed to eight murders at the house, including those of Evans's wife and daughter. By the time that Ruth Ellis was hanged in 1955, the three cases had become inextricably linked in the popular imagination – the crowds gathered outside Holloway the day before her execution reportedly chanted, 'Evans! Bentley! Ellis!'

The story of capital punishment in England had run in largely parallel lines to that of murder down the centuries. Like murder, hanging was an Anglo-Saxon invention and replaced the favoured method of the early Britons, boiling in oil. Before that, the Romans had generally preferred beheading; this practice survived into the 18th century but was reserved for noblemen and peers of the realm, for whom, as we have seen, a swift decapitation was considered more fitting and less vulgar than hanging like a common criminal. This was until the practice came to an end with the hanging of Earl Ferrers for murder in 1760.

As well as class, there were other distinctions applied in the exercise of the law's ultimate sanction. Women were often put to death by drowning or burning, particularly for offences such as witchcraft or adultery. The execution of seafaring criminals usually took place as close to a body of water as possible, derived from the old custom that a criminal should be hanged at or as near as possible to the scene of their crime. The notorious Execution Dock on the bank of the Thames at Wapping was therefore the site of hundreds of hangings during the Georgian era. The bodies were originally left submerged until they had rotted completely and so the wrongdoers had been reclaimed by the sea, but gradually this was replaced by a habit of recovering the bodies after three tides had washed over them. A replica noose and gibbet still stand on the foreshore in front of the Prospect of Whitby pub in Wapping, to commemorate the area's grisly past.

In practical terms, murder had been the only capital offence in England since the 1840s, but the death penalty for crimes

other than murder was not formally abolished until 1861.*
Since that time, any question of reform of the law of murder
had been inextricably bound up with the continued existence
of the death penalty itself. The stirrings of an abolition move-
ment had first begun in the early 19th century, as a reaction to
the Bloody Code. The first Royal Commission on Capital
Punishment was convened in the 1860s, with a remit to:

> inquire into the Provisions and Operation of the Laws now
> in force in the United Kingdom, under and by virtue of
> which the Punishment of Death may be inflicted upon
> persons convicted of certain crimes, and also into the manner
> in which Capital Sentences are carried into execution, and to
> report whether any, and if any what alteration is desirable in
> such Laws, or any of them, or in the manner in which such
> sentences are carried into execution.

The Commission's report of 1866 made two ground-breaking
recommendations. They proposed a two-tier classification for
murder, to differentiate between those cases involving deliberate killings and those resulting from provocation but lacking in
premeditation. The Commission based their proposal on the
degrees of murder that had recently been adopted in some parts
of the United States. Their second conclusion was that the
unedifying carnival of public executions, a feature of British life
for hundreds of years, should be brought to an end. The

---

* The death penalty did remain in force for high treason until the
twentieth century, but cases were rare.

supposed deterrent effects of the practice could no longer be said to outweigh the corrosive influence of reducing the ending of a human life to a pantomime, in the view of the Commission.

The scrapping of public executions had been mooted before but, again, issues of class had raised their head. Opponents of the move believed that such secret executions would give the establishment opportunity to renege on the sentence, particularly if a prisoner was from the upper echelons of society. If the execution was public, at least everybody could be satisfied that it had been carried out. However, the government were persuaded by the Commission's stance, although this was to be the only one of their proposals to be adopted. The last public execution took place in May 1868. From that time, all capital sentences were carried out within the prison precincts, with only a select few people admitted to spectate.

Buoyed by the partial success of the Commission's approach, several MPs during the second half of the Victorian era would try to advance the abolitionists' cause by putting forward Private Members' Bills to legislate for varying degrees of murder, reform of the law on provocation or even abolition of the death penalty entirely. All were defeated. In 1882 Home Secretary Sir William Harcourt proposed a law to restrict capital punishment to murders that involved a clear and wilful intent to kill, but the issue was kicked into the long grass by parliament, where it would remain for the next half a century.

By the eve of the Second World War, the House of Commons was toying with the idea of an experimental period of abolition, and this gained some traction before the business of Westminster was halted by the conflict. When the question was resurrected after 1945, there was still a reasonable level of support for it in parliament but the government persuaded itself that public opinion still remained in support of hanging. A further Royal Commission began consulting on the question of capital punishment in 1948, with the executions of Evans and Bentley intruding upon its deliberations. When it issued its report shortly after Bentley's hanging in 1953, the tide of public opinion had well and truly turned, and by the time of the outcry at Ruth Ellis's conviction, it was clear that the issue could be ducked no longer. Two years later, the Homicide Act 1957 came into force.

The Act's provisions represented the most significant reforms to the law of murder in history. The most revolutionary aspect was the introduction of three partial defences to murder. In cases where there was a clear intention to kill, which would make a murder conviction an apparent inevitability, the successful argument of one of these defences would reduce the offence to manslaughter. The first and most revolutionary was diminished responsibility. This is the younger cousin of the insanity defence and applies only to the offence of murder. Its introduction was a belated recognition of the host of mental conditions or pressures that can drive someone's behaviour but that stop short of meeting the test for insanity under the M'Naghten rules.

To succeed with a diminished responsibility defence, the defendant must prove that they were suffering from an 'abnormality of mind' that substantially impaired their mental capacity to control their actions. Both insanity and diminished responsibility require an underlying medical condition to be established, but the test for the latter is much more subjective. Unlike the insanity defence, diminished responsibility does not raise any questions as to the killer's understanding of the nature of their actions; it focuses instead on the effect of their mental state on their decision to kill.

Defence number two was provocation. Although this had been recognised as a defence by the courts for centuries, the Homicide Act was the first time it had been formally set out in statute. It also widened the definition of provocation set out in Renee Duffy's case (which itself was derived from the rules established back in the 1700s at John Mawgridge's trial) by including the words, as well as the actions, of the deceased in the factors that could be considered by the jury. A killer who had been provoked into losing self-control, by words or actions, could now claim the defence provided that a hypothetical 'reasonable man' would have reacted in the same lethal way in the face of the provocation.

Finally, the Act confirmed that a person was guilty of manslaughter instead of murder if they killed another in furtherance of a suicide pact and then failed to see it through themselves. This seems an odd priority but reflected a hangover of legal attitudes to suicide in the 18th and 19th centuries. Until 1879 suicide was classed as 'self-murder', and attempting suicide unsuccessfully remained a criminal offence until the 1920s.

The Act also restricted the types of murder for which the death sentence would apply. Since the Offences Against the Person Act 1861, capital punishment in the UK had been almost exclusively restricted to murder. Under the new legislation, only certain categories of murder would attract the death penalty, namely killing a police officer or prison officer, killing in the course of a theft or to resist arrest, and deaths caused by firearms or explosives. Multiple murderers, who had either been convicted previously or charged with more than one killing at a time, would also continue to face the death penalty for subsequent killings. Those convicted of murder in any other circumstances would from this point onwards be sentenced to life imprisonment. The Act also amended the law to make another case like Derek Bentley's impossible. In joint enterprise cases, a charge of capital murder could now only be applied to the person who had actually inflicted the lethal force on the victim. The other participant, while still liable to be convicted of murder, could not face the death penalty.

The Homicide Act was a rather muddled attempt to answer the questions posed by three of the most troubling cases of the era. How could Derek Bentley hang for a killing when someone else had pulled the trigger? Why was the abuse suffered by Ruth Ellis at the hands of her victim ignored at her trial? And what faith could be placed in a justice system that had executed the innocent Timothy Evans for the Rillington Place murders while John Christie remained at large for another three years? At the same time, it had to try to keep those on both sides of the capital punishment debate satisfied. Despite the public outcry at the three executions, the government was not yet persuaded that the man in the street was crying out for full abolition. While it had strenuously resisted introducing any form of degree system for murder, the creation of a new category of capital murder in effect created a top tier of murder cases, one based on the nature of the killing rather than the killer's intention.

But it was the introduction of the concept of diminished responsibility that was revolutionary in British law, which had hitherto only recognised cases of full-blown insanity within the M'Naghten rules as being sufficient to give an excuse for murder. Working out how to apply this new piece of law would exercise the courts significantly over the next few years and its first test would come a few short years later, in one of the most horrific cases the country had seen in a generation.

*   *   *

Sydney Stephanie Baird was born in the sleepy Cotswolds village of Bishop's Cleeve. In 1958, at the age of twenty-eight, she moved north to the bright lights of Birmingham to pursue her career as a clerk and typist. In August the following year she moved from her temporary digs to stay at the YWCA in Wheeley's Road in the affluent Edgbaston area of the city. The hostel was housed in a grand mansion built in 1820 by Joseph Sturge, one of those philanthropic industrialists that the big manufacturing cities of the 19th century churned out on a conveyor belt. Sturge's company made industrial chemicals and, like his neighbours the Cadburys, he was a Quaker. The link continued when the heir to the Cadbury business acquired the house in 1901. When he moved out in the late 1920s he donated the property to the YWCA.

In the months since Baird moved into the hostel there was a sense of unease among the residents. Women reported being watched in their rooms and there had been sightings of a prowler in the hostel's still extensive grounds. On the early evening of 23 December 1959 Baird was getting ready to go home to Bishop's Cleeve for the Christmas holidays. Many of her fellow residents had already left for Christmas and those that remained were bustling about the hostel preparing to do so. She had finished work early and had her hair done at a nearby salon in the afternoon. Baird's wing of the hostel was virtually deserted. Opening her bedroom door to head down the corridor to the bathroom, she was startled by a man standing directly outside her door. He told her that he was looking for someone who lived at the hostel and she offered to fetch the warden to help. The man hesitated and then clamped his hands around her neck, pushing her back into the room.

At around 7.30 p.m. Margaret Brown was down in the laundry sorting out her clothes to pack for her trip home to Scotland. Suddenly an intruder loomed out of the basement shadows, swinging something at her head. Margaret's scream stopped him in his tracks and he fled. When the police arrived a short time later they began scouring the house and grounds for her assailant. All seemed in order until they tried the door of Baird's room. It was locked from the inside and she did not respond to their calls. They forced the door open and found her body lying on the floor, alongside her single bed. She had been sexually assaulted, mutilated and decapitated. The cause of death was strangulation. An ordinary table knife was found in the room, bloodstained and broken in two. On top of the wardrobe the police found an envelope on which was written, 'This was the thing I thought would never come.'

The case sparked an immediate national manhunt. The most promising lead came from the many passengers on the number 8 bus, who reported seeing a man board the bus near the YWCA shortly after the time that Margaret Brown had scared away the attacker in the laundry. The man was described as being in his twenties, of average height, thickset, with curly fair hair and, crucially, covered in blood. In the week after the killing, the story was headline news across the country. Any male with convictions for violence against women was questioned and Birmingham Police consulted with Scotland Yard's murder squad. The local newspaper, the *Birmingham Mail*, likened the killer to Jack the Ripper and implored further witnesses to come forward, with the promise of a £1,000 reward from an anonymous donor. Joe Mercer, the manager of the local Aston Villa football club, had to deny reports that the team had cancelled an upcoming training trip to Bournemouth because players were nervous about leaving their wives home alone in the city.

Despite all of this, by the New Year of 1960 the trail had gone cold. The bloodstained man on the bus had not been traced, but the police continued their dogged pursuit. Just over a month after Baird's death a constable was making door-to-door inquiries in Islington Row, a few hundred yards round the corner from Wheeley's Road. The occupant of one house revealed that Patrick Byrne, a jobbing labourer, had been lodging there for a few months but had left abruptly on Christmas Eve to return to his family home in Warrington. Immediately suspicious, West Midlands Police and their colleagues in the north-west traced Byrne to an address in Warrington. When confronted by local detectives, Byrne promptly confessed to

Vera Effigies Viri clariſ EDOARDI COKE
Equitis aurati nuper Capitalis Iuſticiarij
ad Placita coram Rege tenenda aſſignati

R:White ſculpſit

Portrait of Sir Edward Coke (1552–1634), jurist and
author of *The Institutes of the Laws of England*.

Contemporary engravings of Mary Ashford and her
alleged assailant Abraham Thornton.

The 'Brainless Brothers', who formerly crowned the gateway to Bethlem
Hospital in Moorfields. They are now on permanent display in the hospital's
Museum of the Mind in its current location in Beckenham.

Daniel M'Naghten, photographed in around 1856 during his time as a patient at Bedlam's Southwark site.

Depiction of the stabbing of William Terriss in *The Illustrated Police News*, which specialised in lurid and sensational accounts of violent crimes.

The lifeboat in which Richard Parker met his end
at the hands of his hungry crewmates. It was put on
display in Falmouth.

The Old Custom House in Falmouth today. This is where
Dudley, Stephens and Brooks told their grisly tale to
Mr Cheeseman and Sergeant Laverty in 1884.

ALLEGED NEGLECT.

GRAVE CHARGE AGAINST A DOCTOR.

Dr. Percy Bateman, of New Cross-road, was charged at Greenwich on Friday with the manslaughter of Mrs. Mary Ann Harding (38), of Norfolk House, Deptford.

He attended the woman in her confinement, and his treatment was alleged to have been so rough that an organ was torn away from its attachment, and Sir Bernard Spilsbury stated that only an operation could have saved her life, and neglect to carry that out was a serious neglect of duty.

The woman's death, he said, was the direct result of the injuries inflicted and failure to take proper steps rendered it inevitable.

Defendant was committed for trial, bail being allowed.

Dr. Percy Bateman.

Reginald Woolmington

The *Western Mail*'s report on the manslaughter prosecution against Dr Percy Bateman.

Reginald Woolmington pictured in the *Liverpool Echo*'s 'Strange Stories' column, which reviewed the case in the 1950s.

The Magdala Tavern, where Ruth Ellis shot David Blakely, seen in 2020. The tiles beneath the windows in the middle of the building are marked with 'bullet holes', which were actually drilled into the wall in the 1980s.

Stephanie Baird pictured in the *Birmingham Mail*,
alongside a policeman putting up a poster appealing for
information on her murder.

Croydon teenager Derek Bentley, who
was executed for murder under the law
of joint enterprise in 1953.

Cyril Church is taken into custody
by police investigating the murder
of Sylvia Nott.

Kiranjit Ahluwalia (*left*) and her supporters celebrate the quashing of her conviction for the murder of her husband Deepak outside court in 1992.

Protesters march through Cardiff after the murder convictions of Reginald Hancock and Russell Shankland in 1986.

The solitary Yew Tree Farm, near Stourbridge, stood derelict for many years after paperboy Carl Bridgewater was murdered there in 1978. The property has since been renovated.

Rescue and salvage workers stand on top of the wreck of the
MS *Herald of Free Enterprise* in Zeebrugge harbour. The ship's
open bow doors, which led to the ferry capsizing,
can be clearly seen.

It was this question of control that was to prove key to Byrne's defence, leading to the first detailed guidance on how the courts should apply the new concept of diminished responsibility. The evidence of Byrne's doctors was insufficient to give him an insanity defence as per the M'Naghten rules, which required only that he understood what he was doing and that it was wrong in order to be adjudged sane. There was no question that he knew what he had done; his confession to Warrington Police was thorough and almost enthusiastic. As for his comprehension of the wrongness of his actions, there could be no doubt. He had fled the city immediately after killing Baird. The issue that the all-male jury had to determine was whether Byrne's tendencies were an abnormality of mind that had substantially impaired his mental responsibility for the killing. They didn't need to deliberate for long. The trial lasted just a day, and on 24 March 1960 Byrne was convicted of the murder of Stephanie Baird and sentenced to life.

Byrne immediately launched an appeal, hoping to substitute the murder conviction for one of manslaughter and so reduce the prison sentence. This was to be one of the first cases where the courts would have to consider in detail the meaning of diminished responsibility and the circumstances in which it could be established. That persistent, intrusive fantasies about raping, killing and mutilating young women were an abnormality of the mind was not seriously in doubt. It was how Byrne had policed these desires that was the key question. The distinction had to be drawn between an impulse that he could not resist and one that he did not resist.

On this question the Court of Appeal gave him the generous benefit of some considerable doubt. They found that 'the evidence of the revolting circumstances of the killing and the subsequent mutilations ... pointed ... plainly, to the conclusion that the accused was what would be described in ordinary language as on the border-line of insanity or partially insane'. On this basis, the court decided that Byrne was indeed suffering from diminished responsibility and the verdict of murder was changed to one of manslaughter. However, they did not interfere with the life sentence.

The case is not an easy one to reconcile with the new law and the convictions that preceded it. Byrne had been able enough to resist his impulses on previous occasions, when he had caught other residents unawares in their rooms. Luckily for Margaret Brown, he succeeded in controlling his violent urges quickly when she fought back against his attack in the laundry. Such was the ferocity of the attack on Baird, it seems improbable that it was the first that Byrne had committed. One would have expected other, perhaps less brutal assaults, as his urges built into a frenzy towards this ultimate, horrific act. Certainly his note, found at the scene, suggested that the killing was a cumulative, rather than isolated, act. But if there were previous victims, they have never been linked to Byrne and the cases still moulder in West Midlands Police's archives of unsolved crimes. Edgbaston remains one of Birmingham's well-to-do suburbs but the YWCA has long gone. In 1968 it was demolished and replaced by a block of flats.

*   *   *

Despite the media frenzy surrounding the killing of Stephanie Baird, Byrne quickly faded from view after his appeal, failing to enter the public consciousness in the way that both Derek Bentley and Ruth Ellis did, as they gained a notoriety not seen in many post-war killers other than serial murderers like John Christie. The controversies over their convictions continued to rage long after their executions, fuelled by a fervent appetite for information about them and their crimes.

Miranda Richardson portrayed Ellis in *Dance with a Stranger*, director Mike Newell's 1985 retelling of the case, alongside Rupert Everett as Blakely and Ian Holm as Desmond Cussen, Ellis's former lover and Blakely's rival for her affections. The film is a cut above the usual true crime fare, thanks to a classy cast and careful reconstruction of the brittle, dusty glamour of the period, captured in fringed lampshades and bottles of Pernod on glass shelves. The film ends just after Ellis has fired her last bullet into Blakely and is standing, dazed, in the road outside the Magdala.

Richard Attenborough played John Christie in the 1971 film *10 Rillington Place*, shot on location in the Ladbroke Grove cul-de-sac where the murders took place. Elvis Costello's 1989 album *Spike* features the song 'Let Him Dangle', telling Derek Bentley's story in a post-punk folk ballad that combines the lyrics of a Victorian broadside with the bassline of 'Minnie the Moocher', and in 1991 actor Christopher Eccleston made his big-screen debut as Bentley in the film *Let Him Have It*. The film's most powerful scene comes near the climax, when Craig and Bentley are taken down to the cells at the Old Bailey following sentencing. The two share a look of wordless horror that one of them is going to hang for a crime that the other committed.

The cases cast long shadows down the latter part of the 20th century. In 1993 Bentley's family obtained a royal pardon in respect of his capital sentence from then Home Secretary Michael Howard. His murder conviction remained extant, however, until 1998, when the case was belatedly referred to the Court of Appeal for a second time by the Criminal Cases Review Commission. The Appeal Judges concluded that the approach of the trial judge in summarising the case to the jury was flawed and unduly prejudicial to Bentley in particular. Overturning Bentley's murder conviction almost fifty years after the fact, the Court of Appeal's verdict on the judicial conduct of the original trial was damning:

> In our judgment, far from encouraging the jury to approach the case in a calm frame of mind, the trial judge's summing up … had exactly the opposite effect. We cannot read these passages [of the trial transcript] as other than a highly rhetorical and strongly worded denunciation of both defendants and of their defences. The language used was not that of a judge but of an advocate … Such a direction by such a judge must have in our view have driven the jury to conclude that they had little choice but to convict … In our judgment the summing up in this case was such as to deny [Bentley] that fair trial which is the birthright of every British citizen.

Ruth Ellis's family also sought to redress the balance, and in 2003 they also secured a retrospective referral to the Court of Appeal. In 1955 Ruth herself had deliberately chosen not to appeal against her conviction. In the following decades her public image had undergone something of a shift, and she had begun to shed the brassy blonde stereotype that had been such a feature of the contemporary press coverage of her trial, as more information had emerged about her troubled early life and the abuse she had suffered at the hands of Blakely. The role that Desmond Cussen had played in the shooting also came under further scrutiny.

Up until the eve of her execution, Ellis had taken sole responsibility for the shooting, but at the eleventh hour she made a statement to her solicitor that Cussen had given her the murder weapon, taught her how to fire it and driven her to Hampstead to find Blakely on that fateful Sunday evening. Had this been known at the time of the trial, Cussen would most likely have been in the dock alongside Ellis, charged with murder under the same law of joint enterprise that had resulted in Derek Bentley's conviction. Her new statement was sent to Home Secretary Gwilym Lloyd-George in a last-ditch appeal for clemency, but to no avail.

Ellis was to fare no better from the justice system in the 21st century, and her belated appeal was rejected by the Court of Appeal. The Court remained satisfied that the conviction was correctly decided on the basis of the law on provocation as it stood at the time of the murder, and its judgment concluded with a stinging rebuke about the cost and court time consumed by appeals in historic cases. But in spite of the court's criticism, the public interest in the cases shows no sign of waning nearly seventy years on.

In 2016 the BBC broadcast a new adaptation of the Rillington Place story, starring Tim Roth and Jodie Comer. A few months earlier, the Museum of London staged an exhibition called 'The Crime Museum Uncovered'. In conjunction with Scotland Yard, the museum showcased choice artefacts from the Met's semi-mythic archives of crime, better known as its 'Black Museum'. The show ran for seven months and was a blockbuster. Among the exhibits on display were the arrest warrant issued for Edwardian wife-killer Dr Crippen, Ronnie Kray's Mauser handgun and the sawn-off .455 Eley revolver with which Christopher Craig shot PC Miles. The star of the show, chosen to grace the cover of the exhibition guidebook and the posters that advertised it across the city, was the Smith & Wesson revolver used by Ruth Ellis to shoot David Blakely one Sunday evening in the spring of 1955.

* * *

Over a period of just five years in the aftermath of the Second World War, the country had been rocked by three controversial cases that proved to be the tipping point in the quest for reform of the law of murder. The effect of these reforms was to create a two-tier classification of murder, with 'capital' murders being distinguished by the nature of the act, rather than the intention behind it.

But this left the uncomfortable result that Bentley and Ellis were executed as murderers when, a few short years later, Patrick Byrne got away with manslaughter in much more horrific circumstances. Hand in hand with the changes to homicide law came the question of the death penalty; of how, when and even if it should still be applied in Britain in the 20th century. While the Homicide Act represented a hesitant response to the question of abolition, in effect it sounded the death knell for capital punishment. When the question came before MPs again in 1965, they had swung round in support and the Murder (Abolition of the Death Penalty) Act became law, its five-year suspension of capital punishment being made final in 1969. With the threat of such tragic consequences if they erred now lifted, the courts would proceed to wrestle with the question of where the fault lines between murder and manslaughter should lie and who was truly deserving of the label of murderer.

CHAPTER SIX

HIRAETH

'... swiftly and with a jet-like roar ...'

As the stars glittered down on the Moyka River in St Petersburg on a crisp black night at the end of 1916, a car drew up in front of the mustard yellow façade of the Yusupov Palace. From the car stepped Grigori Yefimovich Rasputin, dressed in tall leather boots and his finest silk tunic. The palace on the embankment of the river was the home of the Yusupov family, scions of Russia's ruling class whose wealth surpassed even that of the royal family, the Romanovs. Rasputin, a self-styled *starets* or holy man, was on such intimate terms with Tsar Nicholas II and his wife Alexandra that the extent of his influence on the imperial family was a growing concern in Russian state circles. He was believed to have certain mystical powers, and the tsarina herself seemed to have fallen under some sort of spell. Prince Felix Yusupov and a close circle of his political allies had decided to take matters into their own hands.

When Rasputin arrived at the palace, Yusupov ushered him down the stairs and into a vaulted cellar room that was adorned with religious items and tapestries. A table was set with plates of cakes, a samovar of tea and a carafe of Madeira. To Rasputin's surprise, there was no one else in the cellar, although he could hear music and chatter from the room above. He had come to the palace on the promise of a meeting with the prince's wife Irina; the 'mad monk' had a well-known weakness for female company. Yusupov explained that the princess was hosting a party upstairs and would be down shortly. He encouraged Rasputin to eat the cakes and drink the wine. Yusupov himself ate nothing.

After watching Rasputin eat his fill of cakes, a fidgety Yusupov excused himself and went upstairs, where his co-conspirators were still enacting the sounds of a lively party for the benefit of Rasputin's ears below. One of the group, a Dr Lazovert, was astonished at the prince's report. He had laced the cakes with enough cyanide to kill an infantry battalion almost instantly, and yet Rasputin's only complaint was of mild indigestion. Yusupov headed back downstairs to take another look. When he returned to the cellar to the sight of Rasputin casually admiring an Italian crucifix on the sideboard, his nerves got the better of him. Yusupov pulled out a pistol and shot the *starets* in the back, and he collapsed to the floor. But when Yusupov knelt over his body to confirm that life was indeed extinct, Rasputin sprang to his feet and chased the terrified prince out of the cellar, crawling up the stairs in pursuit, with blazing eyes and a foaming mouth.

Startled by the commotion, the rest of the group emerged from their 'party' just in time to see Rasputin stumbling out of a side door to flee across the palace courtyard. They gave chase and he was felled by a further volley of shots, including at least one to the head. The conspirators battered him with a club for good measure before pitching his body into the frozen River Neva. Written in the 1960s, Robert Massie's account of the downfall of the Romanov dynasty gave weight to the more sensational stories of Rasputin's demise:

> *Three days later, when the body was found, the lungs were filled with water. Gregory Rasputin, his bloodstream filled with poison, his body punctured by bullets, had died by drowning.*

Legend also had it for many years that Rasputin's eyes had fluttered open as he slipped beneath the ice.

In some twisted way, nothing in his life became him like the leaving of it, and the murder of Rasputin has gone down in popular legend as both a masterclass in botching an assassination and a posthumous endorsement of all his putative powers. The historical accounts on the conclusions of Rasputin's autopsy vary widely and the death by drowning story has now been mostly debunked by historians, to be replaced by equally colourful theories about the potential involvement of the British Secret Service in the assassination. But the myth of Rasputin's invincibility remains one of the archetypal good stories that persist unobstructed by truth.

There was of course no question that the killing of Rasputin was murder. It was a carefully plotted act, executed with determination – even if things didn't go to plan in the end. But the political instability in Russia at the time meant that Yusupov and his colleagues never faced a trial, and the tsar's only reaction was to exile the prince and his wife from St Petersburg. Within two years of Rasputin's death, Russia erupted into revolution and the entire Romanov family was executed at Ekaterinburg.

What's more, fifty years after Rasputin died, the strange circumstances of his death would find an unlikely echo in an English murder trial that raised complex questions about how the law should treat those who claim to have killed unintentionally or even unthinkingly. Far from the melancholy grandeur of imperial Russia, the sad death of Mrs Sylvia Nott saw the free-love clichés of the Swinging Sixties mired in the bleak realities of provincial mid-century life. It's the death of Rasputin as it might have occurred in a John Braine novel. But unlike Yusupov and his friends, Mrs Nott's killer would have to face justice, in a case that would epitomise the struggle to find coherent modern meanings of murder and manslaughter.

*   *   *

On the morning of Sunday 31 May 1964 police pulled the body of a young woman from the River Ouse in Buckingham. Her face was battered and bruised; she did not appear to be an accidental drowning victim. The deceased was identified as Sylvia Nott, a twenty-six-year-old mother of three small children who lived to the north of the town centre, not far from where her body had been found. She had not returned home the previous evening.

Parked a short way along the riverbank from where the body had been found was a white van. The police traced the owner of the van in the hope that he would be able to shed some light on what had happened to the woman found in the river. Under questioning by the police, the van owner quickly crumbled. His name was Cyril Church and he worked locally as a labourer. On the Saturday evening, he had met Mrs Nott in the town and they had hit it off. As the evening progressed, they had repaired to his works van, which was parked up on the riverside, just out of the town centre. Of course, there was only Church who was able to give an account of what happened next. He told the police that, when he was unable to perform sexually, Nott was less than sympathetic to his predicament. She allegedly taunted him that she was looking for 'a man and not a mouse'. Church saw red and according to his police statement:

> I got mad, like – and hit her ... I was shaking her to wake her up for about half an hour, but she didn't wake up, so I panicked and dragged her out of the van and put her in the river.

Church's rather anodyne description of his assault on Nott was belied by the results of a post-mortem. This revealed that as well as being beaten about the head, she had suffered a fracture to her hyoid bone, a small horseshoe-shaped bone that sits in the middle of the neck between the chin and voicebox. It is almost impossible to break this bone accidentally, and such an injury is usually indicative of manual strangulation. But the pathologist's report contained a further revelation. While these injuries were likely to have caused unconsciousness and subsequently death, they had in fact been inflicted around half an hour before Nott died. She was alive when she had been thrown into the river and the actual cause of death was drowning.

Church was charged with murder. At his trial at Nottingham just over a month after Nott's death, he pleaded not guilty. His defence was scattergun. There was a half-hearted attempt at claiming a provocation defence on the basis of Nott's taunts, although this was swiftly dismissed by the judge. But Church mainly relied on his confused account of his actions and added one crucial new point to the story he had told the police – at the time that he threw the unconscious Mrs Nott into the river, he thought he had already killed her. To be found guilty of murder, Church must have intended his act to kill Nott; and it is clearly impossible to intend to kill someone whom you think is already dead.

The prosecution argued that the severity of the injuries he had inflicted on her, particularly the strangulation, showed a clear intention to kill or at least cause serious harm, and the fact that it was the river that finally claimed her life was irrelevant. The judge summed up the law to the jury in unambiguous terms:

His case is that he genuinely and honestly believed that she was dead ... If that is his genuine and honest belief, then when he threw what he believed to be a dead body into the river, he obviously was not actuated by any intention to cause death or grievous bodily harm; you cannot cause death or serious bodily harm to a corpse.

Church could not be convicted of murder unless he knew or at least believed that Mrs Nott was alive when he put her into the river – and he denied that this was the case. Regarding the offence of manslaughter, the question as to what Church believed was irrelevant. Throwing a living person into a river was an unlawful act that carried an obvious risk of harm to the person concerned and, when death resulted, this was sufficient to make it manslaughter. The jury accepted that Church had thought he was throwing a corpse into the Ouse and, based on the judge's instructions to them, convicted Church of manslaughter, rather than murder. Sentencing him to fifteen years' imprisonment, the judge commented that it was the worst case of manslaughter he had ever come across.

The conviction of Cyril Church was a turning point in the modern history of the law of manslaughter. Following the Bateman case in the 1920s, a clear dividing line had been established between unintentional deaths resulting from neglectful or reckless actions (known as 'gross negligence manslaughter') and those caused by a standalone illegal act. In the latter cases, the commission of the unlawful act itself was sufficient, if death ensued, to make the killer guilty of manslaughter. But in the Church case, the court introduced a new element – risk – ruling that:

[an] act causing the death of another cannot, simply because it is an unlawful act, render a manslaughter verdict inevitable. For such a verdict to inexorably follow, the unlawful act must be such as all sober and reasonable people would inevitably recognise must subject the other person to, at least, the risk of some harm resulting therefrom.

Notwithstanding Church thinking that he was disposing of a body rather than actually killing someone, his actions carried a clear risk of harm. He could have negated this risk with a quick check of Mrs Nott's breathing or pulse, but he did not do so. His belief that she was already dead was immaterial; he should have made sure, rather than taking the gamble that she was still alive. The extent to which the law should permit someone to take a risk with another's life would become the cornerstone of the controversies and debates around homicide law for the rest of the 20th century. Uncertainties about how to determine a killer's mental state, knowledge and intention, and the point at which these would combine to make them a murderer in the eyes of the law, would continue to plague the law over the coming decades.

Sylvia Nott was the victim of a very intimate and personal horror, in some ways the very essence of what springs to mind when we think of violent death at the hands of another. But in the eyes of the law it was not murder, and Cyril Church's manslaughter conviction would mark the beginning of a period of revision and reappraisal of the law of homicide. In the years following his conviction came a succession of troubling incidents and trials that would challenge the respective meanings of murder and manslaughter, and call into question the traditional notions of what, and who, was deserving of the label of 'murder'. The extent to which we, both as individuals and as a society, should be permitted to knowingly or unknowingly endanger the lives of others would come to the fore in the coming decades, as personal tragedies and public disasters mingled to an unprecedented degree.

*   *   *

Hiraeth is one of those almost untranslatable words that serves to demonstrate how clumsy and inarticulate the English language can be, as it struggles across convoluted sentences or even whole paragraphs to convey something that another tongue can capture in just two syllables. When translated from the original Welsh, it is usually equated to simply 'homesickness' or 'nostalgia', but it goes beyond both and is captured by neither. Everyone will experience their own form of *hiraeth*, but it most commonly conjures up a deeply personal mix of grief, longing, regret and loss. It's sometimes described as a yearning for a place that you cannot return to or a time that has passed. For the people of the South Wales village of Aberfan, perhaps this would be a return to 9 a.m. on Friday 21 October 1966, fifteen minutes before the world ended.

The first shaft at the Merthyr Vale Colliery, situated on the floor of the Taff valley just below Aberfan, had been sunk in 1869. During the First World War the colliery had begun the practice of disposing of the waste products of its mining activities in huge slag heaps or 'tips' on the side of the Merthyr Mountain, which loomed over the valley. Over the next fifty years, seven of these tips built up on the site, forming into an Alpine range of jet-black peaks that encroached progressively closer to the village. By 1966 the seventh tip was over one hundred feet high and contained almost 300,000 cubic yards of mine waste. Four of the tips, including Tip 7, had been built on top of watercourses that sprang from the Aberfan side of the mountain. For over a decade the village had been plagued by flooding problems, and residents reported that the water that had invaded their properties was often black and slimy.

As any child who has ever built a sandcastle will know, there is an optimum amount of water that must be added to the sand to build a sturdy citadel. Too little water and the dry sand particles will not stick together; too much and the structure becomes critically unstable. The same principle applied to the composition of the tip piles, which faced the double threat of the ingress of groundwater from below and rainfall from above. Past a certain point of saturation, the solid waste material in the pile was at risk of liquefying into a loose sludge with twice the density of water, which would fatally undermine the stability of the entire tip.

Shortly after nine o'clock on that terrible Friday morning in 1966, the worst happened. Witnesses described seeing a 'dark glistening wave ... burst from the bottom of the tip'. Directly in the path of this wave lay farms, cottages and, on the edge of the village closest to the tip piles, Pantglas Junior School. The bare facts of what happened that day were succinctly summarised in the report of the inevitable inquiry, which concluded in July 1967:

At about 9.15 a.m. ... many thousands of tons of colliery waste swept swiftly and with a jet-like roar down the side of the Merthyr Mountain which forms the western flank of the coal-mining village of Aberfan. This massive breakaway from a vast tip overwhelmed in its course the two Hafod-Tanglwys-Uchaf farm cottages on the mountainside and killed their occupants. It crossed the disused canal and surmounted the railway embankment. It engulfed and destroyed a school and 18 houses and damaged another school and other dwellings in the village before its onward flow substantially ceased.

The tip-slide occurred at 9.15 a.m., and, despite the frantic efforts of locals and emergency services, no one was rescued alive from the remains of the destroyed buildings after 11 a.m. In total, 144 people lost their lives in the disaster; twenty-eight adults and 116 children, the majority of whom were sitting at their desks inside Pantglas when the slurry engulfed the school building.

The Merthyr Vale Colliery, like all British pits at the time, was run by the National Coal Board (NCB), which had been established in 1946 upon the nationalisation of the mining industry. At the start of the public inquiry into the causes of the disaster, the NCB drew its battle line – the slide had resulted from the unique and unknown geological conditions of the Merthyr Mountain and the catastrophe had been completely unforeseeable. Lord Alfred Robens, the chairman of the NCB, had been caught on camera telling a journalist that it was impossible for them to have known that there were any watercourses underneath the tip; but the evidence of locals and the mine's own staff soon gave the lie to this assertion.

After the inquiry tribunal had heard from 136 witnesses over seventy-six days of evidence, the NCB was forced to belatedly accept that its stringent denial of liability was not a tenable position. The tribunal concluded that the Board's failure to put in place any policy for the management of tipping was the root cause of the disaster. Despite several previous tip slides at both Merthyr Vale and other collieries, there was no system for monitoring or inspecting tips, no surveying of ground conditions before tips were built, nor any real understanding by the NCB of the risks posed by a slip.

Tip 7 itself had suffered a significant slide just three years earlier, but this had not prompted any remedial action or investigation; remarkably, the NCB claimed to have no records of the incident at all. And while local residents and the borough council had raised concerns about the proximity of Tip 7 to the village and the school, these were never acted upon by the NCB. There was a collective blindness in the organisation to the real risks of disaster posed by the tip. But even among those who were concerned, most believed that in the event of a slide there would be sufficient time to warn the village and evacuate the area. The speed and scale of the catastrophe had taken everyone by surprise.

Although the inquiry laid the blame for the disaster at the door of the NCB as an organisation, it also proceeded to single out several individuals from the middle to lower echelons of the regional management. While it was acknowledged that the byzantine organisational structures of the NCB made effective communication and dissemination of information difficult, none of the top brass were named and shamed in the final report, no legal action was taken against the NCB or any of its employees, and no one from the NCB lost their job or resigned. In fact, in 1970 Lord Robens was entrusted by the government with conducting a review into workplace hazards and accidents. His ensuing report, which made only fleeting references to the catastrophe at Aberfan, led directly to the overhaul of health and safety legislation that was undertaken in the 1970s.

In November 2019 Netflix released the third season of *The Crown*, its blockbuster biopic of the royal family. Episode three was titled simply 'Aberfan' and focused almost exclusively on the events of October 1966, paying particular attention to the muted response of the Queen (played by Olivia Colman) to the disaster. The episode marked the first time that the catastrophe had ever been dramatised on film or television. The ominous opening sequence has the mine looming large over the village and its inhabitants, dominating both the area's landscape and its economy. Lives, livelihoods and the very existence of the village were dependent on the pit. Village life on the eve of the tip slide is soundtracked by a continual rumble of digging and blasting, which contrasts with the silence in the valley in the scenes showing the aftermath of the disaster. The chaos of the rescue effort is seen through the eyes of Prime Minister Harold Wilson, who abandons his ministerial car to walk the final stretch up to the village along a road choked with emergency vehicles and cloaked in a haze of coal dust.

The episode pulled its punches on what lay behind the tragedy, and the only hint of the heartache to come for families searching for answers is in a short and clichéd scene of a public meeting, with angry villagers shouting at the emotionless officials sitting on the stage of the village hall. But this episode of *The Crown* has been credited with reviving public interest in the events at Aberfan, which were hitherto almost unknown in the US and rarely feature even in British media outside of the coverage of the anniversary of the disaster.

The Merthyr Vale Colliery closed in 1989 and the site has been extensively redeveloped, with a new housing estate springing up to reclaim the mine's location for the village. The ruined school buildings of Pantglas were demolished and the area has been landscaped into a memorial garden in remembrance of the tragedy. The floorplan of the school is laid out in lawns and stone paths, edged by borders of flowers and dotted with small trees. The line of the railway that ran behind the school and was swept away by the slide is now a track for cyclists and walkers. A little further down the valley from the school is the village cemetery; high on the sloping hillside is a section dedicated to the victims of Aberfan. The memorials, rows of bright white arches, stand out against the green hillside; and the deep rumble of the pit has been replaced by the faint buzz of traffic on the road across the top of the valley.

The lack of any criminal accountability for the disaster has never been forgotten, either. In the wake of Aberfan, a succession of disasters resulting in loss of life on a large scale would result in a paradigm shift in how the law treated organisations who injure or kill innocent members of the public. The prosecution of faceless corporate killers for homicide on a big or small scale was still fifty years away, but twenty years after the horrors of 1966, the mining communities around Aberfan would be thrust back onto the front pages following another tragedy in the valleys. The ensuing trial would be politicised to an extent never seen before in a murder case and would have far-reaching consequences for the law of homicide.

*   *   *

In 1984 the Merthyr Vale Colliery – like mines up and down the country – was embroiled in the miners' strike. In the eighteen years since the valley had been rocked by the Aberfan disaster, the mining industry as a whole had been engaged in a fight for its life. By the early 1980s Margaret Thatcher's government was set on a collision course with the miners' union over her plans to streamline and economise the entire structure of British coalmining. The NCB announced a series of job losses and pit closures in March 1984. The National Union of Mineworkers (NUM), led by anti-Thatcher firebrand Arthur Scargill, believed that these were the thin end of the wedge and would inevitably lead to the decimation of the whole industry. At collieries across England, Wales and Scotland, miners downed tools and came out onto the picket line in protest at the planned cuts.

However, support for the strike was not universal across the mining industry and the NUM avoided calling a national ballot of its members on the action for fear that it would be unsuccessful. They had anticipated – correctly – that there would be a domino effect as local pits came out in favour of industrial action, which would spread the strike nationwide. This approach led to two challenges in the High Court to the overall legality of the strike in the absence of a national ballot; but the NUM were undeterred and the strikes continued.

The action dominated the news for months on end, its profile aided by Scargill's knack for dressing up revolutionary rhetoric in a snappy soundbite. Journalist and broadcaster Andrew Marr neatly summarised the success of the union's positioning of the aims of the strike:

> From the start, Scargill emphasised the [pit] closures. To strike to protect jobs, particularly other people's jobs, in other people's villages and other counties' pits, gave the confrontation an air of nobility and sacrifice which a mere wages dispute would not have enjoyed.

But the NUM was not held in universal regard, even on its own side. Labour Party leader Neil Kinnock had only been in post for six months when the strike began and, while he was in support of the principles of the action, he was no fan of Scargill and his more militant tactics. Regardless of the infighting on the left, and the violent clashes between police and pickets at some pits, public opinion remained robustly in favour of the striking miners.

Levels of support for the strike in South Wales were among the highest in the country, and strike-breakers were few and far between. So-called 'scabs', who refused to participate in the strike, sometimes objected to the ideology of the industrial action, or were simply unable to afford to go without their wages for the duration of the walkout. The NCB tried to tempt people back to work with the offer of a cash bonus, on top of the resumption of payment of their salary, but even so, only two Merthyr Vale miners continued going to work. One of them was David Williams, and his decision did not make him popular with his colleagues who had stayed out on strike in the local area. Missiles were thrown at his house and colliery bosses arranged for him to travel to work in a taxi, accompanied by a police escort. The convoy took to varying the timing of its journey and route in order to avoid any disgruntled pickets who might try to intercept it.

On the morning of 30 November 1984 Williams had been picked up from his home shortly before five o'clock and the taxi made its way along the Heads of the Valleys Road towards Merthyr Tydfil. As the convoy approached the turn-off for the village of Rhymney in the gloomy pre-dawn, no one spotted the figures that had appeared on the deck of a bridge spanning the road a few hundred yards ahead of them. Just as the taxi was about to pass underneath the bridge, something smashed through its windscreen with tremendous force. The accompanying police vehicles screeched to a halt and could only watch as the taxi veered out of control and crashed into the embankment at the side of the road.

From his seat in the rear of the vehicle, Williams was shaken but unhurt. But David Wilkie, the taxi driver, was unresponsive and pinioned in his seat by the weight of the twenty-kilogram concrete block that had been hurled through the windscreen. He suffered head and chest injuries, and was pronounced dead on arrival at hospital. He was a father of two and his girlfriend was almost eight months pregnant. When police arrived at their home to tell her about the crash, she collapsed and had to be taken to hospital.

Arrests were swift. Two striking miners from other collieries in the Merthyr area – Reginald Dean Hancock and Russell Shankland – admitted to being on the bridge as Wilkie's taxi drove underneath it. Hancock had pushed over the concrete block that killed Wilkie and Shankland had launched a cement post off the bridge that struck the side of the taxi.

The death of David Wilkie was front-page news up and down the country, and was mired in political controversy almost from the moment that it happened. The strike itself was entering a crucial phase. After over eight months on the picket line, miners were beginning to drift back to work in low but increasing numbers. While South Wales was a stronghold of NUM support and the taxi's passenger David Williams was one of only two miners to carry on working at Merthyr Vale, the tide was beginning to turn. David Wilkie's death proved to be a tipping point on the finely balanced scales of public opinion regarding the strike. He was a completely innocent victim, who had just been going about his job when he was killed, and had nothing to do with the mine or the dispute. Even among those supportive of the strike, sympathy for Hancock and Shankland was in short supply in the immediate aftermath of the tragedy.

Opponents of the strike peddled a conspiracy theory that the incident was in fact a hit by the local union branch, planned to deter other 'scabs' from breaking the strike. Prime Minister Margaret Thatcher was quick to condemn Hancock and Shankland's actions. Labour leader Neil Kinnock appeared on stage alongside Arthur Scargill at a Stoke-on-Trent campaign rally on the evening of 30 November and described Wilkie's death as 'an outrage'. Scargill, however, said nothing. In an editorial published two days after the incident, even the left-leaning *Sunday Mirror* rounded on Scargill for his silence:

> *The awful, simple truth is that by his refusal to condemn violence on the NUM picket lines, Mr Scargill is guilty of complicity in the killing of Mr Wilkie … If Black Friday [as the paper had termed the day of Wilkie's death] is the turning point in this dreadful dispute, Mr David Wilkie will not have died in vain.*

Although this febrile atmosphere was still persisting when the two miners stood trial for murder in May 1985, the strike that had spawned the case was not. Following a vote to return to work by the NUM two months earlier, the most divisive industrial dispute in British history had come to an end. But Hancock and Shankland were to find themselves at quite a different coalface from the one that they were used to, as the arguments put forward in their defence would have to work hard in order to change one of the most controversial aspects of the law of murder – the difficult question of intent.

Both denied any intention to kill Wilkie on that bleak November morning. Their plan, they claimed, was simply to block the road and prevent David Williams from getting to work. They had been aiming to throw the block and pole into the middle lane of the carriageway, so that they would land clear of the nearside lane in which the convoy was travelling, but would still bring it to a halt. The local police had dealt with several incidents over the preceding months where pickets had blocked deliveries to mines with similar tactics. Hancock and Shankland maintained that they had not intended to harm either David Wilkie or his passenger. In the course of the police investigation before the prosecution commenced, both indicated that they would be prepared to plead guilty to manslaughter but the prosecution decided to press ahead with a murder charge. The miners accepted that they were guilty, but the question was – of what crime?

On 16 May 1985 Reginald Hancock and Russell Shankland were convicted of murder at Cardiff Crown Court and jailed for life. Reactions were vocal and immediate. Labour MP Tony Benn came out in defence of the two miners and drew opprobrium from the press when he told an audience of teenagers on the BBC's *Open to Question* programme that 'the tragedy of the taxi driver in Wales was a horrible tragedy but it was not a crime. It was a tragedy that arose out of the dispute.' When news of the conviction reached the local pit, seven hundred miners walked out in protest. Ten days later, protesters marched through the centre of Cardiff to hold a vigil outside the city's jail, where Hancock and Shankland had just started to serve their sentences. In the middle of June the Workers' Revolutionary Party rallied a group of three hundred people to march from Swansea to London to demand the immediate release of the two miners.

The notoriety of the case and its deep entanglement with the strike proved to be an enduring headache for the Labour Party. Leader Neil Kinnock's distaste for Scargill and his conduct of the entire dispute had set him at odds with some of his own MPs, particularly veteran left-winger Tony Benn. In the summer of 1985 Benn introduced the Miners' Amnesty (General Pardon) Bill to the House of Commons, which proposed a full pardon for miners convicted of any criminal offence during the strike. The potential ramifications of the policy for the killers of David Wilkie led one Tory MP to ask a caustically rhetorical question in the course of the Bill's debate:

> *What would be the likely effect on the level of crime if the Miners' Amnesty (General Pardon) Bill in the name of the Right Honourable Member for Chesterfield [Tony Benn] were to be passed, given that the burden of that Bill is that people will be entitled to commit murder provided it is in pursuit of objectives that are central to those of the national executive of the Labour Party?*

Both Benn and Scargill lent their support to the campaign by the miners' families to overturn the murder convictions, and by the autumn of 1985 they had been successful in securing permission to appeal against the verdict of the Cardiff jury. The main question for the Court of Appeal to consider was whether or not Hancock and Shankland had the requisite intention to kill or harm David Wilkie, so as to make them guilty of murder.

In cases such as theirs where a direct intention is denied, the law can subsequently construct one in certain circumstances. Up until the end of the 19th century, defendants in criminal cases were extremely limited in the evidence that they could give in their own defence. Other than when putting forward an insanity defence, they were not permitted to testify, and so questions about a person's mental state and true intentions at the time that they had killed did not arise. But as the 20th century progressed and the law began to explore more expansive interpretations of the mental element of manslaughter, particularly in the wake of Cyril Church's conviction, there was an inevitable blurring of the line that separated it from murder – and a huge potential for overlap.

Just two years before Hancock and Shankland's trial, Alistair Moloney had been convicted of murder in a similar legal quagmire of intention, accident and foresight. Moloney had been celebrating his parents' wedding anniversary at a party at the family home in Huntingdon, Cambridgeshire. The drink had been flowing and he sat up late to talk with his stepfather Patrick. The pair were close and, in a drunken game initiated by Patrick, they decided to see which of them could load a shotgun the quickest. At the time, Moloney was serving in the Gordon Highlanders and was on leave from a deployment to Belize; as would be expected, he was quickest on the draw.

According to Moloney's statement to police, Patrick then dared him to fire it; he did so, apparently without stopping to think or check where the gun was pointing. A split-second after firing, Moloney realised that he had blown his beloved stepfather's head off his shoulders. He claimed at his trial that he had no intention of shooting Patrick and he had not aimed the gun at him, but simply pulled the trigger, almost as a reflexive action. He was convicted of murder in September 1982 at Birmingham Crown Court and was sentenced to life imprisonment. In June 1984 the conviction was upheld by the Court of Appeal and it was this that cemented Hancock and Shankland's fate. The basis of Moloney's murder conviction was that, even if he had not directly intended to shoot Patrick, the gunshot wound was a natural consequence of firing the gun without checking where it was aimed. In such circumstances, a killer should have foreseen the result and so the jury was entitled to infer a lethal intention from Moloney's actions, even if he were not conscious of it himself. The same approach had been taken by the court at Hancock and Shankland's original trial.

Arguing their case at the Court of Appeal, the miners' lawyers challenged the Moloney verdict on the grounds that it had effectively created a new category of 'murder by reckless-ness', which should in fact be classed as manslaughter. The Court of Appeal was persuaded; they overturned the murder convictions and substituted ones of manslaughter. For Hancock and Shankland to be guilty of murder, it was not enough that they should have foreseen the consequence of their actions. The prosecution must also prove that the death of David Wilkie was a probable result of these actions – and they had not done so. The life sentences were replaced with eight-year terms. Hancock and Shankland were finally released from jail on 30 November 1989, the fifth anniversary of Wilkie's death.

*   *   *

Reginald Hancock, Russell Shankland and Alistair Moloney all shared one important belief. Under pain of death, they would never have considered themselves to be murderers. They accepted that their actions were reckless, selfish and stupid, and they even acknowledged that they were deserving of punishment under the law. But what they disputed was the label that was attached to their crime; and hapless young men who do monumentally idiotic things without thought for the consequences do not correspond to most people's idea of a murderer either. The intricacies of these cases posed uncomfortable questions about whether the law of homicide had kept pace with the lethal realities of modern life or whether it was now too blunt an instrument to properly administer justice.

Just three years before Hancock and Shankland killed David Wilkie, the six-year reign of terror of the Yorkshire Ripper had come to an end in Court Number One of the Old Bailey. Peter Sutcliffe had been convicted of the murders of thirteen women and was sentenced to multiple life sentences. The judge, Mr Justice Boreham, recommended that he serve a minimum of thirty years and expressed the hope that in Sutcliffe's case life would indeed mean life. Covering the trial for the *Guardian*, journalist Nick Davies noted:

> *The prison officers turned, and at 4.22pm, Sutcliffe, his face still expressionless, descended the steps into the cells to begin his sentence at Wormwood Scrubs, London. He will later be moved to Wakefield.*

Sutcliffe's conviction marked the conclusion of one of the longest manhunts in British policing history. Between 1975 and 1980 he killed thirteen women and viciously attacked at least nine more in West Yorkshire and Manchester. Sutcliffe pleaded not guilty to murder on the basis of diminished responsibility, and the trial got off to a controversial start when the Attorney General Sir Michael Havers,* who was prosecuting the case, suggested to the judge that he was prepared to accept a guilty plea to manslaughter. The judge overruled this and ordered that the prosecution for murder must proceed – it would be for the jury to decide whether Sutcliffe was suffering from diminished responsibility or not. His evidence, supported by testimony from psychiatrists, was that his killing spree had been prompted by hearing a holy voice emanating from a tombstone while he was working as a gravedigger at a cemetery in Bingley, near Bradford. The divine speaker had apparently told him to kill. The defence psychiatrists were satisfied that such a delusion was sufficient to support a finding of diminished responsibility, subject to one important caveat – that Sutcliffe genuinely believed that he had heard the voice.

The prosecution's version of events cast considerable doubt on the plausibility of Sutcliffe's story of mental disturbance. He did not mention hearing the voice when interviewed by police after his arrest in January 1981. He had also made an apparently calculated decision to move his hunting ground across the Pennines to Manchester when he considered that he was a greater risk of apprehension due to the publicity attracted by the murders in the Leeds area. This was hardly the action of a disciple convinced he was doing the Lord's work. Prison officers who had supervised Sutcliffe on remand also testified

* Sir Michael's father Cecil Havers was the judge who sentenced Ruth Ellis to death, while his son Nigel eschewed the law for an acting career.

Physically, he was a strikingly good match for the descriptions given by those women who survived his brutal attacks. Most chillingly of all, between 1977 and 1980 he was interviewed by police on nine separate occasions in connection with four of the murders, but the dots were never joined. Sutcliffe was never identified as a suspect and his eventual apprehension was down to dumb luck, when two constables on a routine patrol in Sheffield caught him in a car with stolen number plates, with a woman whom he intended to become his next victim.

From a legal perspective the case was relatively straightforward. It was, as one judge described it, 'an all or nothing case': either Sutcliffe was genuinely disturbed enough to make him guilty of manslaughter only; or he was not, and so the only correct verdict was murder. The verdict has overshadowed several other cases of the era that tangled with fundamental points going to the heart of the law of murder itself. During the 1970s and 1980s, the Court of Appeal and House of Lords saw a succession of complex cases that sought to challenge the received wisdom on how to define murder itself. There was a growing dissatisfaction from elements within the judiciary with the current state of the law, and several senior judges were keen to see the crime of murder restricted to cases where there was a clear intention to kill. Those defendants who, like Cyril Church or the South Wales miners, took a risk with another's life could not be sure which side of the dividing line between murder and manslaughter their actions would fall.

It was a turbulent couple of decades for the law of homicide and there was considerable uncertainty from the courts about the proper scope of the offence of murder. When set against the dark deeds of a killer like Sutcliffe, the murder convictions of the likes of Hancock and Shankland are thrown into sharp relief. Was justice really served by categorising them and punishing them in an identical manner to such a monster? They were convicted of the same crime and, until their successful appeals, faced the same mandatory life term. Had they been tried and convicted just twenty years earlier, they would have faced execution. These borderline cases were instrumental in shaping this complex area of the criminal law.

But it is the image of Sutcliffe and his crimes, perhaps more than any other murderer in the late 20th century, that has bled into the depictions of murder and crime in popular culture today. So many features of the case – the bodies dumped on waste ground, the slow stalking of a woman down a street at night, the drawn-out manhunt – have become common tropes in crime fiction. You can trace a direct line from Sutcliffe's crimes to the stylised and sometimes glamorised depiction of serial murder, particularly of women, that is now such a recurring feature of film and TV drama. But the Yorkshire Ripper is not representative of most of the killers that come before the courts in trials for murder and manslaughter in Britain. Indeed, it is perhaps the very rarity of serial murderers in this country that helps drive our collective fascination with them. While the reality of modern homicide is less dramatic than film and TV would have us believe, the consequences for all concerned are no less devastating.

In 1981, the same year that Peter Sutcliffe was convicted, the House of Lords upheld the murder conviction of Anthony Cunningham, who had killed Korosh 'Kim' Natghie in a pub fight in Margate. Cunningham claimed that his attack had been prompted by jealousy as he believed that Natghie was involved with his former girlfriend, but he denied that he had ever intended to kill Natghie. The Law Lords confirmed that the murder conviction was correct, on the basis that Cunningham had clearly intended to cause serious harm to his victim, even if not to actually kill. This was sufficient to satisfy the mental element of the offence of murder, and an intention to kill or cause grievous bodily harm was thus established as the modern meaning of Sir Edward Coke's malice aforethought.

There was a stark contrast between, on the one hand Sutcliffe, a serial killer who planned and executed a string of horrific attacks that had escalated in violence and depravity, and on the other Cunningham – a pub brawler who in the heat of the moment took things too far. In delivering their judgment in Cunningham's case, the Lords expressed their dissatisfaction with the confused state of the law of murder as they saw it in the late 20th century. Lord Hailsham made a pointed note that piecemeal development of the law of homicide through case law, rather than statute, had left it in dire need of clarification and simplification. He posited one possible solution:

> Or, are we to … create a single offence of homicide and recognise that homicides are infinitely variable in their heinousness, and that their heinousness depends very largely on their motivation, with the result that the judges should have absolute discretion to impose whatever sentence he considers just from a conditional discharge to life imprisonment?

The suggested approach would remove the uncertainties over how to determine intent, knowledge or foresight from the jury, who would simply have to decide whether a defendant was the cause of another's death. The particular circumstances of the killer and the killing would be considered by the judge, who would determine how to reflect them in the severity of the sentence that they passed. But the Lords acknowledged that this decision was not one that the judiciary was empowered to make and that such a comprehensive change would require legislative intervention from parliament. The judgment in Cunningham's case ended with a plea from the House of Lords to the House of Commons to grasp the nettle and undertake a root-and-branch review of the English law of homicide.

The latter half of the 20th century had highlighted the shortcomings of the law of murder, most notably in cases where the circumstances of an unlawful death were more nuanced than the traditional parameters of a coldly premeditated killing. Disasters such as Aberfan also called into question the ability of the law as it stood to properly criminalise and sanction those who posed a risk to public safety. This would only continue in the following decades as controversial cases further challenged society to think twice about what really does make a murderer, particularly when the killer turns out to be more sympathetic than their victim.

CHAPTER SEVEN
LIPSTICK ON THE MIRROR

'The law must take its course'

For those driving down the A449 near Stourbridge, the redbrick farmhouse is easy to miss. It stands on the corner of a country lane, set back a little from the main road, on a rise before the carriageway dips down through wooded slopes. The towns that make up the post-industrial heartlands of the West Midlands lie just to the east, but the house looks out to the west, over the open fields and rolling hills of South Staffordshire and Shropshire beyond. Even on days when the traffic is streaming past the door, it's a lonely spot. For many years, the property stood empty and derelict, as if in remembrance of what had happened there. Its windows were broken, the grounds around the house overgrown, with the curving gable ends and the crumbling chimney stacks just visible from the road through the tall trees that gave the house its name – Yew Tree Farm.

The last time thirteen-year-old Carl Bridgewater was seen alive was late on a Tuesday afternoon in September 1978, as

208

he cycled along Lawnswood Road towards the farmhouse on his regular paper route. A couple of workers from the water board waved to him as he whizzed past them on his bike. An hour later, at about 5 p.m., the local doctor called at the farm to check up on its elderly occupants. Unbeknownst to Dr Angus Macdonald, his patients had gone out for the day. He swung his car into the farmyard and walked up to the farmhouse. He later recalled, 'I felt as I walked up there that something was very strange about the place. It was something to do with the wind, I don't know.'

The doctor's premonition was correct. As he approached the front door he saw that it was ajar and had clearly been forced open. When he went inside he found that the house had been turned over. On the sofa in the living room Carl lay dead from a shotgun wound.

The obvious conclusion was that the young paper boy had inadvertently disturbed a robbery at the farmhouse when he arrived to deliver the paper; the house was chock full of antiques, and some were found scattered in the yard and outbuildings, where they had presumably been dumped as the robbers had fled the scene. When the elderly residents of a similarly isolated farmhouse in Worcestershire, just half an hour's drive from Yew Tree, were robbed at gunpoint by a masked gang a couple of months after Carl's death, the police were convinced that there was a connection. The gang, comprising James Robinson, Patrick Molloy, and cousins Vincent and Michael Hickey, were small-time Birmingham crooks who the police quickly fingered for the second robbery. In October 1979 they found themselves convicted of both the Worcestershire robbery and the murder of Carl Bridgewater.

The Bridgewater Four, as they would come to be known, loudly and consistently denied any involvement in Carl's death from the moment they were convicted; and there was no let-up in their vocal protests as their life sentences wore on. In the cold light of day the case against them certainly seemed less than watertight. There was no physical or forensic evidence that tied them to Yew Tree Farm and eyewitness evidence was limited. None of their fingerprints matched those found at the farmhouse. Although Robinson admitted owning a sawn-off shotgun of the type that the police believed had been used in the shooting, the ballistics evidence did not tally with the cartridges found at the scene and the actual murder weapon was never identified. Several people had seen a blue car on or in the vicinity of the farmhouse drive in the afternoon, but there were question marks over whether they could positively identify one or more of the four men as being present. The only photofit produced in the investigation, based on the account of one witness who had passed a car near the farmhouse that afternoon, bore little resemblance to any of the men convicted.

In large part, therefore, the prosecution's case rested on alleged confessions made by two of the gang, Molloy and Vincent Hickey. The original information was volunteered by Hickey, in an apparent ploy to negotiate his way out of charges for the second burglary, in which he was definitely involved. When he was told by police that Hickey had pointed the finger, Molloy retaliated with a detailed statement, describing how the gang had been ransacking the house when they were interrupted by Carl Bridgewater. Molloy claimed that he was upstairs when he heard the gun go off.

But almost as soon as these confessions were made, they were retracted by the two men amid claims that they had been pressured, coerced and even beaten into submission before they made the incriminating statements. Michael Hickey, the youngest of the four and only eighteen at the time of his conviction, was particularly strident in his own defence. Four years into his sentence, he mounted a rooftop protest at Gartree Prison in Leicestershire to proclaim the Four's innocence. He stayed on the roof for three months, surviving the winter on food parcels passed up to him by fellow inmates from their cell windows, most of whom had become convinced that Hickey and the other men were innocent of Carl's murder.

The Bridgewater Four's campaign to clear their names involved an exhaustive and exhausting process of appeals against their convictions – and they weren't alone in such a struggle. Placards and protesters outside court buildings and government offices became a recurring feature of news reports in the last decades of the 20th century. A string of controversial murder convictions would highlight the shortcomings of the legal system and the risks of injustice, thrusting the Court of Appeal and its role in righting historic wrongs into the public and media spotlight.

The stakes are always highest in murder cases. For many years, an overturned verdict was literally a matter of life and death for those facing a capital sentence. Even after the abolition of the death penalty, the avoidance of the automatic life sentence for murder has become a powerful incentive to pursue an appeal. The part played by the government of the day in deciding which cases should be reviewed meant that politics became embroiled in the law to an extent not seen since the 1950s, when the pleas to the home secretary for clemency for Ruth Ellis and Derek Bentley fell on deaf ears. As these cases and campaigns dragged on, sometimes for several years, the 1990s would end up being a decade of reckoning for the English legal system, with the law of homicide being shaped by political, as well as legal, judgments.

*   *   *

The Bridgewater Four's quest for justice ran almost in parallel to that of another group of men, also labelled with a name and a number, who were protesting their innocence regarding another Midlands tragedy of the 1970s. On the evening of 21 November 1974, at 8.18 p.m. precisely, a blast ripped through the Mulberry Bush pub in Birmingham city centre, which was packed with Thursday-night drinkers. While the debris was still falling, and with the ear-shattering blast still ringing in the ears of the people trapped in the pub, another explosion was heard, further away but still terrifyingly close. A couple of hundred yards round the corner from the Mulberry Bush, a second bomb had just detonated at the Tavern in the Town, a cellar pub on the city's main shopping thoroughfare of New Street. Twenty minutes before the explosions, a group of five men with Irish accents had boarded a train at New Street station while a sixth man waved the group off from the platform. The train was bound for Heysham in Lancashire, where it connected with the ferry to Belfast. New Street station was within a couple of minutes' brisk walking distance of each of the pubs.

Twenty-one people died in the Birmingham pub bombings and almost two hundred were injured. The events of that November evening were the culmination of a campaign of attacks across the Midlands over the previous year. The city was already on high alert after another explosion in Coventry the previous week, in which a member of the Birmingham branch of the IRA was killed when the bomb he was planting went off prematurely. So the station staff were immediately suspicious of the group of Irish men leaving the city straight after the explosions. They tipped off the Birmingham police, and when the train reached the north-west the men were intercepted by British Transport Police, arrested and, within three days of the explosions, had all given either written or verbal confessions.

Together with the man on the platform, they would quickly become known as the Birmingham Six, and their 1975 trial was one of the most controversial murder cases of the late 20th century. The trial took place in Lancaster, in the castle that sits in the heart of the old stone city. At that time, the castle still housed both a working prison and a Crown courtroom; the impregnability of the complex meant that it was often used for criminal trials that posed a security risk or potential terrorist threat, and the Six could be held securely in the Victorian prison cells in the heart of the castle throughout the three months of the trial.

In addition to their alleged confessions, the case against them had rested on scientific evidence of the presence of nitroglycerine detected on the hands and clothes of several of the men – a component of the commonly used explosive gelignite. At the trial, the defendants all pleaded not guilty and argued that the confessions had been beaten out of them by police officers, but the judge ruled that the admissions had been made voluntarily. On 15 August 1975 all six were convicted of twenty-one counts of murder.

Sixteen years later, on their third attempt at an appeal, the murder convictions of the Birmingham Six were quashed and they walked free from court. The public outcry over the case, and their long road to securing the reversal of their murder convictions, highlighted the shortcomings of the Court of Appeal and its role in the justice process. The right to appeal and the circumstances in which that appeal could be successful were so rigidly prescribed in English law that there was no real opportunity within the system to proactively investigate and remedy miscarriages of justice. In any cases involving a murder verdict there was the added complexity that, just a few decades before, the defendants would have been executed and so the safety of the convictions would have become moot many years earlier.

The Court of Appeal was a relatively modern invention and had only been created at the turn of the 20th century. Prior to this, a convicted murderer's only hope of changing a guilty verdict was if the case was referred up to the Court of Crown Cases Reserved. This higher court had a very limited ability to review and overturn judgments. The Victorian judiciary believed in the supremacy of the jury's decision and the deterrent effect of carrying out death sentences swiftly, without getting bogged down in appeals. But the Edwardians were more alive to the possibility that the courts sometimes got things wrong and so, in 1907, parliament established a court of criminal appeal to replace the Court of Crown Cases Reserved.

In the years that followed, this Court of Appeal would play a central role in some of the most notorious and important murder cases in history, and 'in the twentieth century, the criminal appeal court came to occupy a central position in the criminal justice system and to be viewed as an indispensable safeguard against injustice'. The other such bulwark was the ability of the government to interpose and reprieve condemned prisoners before their sentence was carried out. For centuries, the power to commute a death sentence had been exercised by the monarch under the 'royal prerogative' of mercy, but for the last hundred years or so it has been delegated to the home secretary.

The twin safeguards of appeals and political intervention were not, however, always as effective as one would hope. In the 1950s Derek Bentley and Timothy Evans both had their cases rejected by the Court of Appeal – in Evans's case, the appeal judges expressly rejected his assertions that the real monster of Rillington Place was John Christie, who would go on to be convicted of the murders just three years later. Ruth Ellis did not contest her murder conviction but, like Bentley and Evans, she did ask the home secretary for a reprieve. In all three cases the pleas were refused, and in each case they were damned to hang with the dreaded words 'the law must take its course' written across the case papers by officials at the Home Office.

The placing of this power of life and death in the hands of one politician also ran the risk of inconsistent results. In 1916 Canadian soldier Georges Codere had escaped the noose for the murder of Henry Ozanne in a decision that owed as much to political expediency as it did to the application of the law. Ruth Ellis had hanged when Renee Duffy had been reprieved for a remarkably similar murder just a few years earlier; but at the time of Ellis's crime the government feared that a display of mercy would undermine the death penalty in its entirety.

After the death penalty was outlawed, the home secretary would continue to play a central role in difficult cases. Following the abolition of capital punishment, the home secretary was given the power to refer cases to the Court of Appeal on their own volition, even when previous appeals had been rejected. This power was usually exercised in cases where new evidence had been uncovered, and up until the 1990s it had been only been deployed on rare occasions. But this decade saw a glut of crusades against controversial convictions, including those from the IRA bombing campaigns of the 1970s. Not all were murder convictions, but the most hotly contested verdicts were for homicide offences.

It was this process that enabled the Birmingham Six to return to the appeal courts on two further occasions, after their first attempt just a year after their conviction had been unsuccessful. Over a century on from its establishment, the remit of the criminal appeal court remained very strictly prescribed, and in the Birmingham Six's last appeal the court was keen to stress that:

Nothing ... obliges or entitles [the Court of Appeal] to say
whether we think the appellant is innocent. This is a point
of great constitutional importance. The task of deciding
whether a man is guilty falls on the jury. We are concerned
solely with the question of whether the verdict can stand.

A conviction can only be overturned on appeal if the court is satisfied that overall it is unsafe and unsatisfactory, or that the original trial was subject to a significant irregularity or an error in the law as it was applied in the case. The power of the court to order a retrial after quashing a conviction was only introduced in the 1960s.

In the Birmingham Six's case, the Court of Appeal had ruled that on the basis of the new evidence presented to it, the verdict from the original trial was neither safe nor satisfactory. Fresh evidence was produced indicating that the trace substances found on the men's hands could have been picked up from everyday objects or even have been the result of contamination by the scientists conducting the original tests. Furthermore, and most notoriously, a subsequent review of the case by an independent police force raised several red flags about the original investigation. Custody and charging records were incomplete, and the confessions themselves contained enough inconsistencies to cast considerable doubt on their reliability.

On 14 March 1991, on the same day that the Birmingham Six walked free from court, the government announced the establishment of a new royal commission to conduct a root and branch review of the entire criminal justice system. Heavily grounded in the controversies surrounding the investigations

into the bombing cases, the commission spent two years looking at all facets of the lifespan of a criminal case, from the
initial police inquiry to the role of the appeal courts in reviewing unsafe convictions. There were specific sections of the
commission's report dedicated to the use of confession
evidence, the conduct of interrogations of suspects and the
risks of miscarriages of justice presented by the system as it
stood. The commission's guiding principle boiled down to one
simple statement, as set out in its eventual report:

> All law-abiding citizens have a common interest in a system
> of criminal justice in which the risks of the innocent being
> convicted and of the guilty being acquitted are as low as
> human fallibility allows.

On the question of the appeals process, the commission
concluded that it was no longer tenable for the home secretary
to stand as the final arbiter on whether criminal cases could
and should be referred back to the judiciary. This process effectively placed a government minister, whose day job required
no legal experience or qualifications, in the role of judge and
jury. The home secretary's power to refer was wholly discre-
tionary and there was no obligation to refer cases back to the
Court of Appeal even where a prima facie miscarriage of justice
had occurred. In an average year, seven hundred cases were
referred to the government; of these, only four or five made it
to the Court of Appeal and it remained the case that some of
the most troubling convictions were not getting past the
government gatekeeper and back to the courts. In the same

year that the commission's report was published, Home Secretary Kenneth Clarke rejected a new plea from the Bridgewater Four to send their case back to the Court of Appeal.

Instead the commission proposed the establishment of an entirely new body independent of both government and the courts, which would have the power to proactively investigate such cases and direct the courts to reconsider them on appeal if it was satisfied that there were grounds to do so. It was hoped that an independent body would counteract the perceived reluctance of the courts, in some cases at least, to admit that the judicial process may have veered off course, even when such errors were historic.

These proposals were still being mulled over by the government in the summer of 1992 when the legal establishment was rocked by another alleged miscarriage, which showed that men didn't have the monopoly on injustice. This case would revisit some of the most controversial aspects of the law of murder, illuminating the law of homicide in all its infinite and awful variety, and lending new weight to the calls for reform of the offences of murder, manslaughter and everything in between.

*   *   *

To the civil servants hurrying through Westminster on their lunchbreak, or the tourists taking the scenic route from Westminster Abbey to Buckingham Palace via St James's Park, the women had become a regular sight that summer. Every Wednesday they would gather, packing the pavements on Queen Anne's Gate in the shadow of the hulking high rise that housed the Home Office. The shouts, whistles and jeers would gradually come together into a chorus as they took up their song. Sometimes it was an improvised sea shanty entitled 'What shall we do with Kenneth Baker?', with the serving home secretary replacing the drunken sailor of the traditional version. On other occasions it was a robust chanting of 'We'll free all the women, yes we will' to the tune of 'She'll be coming round the mountain'. Some carried homemade placards, lending the scene the aura of a picket line. And if Mr Baker had been moved by the noise on the street below to look out of his office window, he would have seen one slogan emblazoned across the placards: 'Free Kiranjit Ahluwalia'.

Early on the morning of 8 May 1989 the fire brigade were called to a house in the Langley Green area of Crawley, West Sussex. When they arrived they found a crowd of people gathered on the front lawn shouting and gesturing wildly at a figure in the living-room window. It was a young woman, clutching a child in her arms, seemingly insensible to the cries of her neighbours outside, who were imploring her to leave the burning building. Finally, she ushered her small son out of the house and stood on the grass, looking up with a glazed expression at the flames licking out of the window on the first floor. Behind her, wrapped in a blanket and drifting in and out of consciousness, her husband was loaded into an ambulance.

As the ambulance made its way to the hospital, thirty-four-year-old Deepak Ahluwalia told the paramedics through teeth gritted in pain what had happened. He said that he had fought with his wife Kiranjit on the previous evening, over money owed to them by her family. While he was sleeping in the couple's bedroom that night, she had come into the room and set the bed alight, before dousing him in a solution of caustic soda. Upon arrival at Crawley Hospital, Deepak was found to have burns over 40 per cent of his body, including his face, neck, chest and thighs. He was transferred to a specialist burns unit at Roehampton Hospital, where he received a large blood transfusion. Despite his injuries, he remained conscious and coherent enough to give a statement to the police, in which he repeated the version of events he had given to the paramedics on the night of the fire. But he developed septicaemia, which led to organ failure, and a week after the fire Deepak suffered a fatal heart attack. Kiranjit, already on remand at Holloway Prison for attempted murder, was told of her husband's death in her cell and that she would now face trial for his murder.

One of nine children, Kiranjit was born in the Punjab village of Chak Kalal in 1955. In her early twenties she moved to Canada to live with her brother and his family, who had emigrated there several years before. She studied sociology and law at college in India, and had dreams of pursuing a career in one of those fields. But her family persuaded her into an arranged marriage and, in 1979, a friend in London suggested his acquaintance Deepak as a suitable match. On the advice of her brothers, and having only seen a photograph of her would-be suitor, Kiranjit agreed to marry him. Within days, Deepak flew to Toronto and the couple were legally married in a brief ceremony at a register office. The full religious wedding was to take place in England the following month; Deepak flew home and his bride joined him some weeks later to begin her new life in Crawley at Deepak's family home.

Almost immediately, Kiranjit regretted her decision. Within days of her arrival in England, and before the wedding had even taken place, Deepak's temper had flared on several occasions and, in a troubling sign of things to come, he had pinned her against a wall and brought his fist down on top of her head. He claimed it was done in jest. After the wedding, Kiranjit found herself trapped in the toxic family environment of her new in-laws' home with a husband who was volatile and violent. She described the early weeks of her married life in fraught terms:

> He wanted complete control – to hit me, to have sex, to take me out, to keep me in, to take me upstairs. I couldn't watch TV, I couldn't eat or drink – not a thing could I do without his approval.

Deepak subjected his new wife to a routine of verbal, physical and sexual abuse. His family were not immune from his outbursts and he often exploded at them as well. But he saved the worst of his rages and attacks for his wife, with his parents and siblings often watching on without intervening – Kiranjit observed that 'it was as if the son of the family was simply torturing the family cat'. But when he pulled a kitchen knife out and threatened to kill his mother during a particularly explosive row, his parents kicked the couple out. Too afraid of what Deepak would do and what her family would say if she tried to leave, Kiranjit remained with her husband. But worse was to come.

Kiranjit stayed in the marriage for a decade. During that time, she and Deepak had two sons. She attempted suicide at least once and tried to leave a couple of times. The abuse and threats from her husband continued largely unabated. On one occasion he held a knife to her throat at a family party and then tried to run her over with his car when she fled into the street. This prompted her to take court action to obtain an injunction against him, but it had little effect. He remained living in the marital home and the violence continued. Kiranjit also suspected that he was having an affair with a work colleague.

Matters came to a head on the evening of 7 May 1989. The couple argued about the repayment of money that a family member had borrowed from them, the fight turned physical and Deepak burned Kiranjit's face with a hot iron. In bed later on, Kiranjit recalled, 'As I lay there, the last ten years flashed through my head ... As the scenes of violence rolled by, one after another, I fell asleep.'

She awoke at around 2.30 a.m., went downstairs and returned to the bedroom with a bottle of petrol and a pan of caustic soda solution she had mixed in the kitchen. She entered their bedroom, showered the petrol around the bed and threw in a lighted candle. She later claimed that she had left the pan of soda in the bathroom and that Deepak must have accidentally thrown it over himself when he tried to put out the flames on his body with water from the bath. In a letter to her mother-in-law written while she was on remand – and before Deepak died – Kiranjit said that she had given him an *agni-ishnaan* (the Hindi term for 'firebath') to wash away the sins of his violence and adultery. The prosecution would rely heavily on this letter as evidence of the premeditated and retaliatory nature of Kiranjit's act.

At her trial for Deepak's murder she claimed that she had not intended to kill him when she started the fire, but she also relied on Deepak's behaviour during the course of their marriage as grounds for a provocation defence. The problem was that the two arguments were to some extent mutually exclusive: she could only have been provoked into doing an intentional act, and if she had killed Deepak accidentally, then the issue of provocation was irrelevant. By a majority of ten to two, the jury convicted her of murder.

That could have been the end of her story, but for the involvement of the Southall Black Sisters, a women's campaign group who had heard about Kiranjit's conviction in the press. The Sisters were more accustomed to focusing their campaigns on the plight of women who had been injured or killed by abusive partners, but founding member Pragna Patel observed that 'we took [Kiranjit's case] on precisely because here was a woman who, instead of being on the receiving end of violence to the point where she gets battered to death, which was our experience, commits the ultimate act of survival'. The group secured a new legal team for Kiranjit and in 1992 her case came to the Court of Appeal.

In some respects the courts' treatment of women who killed their partner after suffering domestic abuse had improved since the days of Ruth Ellis; in 1955 the judge at Ellis's trial had refused to let the defence even raise the possibility of provocation, whereas Kiranjit was at least allowed to argue this defence, even though the jury ultimately rejected it. And the Court of Appeal was prepared to look again at an aspect of the provocation defence that had proved a hurdle for both women

– the question of whether their loss of self-control had been sudden and temporary. In Ruth Ellis's case this had been a non-starter, as she had brooded on David Blakely's abandonment of her over a whole weekend before finally shooting him. And for Kiranjit too, there had been a lapse of time between the row with Deepak and her decision to set his bed alight.

The Appeal judges were at least open to the idea that, in some cases and for some defendants, a time gap may be indicative of a 'slow burn' form of provocation. But they were not prepared to make a conclusive statement to this effect and were wary of the risks of widening the boundaries of the provocation defence too far:

> Where a particular principle of law has been re-affirmed so many times and applied so generally over such a long period, it must be a matter for Parliament to consider any change. There are important considerations of public policy which would be involved should provocation be re-defined so as possibly to blur the distinction between sudden loss of self-control and deliberate retribution.

Sympathetic as they were to Kiranjit's appalling domestic situation, the judges were not prepared to deviate too far from the longstanding definition of provocation, which dated back to the Duffy case of the 1940s. They concluded that she had not been provoked. But they took more of an interest in new psychiatric evidence regarding the effect of Deepak's abuse, which had not been produced at the original trial. The Court of Appeal concluded that it was at least arguable that she had been suffering from diminished responsibility at the time of the fire and, as a result, the murder conviction was unsafe. The guilty verdict was quashed, and in September 1992 Kiranjit Ahluwalia walked free from court.

Following her release, Kiranjit acknowledged that, in the cold light of day, her appeal had failed on its own terms, which was the aim of getting the law of provocation redrawn in support of women who kill abusive partners:

The only way the justice system can accommodate women who say 'enough is enough' is if they can be shown to be not in full control of themselves when they did it, if they can be seen as mad, so as not to upset the social order.

It was the long-term effect of the abuse on her psyche that was key to securing her freedom, not the reasonableness of her reaction to one final instance of it.

*   *   *

While serving her sentence at Bullwood Hall women's prison in Essex, Kiranjit Ahluwalia had met another husband-killer who had become the focus of an intense public campaign. Sara Thornton had been convicted of murder just three months after Kiranjit's trial and both women's cases quickly became linked in the public imagination. Late one evening in June 1989 Sara had slowly and deliberately lowered a kitchen knife into her husband Malcolm's stomach as he lolled drunkenly on the sofa at their home in Warwickshire. The couple had argued earlier in the evening and Sara had gone out to the pub; before leaving the house she had written 'Bastard Thornton I hate you' in lipstick on a mirror in the bedroom.

Drink had paid a large part in the Thorntons' short but volatile marriage, which was less than a year old. It was the second time around for both of them and both had children from their first marriages. Malcolm was ten years Sara's senior and worked as a security guard, but his personal and professional life was overshadowed by his increasing dependence on alcohol. Despite attempts at drying out he had lost his driving licence – and consequently his job – about a month before what a judge described as 'the fatal dénouement' to the couple's relationship.

Sara had her own struggles as well. She had made several attempts at suicide after the end of her first marriage and had at one stage been sectioned under the Mental Health Act, resulting in a short stay in hospital. She was later diagnosed as suffering from a personality disorder, to which problems dating back to her schooldays were attributed. A few weeks before he died Malcolm had punched Sara in the face during an argument and had been charged by the police. He had tried to persuade her to drop the case, which was due in court towards the end of June. But the rows continued. In the days leading up to the stabbing Malcolm had kicked his stepdaughter out of the marital home while Sara was away at a work conference. She had returned in a fury and their animosity increased, with Malcolm throwing furniture around at one point.

Sara said at her trial that their fights had frequently turned violent and Malcolm had threatened to kill her on several occasions. On the evening in question, she claimed that she had only intended to frighten Malcolm; to show him that she would not be cowed any longer. She said that he called her a whore and threatened to kill her again when she came home from the pub. In her evidence to the court, Sara 'repeated on several occasions that she had no intention whatever of stabbing him or hurting him at all. She had not brought the knife down fast. She had done it slowly. She ... had plenty of time to stop ... she had stabbed him but had not meant to.' This rather remarkable account was contradicted by the evidence of the police officers and paramedics who rushed to the house, all of whom reported Sara telling them with a preternaturally calm demeanour that she had stabbed Malcolm deliberately and had wanted to kill him. Her defence was largely based on a diminished responsibility argument but, like Kiranjit Ahluwalia before her, Sara Thornton was convicted of murder and sentenced to life.

The two women became close confidantes in prison, sharing a sense of gallows humour about the predicaments that had landed them both in jail. In her memoir, Kiranjit remembered:

Sara and I used to fantasise about our husbands. We would imagine them sitting on a bench in the exercise yard which we could see from a window in the prison corridor. Sara would make me laugh by saying that Deepak and Malcolm had become friends on the other side, and spent their time discussing their respective wives.

After her conviction, Sara's case was picked up by the campaign group Justice for Women, who were also working with the Southall Black Sisters on Kiranjit's appeal. Sara's case was first to reach the Court of Appeal, where her lawyers argued that there had been insufficient consideration at her trial of the possibility of a provocation defence. While the Court of Appeal were prepared to acknowledge the possibility that the abuse that Sara had suffered had coloured her reaction to Malcolm's threats and insults, they concluded that it was insufficient to reduce the conviction to manslaughter. On her return to prison, Sara went on hunger strike for almost a month in protest at her unsuccessful appeal.

When Kiranjit was freed on appeal a year later, the disparity in the court's approach to the two cases galvanised Sara and her campaign team. They petitioned the home secretary to refer the case back to the court for a further appeal. Eventually, in 1995, their persistence paid off and Sara's case went back to the Court of Appeal for a second time. This time the court was prepared to be more understanding. The abuse that Sara had experienced during the marriage could and should have been taken into account when assessing her actions on the night of Malcolm's death. Although the behaviour that had actually precipitated the stabbing was comparatively mild compared with his physical attacks on her, there was a cumulative effect that could be applied to a defence of provocation. The murder conviction was quashed and the court ordered a retrial. But while provocation had been a mainstay of the appeal, Sara's defence at her second trial focused heavily on her mental health issues and personality disorder. She was acquitted of murder and convicted of manslaughter on the grounds of diminished responsibility. As she had already spent five years in prison, she was immediately released.

The Ahluwalia and Thornton cases had turned the spotlight on the issue of domestic violence and the courts' treatment of victims who suddenly become aggressors after sustained periods of abuse, with fatal consequences for their abusers. Some were afraid that the rulings would give women carte blanche to kill husbands on the flimsiest of grievances and then avoid being convicted of murder. Kiranjit's own memoir, co-written with Rahila Gupta of the Southall Black Sisters, is titled *Provoked*, as was the film adaptation that her story inspired. But while the case itself did little to change the actual law on provocation (her murder conviction was actually quashed on the grounds of diminished responsibility), it did kickstart a long-overdue reappraisal of this aspect of the law and pave the way for future reform. Barrister Helena Kennedy QC, who has represented many female domestic violence victims in the criminal courts, observed:

> *[these cases] educated the judiciary and the public about the law's shortcomings. As a result, the jury is now directed to put themselves in the shoes of the woman on trial and to consider the context of events. There is recognition that the courts must acknowledge cumulative provocation, where after a history of abuse the final act which tips a woman over the edge may not seem very grave but may be the last straw.*

*   *   *

While the Birmingham Six and Kiranjit Ahluwalia celebrated their freedom after success at the Court of Appeal, the men convicted of killing Carl Bridgewater continued to languish in jail. Their first attempt to contest their convictions in 1981 fell at the first hurdle and they were refused permission to appeal by the court. In the years since they were found guilty at Stafford Crown Court, the men's families and friends had united into a powerful campaigning force that attracted some significant support. Investigative journalist Paul Foot covered the case extensively in his *Daily Mirror* columns, and in 1986 his book *Murder at the Farm* was published, which argued forensically and persuasively that the men had been wrongly convicted. Foot's investigations spanned almost six years, and in the final chapter he summed up his conclusions in unequivocal terms:

> What seems to me quite certain is that Carl Bridgewater was not shot by Vincent Hickey, Michael Hickey, Jimmy Robinson or Pat Molloy; and that none of these four men were at Yew Tree Farm on 19 September 1978 or at any other time.

The book, and the publicity surrounding it, played a role in persuading then Home Secretary Douglas Hurd to refer the case back to the Court of Appeal in 1987 – but the appeal itself was unsuccessful. Hurd's successor Kenneth Clarke refused a second request for an appeal in 1993. By that time, the case and the campaign had been picked up by the BBC, which commissioned a dramatisation of the trial and the group's thwarted appeals entitled *Bad Company*. This was followed up in 1996 by an episode of the channel's influential *Rough Justice* documentary series, an early foray into the true crime genre, which sought to reopen cases involving alleged miscarriages of justice.* The publicity generated by the TV coverage lent fresh impetus to the campaign to free the Bridgewater Four, which was spearheaded by Michael Hickey's mother Ann Whelan.

The pressure on the government was growing, and several MPs threw their weight behind the campaign to free the men, resulting in a debate on the case in parliament in February 1996. While Home Secretary Michael Howard had prevaricated over their third application for an appeal, he finally relented and referred the case back to court again in the latter half of 1996. By this time, the Four had become the Three; the oldest member of the gang, Patrick Molloy, had died in prison some years earlier, still protesting his innocence. At a hearing at the High Court in February 1997 the prosecution announced that they would not contest the case any further and the three men were freed on bail, pending a full hearing of the appeal. To jubilant scenes amid the crowds of press, supporters and members of the public gathered outside the Royal Courts of Justice in the Strand, Michael Hickey, Vincent Hickey and James Robinson set foot in the outside world for the first time in almost eighteen years.

Five months later, after a hearing lasting several weeks, the Court of Appeal delivered its judgment:

* *Trainspotting* actor Jonny Lee Miller played Michael Hickey in both *Bad Company* and the dramatic reconstruction portions of the *Rough Justice* episode.

The unhappy conclusion that we have reached is that the criminal justice process did not operate fairly in this case as it should have done.

Placing particular weight on the new evidence that the police's account of how the confessions from Molloy and Vincent Hickey had been obtained was 'most improbable, if not impossible', the court quashed all of the murder convictions. Overnight, the Bridgewater Four were exonerated, which left the obvious question – who *had* killed Carl back in 1978?

The investigation had largely halted at the point when the Four entered the frame; from then onwards, the police operated on the assumption that they had got their men. But before the gang had been caught after the second robbery, a local man had been of significant interest to the inquiry. Bert Spencer was an ambulance operative at a nearby hospital whose vehicle and work clothes fitted the description given by one witness, of seeing a man in uniform in a blue car on the access track to the farm on the afternoon that Carl died. He also had an interest in antiques, and knew Yew Tree Farm and the land surrounding it well, as he used to go shooting over the fields behind the farm. But when the Birmingham men were arrested, Spencer dropped out of the picture. There was a resurgence of speculation when, just a month after the Bridgewater Four were convicted, Spencer shot and killed a friend in a crime that bore striking similarities to Carl's death and which took place at a red-brick farmhouse just a couple of hundred yards to the west of Yew Tree Farm, across the other side of the A449.

Spencer was convicted of his friend's murder, and the coincidences between the two incidents featured heavily both in Paul Foot's writings about the case and in the Bridgewater Four's appeal submissions down the years, as well as being referenced in the parliamentary debate prior to their final appeal. The police's initial suspicion of the ambulance man and the second farmhouse murder were prominent subplots in the *Bad Company* film and were also covered in *Rough Justice*'s analysis of the case. But four independent police inquiries conducted in the years after the trial did not implicate Spencer and the police have never pursued any further action against him. He has consistently denied any involvement in Carl's shooting but suspicion regarding the tragedy continued to dog him, even after his own release from prison shortly after the Bridgewater Four were freed. Like the Birmingham pub bombings the case remains open and Carl's murder remains unsolved, over forty years on from when it happened.

*   *   *

The release of the men wrongly convicted of murdering Carl Bridgewater, almost two decades earlier, was to be one of the last times that a home secretary would be the final arbiter on the right to appeal against miscarriages of justice. In April 1997 the brand new Criminal Cases Review Commission opened its office. It had taken almost five years but the government had finally acted on the recommendations made in the aftermath of the Birmingham Six appeal and established an independent body to investigate alleged miscarriages of justice.

The Commission was empowered by statute to examine individual cases, and, if it found new evidence that gave rise to a real possibility that the conviction would be overturned, to refer the case to the Court of Appeal, taking over the home secretary's power to do so.

The Commission's role was intended to be much more comprehensive than the home secretary's. It was given wide-ranging powers to investigate all aspects of a case, including the right to seize documents from parties or bodies involved and to interview witnesses. In particularly complex cases it was able to instruct the police to open investigations into issues that it uncovered. As well as its role in the appeals process, the Commission was also to advise the home secretary when a pardon was being considered – the government retained this power, but the Commission was often asked to provide a recommendation in such cases.

There was no time limit on referrals to the Commission for investigation; one of its early successes was the posthumous referral of Derek Bentley's conviction back to the Court of Appeal in 1998. In 2020 the Commission was given its most historic assignment to date when the government asked it to review the 170-year-old murder conviction of Sarah Chesham, with a view to granting a pardon. Christened 'Sally Arsenic' by the Victorian press, Sarah had been hanged at Chelmsford in 1851 for the murder of her husband Richard, a farmer. He had died unexpectedly, and when traces of arsenic were found in his stomach at a post-mortem, suspicion immediately fell upon his wife. Unhappily, a couple of years before Richard's death, Sarah had also been accused of poisoning her two young sons and another local boy, but she was acquitted in court. At her trial for Richard's death she was not so lucky.

The Victorians had a morbid obsession with domestic poisonings, fed by the sensational newspaper accounts of the agonising deaths of victims like Richard Chesham. According to historian Judith Flanders, one toxic substance was feared above all others:

> Arsenic was colourless, odourless, tasteless and most of all, cheap. It was also found in dozens of household items: in paints, dyes, soaps and patent medicines. It was used for pest control, as a fertiliser and weedkiller, in stables as a wash for horses' coats and on farms as sheepdip.

A re-examination of the case by Sarah's descendants had led to the call for a pardon. With the benefit of modern analysis – and given the prevalence of arsenic in most Victorian homes – many 19th-century 'poisonings' have been attributed either to accidental ingestion or simply small amounts entering the body from medicines or cosmetics. The Commission's review into Sarah's case is ongoing.

The creation of the Commission was intended to prevent the battles for justice fought by the likes of the Birmingham Six and the Bridgewater Four, sometimes over many years. It was the controversies over these and other murder convictions that highlighted the problems with the legal system and its failures to address its own mistakes. While the government was still the ultimate gatekeeper to the Court of Appeal, there remained the risk of inconsistencies and injustices, like those seen in the infamous cases of the 1950s. The introduction of the Commission was intended to address these concerns; but it has not been immune from criticism itself, with questions being raised over the continuing ability of the criminal justice system to own up to and rectify miscarriages of justice. In 2019 the All Party Parliamentary Group on Miscarriages of Justice commenced a new inquiry to examine the effectiveness of the Commission and, if needed, propose further reforms. The fight, it seems, goes on.

*   *   *

Wrongful convictions, especially for murder, are thankfully rare but no less devastating for all involved. And it is important to remember that there are still two sides to every story. In all of the jubilation surrounding the vindication of those like the Bridgewater Four, the victim of the murder is often eclipsed by the victims of the miscarriage of justice, both in the press and in the public consciousness. In the parliamentary debate on the Four's appeal, one MP made the pointed observation that it would have been more sensitive to Carl and his family if the press had alighted on the 'Yew Tree Farm Four' as a nickname instead. But it was too late – the name had stuck.

In a similar vein, terrorist atrocities like the Birmingham pub bombings are often overlooked as murder cases. They are so bound up in their wider context that they somehow become divorced from the crime that they actually involve. Such incidents are viewed as primarily political acts, and the realisation that those who have died are also murder victims is sometimes secondary. Whoever blew up the Mulberry Bush and the

Tavern in the Town was at a considerable remove when their attack took place and they had no idea who or even how many people they had killed. But the word 'murder' evokes something personal, in some strange sense more intimate and emotive; there is an expectation of some form of relationship between the killer and the victim, however fleeting.

Killing on a mass, almost industrial, scale in incidents like bombings or other catastrophes was at risk of becoming a blind spot for the law of homicide. In the years following the Birmingham pub bombings the images of shocked survivors and walking wounded would come to be a regular feature on television news reports. More often than not, however, these weren't cases of terror attacks or other deliberate atrocities, but were public disasters that were often brushed off as accidents.

From the late 1980s, Britain was rocked by a series of tragic incidents that involved loss of life on a huge scale but without an obvious 'murderer' to prosecute. The law of homicide seemed incapable of properly punishing those who killed, not with malicious or evil intent, but with neglect, indifference or mismanagement. Applying the law of murder to these cases, where the killer was a company or other organisation, was doomed to failure – only a human being is capable of forming the necessary mental intention required to commit murder. But the alternative – a complete absence of any legal accountability for incidents that killed hundreds of innocent people – was equally unsustainable. Something had to be done.

CHAPTER EIGHT
THE BODY CORPORATE

'... there's plenty of air'

The Piper Alpha oil and gas platform stood a hundred miles or so out into the North Sea, off Aberdeen. Along with two other platforms, appropriately named Tartan and Claymore, Piper extracted oil and gas from under the sea bed and piped it back to a terminal at Flotta in the Orkneys. On the evening of 6 July 1988 there were over two hundred men stationed on the platform. Sixty of them were working on shift that night, while most of the rest of the crew were eating, sleeping or just relaxing in the accommodation deck, 170 feet above the sea on top of the oil and gas production areas. Shortly before 10 p.m., operators in the production workshop were startled by a high-pitched noise in the air around them. To one it sounded like someone being strangled; another likened it to the wail of a banshee. In Celtic myth, the scream of this malevolent spirit is said to be an omen of impending death.

At about the same time, a member of the rig's diving team was standing at the bow of one of the support boats, which was anchored a few hundred yards away from Piper. He had come out on deck to take photographs of the platform for his son, who was working on a school project about energy sources. As the diver raised the camera up to his eye he saw jets of flame suddenly shoot out of Piper's upper deck, followed by plumes of black smoke. Realising the import of what he was seeing, he began to photograph the scene before him.

Over the next hour the platform was rocked by two further massive explosions, as the gas risers that connected Piper to the other two rigs in the oil field ruptured. Some of the workers managed to get down to the lower decks and from there on to the support boats that had pulled up as close to the rig as they dared. But many more were trapped, above the fire, in the accommodation block. Over the radio to *Tharos*, one of the other support boats, a Piper crewman described the chaos inside in a garbled message: 'People majority in galley area. Tharos come. Gangway … Hoses. Getting bad.' The billowing black smoke meant that the helicopters that had been scrambled from RAF Lossiemouth on the Scottish mainland were unable to land on the helipad right at the top of the platform, where some workers had managed to gather. Men began to take their chance and jump from the landing pad into the sea below.

By 11 p.m. the flames had eaten through much of the supporting superstructure and Piper Alpha began to collapse into the sea. The next morning, as the helicopters circled above, searching in vain for more survivors, only the skeletal remains

Part of the government's reluctance to take the matter further can perhaps be explained by the questions raised in the inquiry report about its own contribution to the disaster. At the time of the Piper Alpha tragedy the management and operation of offshore energy installations were regulated by the Department of Energy. The inquiry had found that the department's inspection process was little more than superficial, in large part due to its shortage of suitably qualified inspectors. Piper had in fact been visited by a DoE inspector just over a week before the explosions and the inspection had been signed off as satisfactory. The risk of leaks posed by missing valves and the lack of processes to ensure that crews were aware of problems when handing over jobs at shift changes went unnoticed by the inspector. Had a prosecution gone ahead, it would almost certainly have highlighted the shortcomings in the government's management of such a dangerous industry.

But the kind of disturbing catalogue of errors and oversights that led inexorably to disaster on Piper Alpha was not unique to offshore oil. In the late 1980s a spate of public disasters, each occasioning huge losses of life, meant that a frightening number of people had boarded a train, attended a party or simply gone about their normal working day and had never come home. Thirty-one people died in November 1987 when King's Cross underground station was engulfed in flames from an escalator fire started by a discarded match. A similar number were killed in a rail crash at Clapham Junction just over a year later. Within a matter of days of the Lockerbie bombing, which killed all 259 people on Pan Am Flight 103 in December 1988, a passenger plane crashed onto the M1 as it tried to make an emergency landing at East Midlands Airport, killing 47 of the 126 people on board. And in August 1989 fifty-one people at a party on the Thames pleasure cruiser *Marchioness* died when the boat was struck by a dredging vessel and sank near Southwark Bridge.

Speaking in a 2008 House of Commons' debate to mark the twentieth anniversary of the Piper Alpha disaster, Aberdeen MP Frank Doran spelled out the ripple effect of the human toll of these kinds of huge public catastrophes:

The roll-call of honour for Piper Alpha is long. It takes in the survivors; the rescue crews who operated in such difficult conditions to bring both survivors and bodies home; the medical teams who waited in Aberdeen for the helicopters to bring in the most seriously injured ... the crews of the lifting vessels who recovered from the wreckage the accommoda-tion module that contained the bodies of many of the victims; the police and others who went into the module after it was removed and brought ashore to recover the bodies; and the psychiatrists, psychologists, social workers and counsellors who worked not only with the survivors and the families, but with many of the rescuers.

When the effect of such incidents is so damaging and so wide-ranging, both in terms of lives lost but also lives forever altered by what has happened, there is a natural desire to see that somebody – or some body – is held accountable. But none of the horrific disasters that filled the airwaves over such a short period of time at the end of the decade resulted in prosecutions, even under the health and safety legislation that had been part of the law since the mid-1970s. The inquiries that inevitably followed most of these tragedies lacked the ability to attribute criminal responsibility. In his report into the Clapham Junction rail crash, Anthony Hidden QC summarised the aims but also the limitations of the inquiry process:

> An inquiry [into the crash] is not a trial: it is not a test of legal liability, whether civil or criminal. Its procedures are not accusatorial: no one is put in the dock ... Its procedures are instead inquisitorial, it is an investigation with the object of discovering the truth.

However scathing an inquiry's conclusion, it had no power to indict anyone or even to recommend prosecutions. From a criminal perspective the cases were treated as if they were, to all intents and purposes, accidents. There was a growing sense of unease that the law as it stood did not adequately address the situation when fatalities were caused on a big organisation's watch. The law on health and safety was seen primarily as a regulatory issue, part and parcel of the bureaucracy of running a business. A breach of these laws, while undoubtedly a criminal offence, was not seen as a 'real' crime. Even on the occasions when they actually happened, convictions for health and safety offences did not carry an appropriate level of stigma, and campaigners maintained that the behaviour of culpable companies should be called out for what it was – corporate manslaughter.

* * *

Just over a year before the Piper Alpha disaster, at around six o'clock on a spring evening in 1987, the passenger ferry MS *Herald of Free Enterprise* pulled away from its berth at the Belgian port of Zeebrugge, on what should have been a routine crossing to Dover. Four hundred and fifty-nine passengers were on board, many of whom were British tourists taking advantage of a ticket deal in the *Sun* newspaper to have a cheap day out in Belgium. The weather was good and the sea was calm as the ship eased past the outer harbour wall and out into the open sea shortly before 6.30 p.m.

Less than five minutes later the *Herald* suddenly capsized, its port side grounded in the shallow water of the harbour. For the passengers, many of whom had headed to the restaurant in the middle of the ship as soon as it sailed, the world quite literally turned upside down. Below the surface the ship was rapidly filling with water, and it had rolled over so suddenly that there was no time for the crew to launch lifeboats or even pass out lifejackets. As the ferry was not even out of sight of the harbour when it tipped over, the rescue effort was swift. Alongside Belgian and French rescue vessels, RAF helicopters swarmed across the English Channel from bases on the south and east coasts, to airlift survivors from the freezing water.

The initial news reports of the disaster were confused and understandably, but crushingly, optimistic. The BBC evening news that night led with the incident and relayed initial casualty figures that were far below the true toll. Reporter Christopher Morris tried to reassure viewers with the news that 'there are clear signs of survivors inside [the hull of the ship] and there's plenty of air'. But rescue teams estimated that those trapped alive inside the ship could only survive for a maximum of thirty minutes, probably less, in the frigid water that had flooded the hull. The report also erroneously stated that all of the eighty crew members had been rescued – in reality, thirty-eight lost their lives and ultimately, 193 people would be found to have died in the sinking.

Reporters also grasped for an explanation as to why the ship had foundered so suddenly. In the immediate aftermath of the capsizing, it was suggested that the ferry may have struck the harbour wall as it sailed out of Zeebrugge or run aground on the sandbank on which it had come to rest. What was immediately apparent to all those on the scene was that the huge doors in the ship's bow, which allowed cars to drive onto and off the vehicle deck of the ferry, were open. Initially it was assumed that this was a consequence of the *Herald* foundering, that the doors had burst open as a result of whatever collision or force had tipped the ship onto its side. But by the following morning there were more disturbing explanations. Some of the crew members that had been rescued told investigators that the ferry had actually put to sea with the bow doors still open. If this had indeed been the case, then the implications were troubling.

The *Herald* was a type of ferry known as a 'roll-on/roll-off' or, more colloquially, a 'RORO'. The vehicle deck ran the length of the ship, with huge doors at both the bow and stern to allow cars to 'roll on' to the ferry when boarding and 'roll off' from the opposite end of the boat when it docked. This meant that the ferry did not need to waste time turning around to enable cars to disembark when it came into harbour at the end of a crossing, making for a speedier run across the congested and competitive cross-Channel routes. The design of RORO ferries meant that the vehicle deck effectively created a tunnel straight through the hull of the ship, secured only by the closing of the doors at each end of the ferry. If the ship had set sail with the bow doors open, a new theory to explain the accident presented itself; as the ship moved forwards, water would have rushed in through the open doors, flooding the car deck and quickly destabilising the whole vessel.

For a month after the capsizing, the *Herald* lay at the entrance to Zeebrugge harbour like a giant beached whale with its red and white flank turned up to the sky. In early April the enormous task of salvaging the wreck began. A fleet of huge barges pulled the boat into an upright position and it rested on its keel on the sandbank, while divers ventured inside the hull to examine its condition and begin the search for victims. A week or so later it was pulled into the harbour and the grim process of removing the bodies began. Calculating the final number of fatalities would take several months and some passengers remained unaccounted for even after the ferry was cleared. The body of one man was only found several months later, during a dredging operation on the seabed around Zeebrugge.

In the weeks following the sinking the Department of Transport convened an inquiry into the disaster, and such tribunals would become a regular occurrence in the late 1980s and early 1990s on the back of the slew of public catastrophes that would follow in the *Herald*'s wake. The inquiry heard that, far from being an isolated incident, the ferry was not the first RORO to set sail with its doors open. Incredibly, it was not even the first ferry with the words 'Free Enterprise' in its name to do so; four years before the Zeebrugge tragedy, the *Herald*'s sister ship the *Pride of Free Enterprise* had sailed all the way from Dover to Calais with its doors hanging open.

The inquiry was swift to identify the causes of the catastrophe, which were a catalogue of human errors, exacerbated by gaps in the ship's monitoring and safety systems. The job of closing the vehicle decks doors before a sailing fell to the assistant bosun – but as the ferry readied itself for departure, he was resting in his cabin and slept through the Tannoy announcement summoning the crew to their stations. None of the other crew members that had been loading cars on to the deck saw it as their job to check whether the doors had been closed. There was nothing built into the loading protocols that required anyone to double-check the doors. Up on the bridge, from where the *Herald*'s captain had given the order for the ship to set sail, there was no means of checking that the bow doors were closed – no indicator lights nor system checks. The captain relied on crew members reporting any problems to him, and, if there were no such reports, he effectively assumed that all was safe for departure. The dangers of this assumption were clear when viewed in the context of the previous incidents involving open bow doors on crossings.

There were other factors identified by the inquiry as well, which individually would not have been sufficient to wreck the ship, but, as is usually the way in these kinds of catastrophe, were part of the fatal combination of events that led to the disaster. The *Herald*'s usual route was Dover to Calais and the

In the inquiry's analysis, it was the very pursuit of 'free enter-prise' that had led to the *Herald*'s sinking, as the company had prioritised its profits by cutting corners to speed up its sailings with scant regard for passenger safety. The criticism was sting-ing; but the government stonewalled. At the parliamentary debate on the publication of the report, under heavy fire from the opposition benches, Transport Secretary Paul Channon was adamant that there would be no criminal charges brought against the ferry company. Manslaughter was conspicuous by its absence in the discussion, and the government maintained the ludicrous position that sailing a large passenger ferry with a gaping hole in its bow was not a criminal offence. The sections of the Merchant Shipping Act that governed the seaworthiness of ships referred only to the 'condition' of the parts of a boat when it set sail, not the position of such parts.

This led to the absurd situation, maintained and promoted by the Department of Transport in the House of Commons debate, that because its bow doors were in good working order at the time of the sinking, the *Herald* was not unseaworthy, conveniently overlooking the fact that they were hanging wide open. John Prescott, the then Shadow Transport Secretary, fumed in the House of Commons that the ship's owners' co-operation with the inquiry had been bought by a promise from government that they would not face any prosecution.

But the pressure on the government would continue to grow in the months following the disaster. In October 1987 the inquest into the deaths of the victims of the *Herald*'s sinking concluded with a verdict that they had been unlawfully killed. The coroner had resisted an argument from the families' lawyers that a verdict of corporate manslaughter should have been returned against Townsend or P&O. Nevertheless, in light of the coroner's verdict, the Director of Public Prosecutions had no option but to order the police to investigate the incident to ascertain whether any criminal offences had been committed; and the police were not interested in technical breaches of maritime legislation – they were looking at the possibility of homicide charges.

The day after the coroner's verdict was announced, P&O went on the attack. Its chairman, Sir Jeffrey Sterling, told the press that the tragedy was entirely the fault of the ferry's captain and crew, and that any suggestion that the company bore any responsibility was 'far-fetched'. The arrogance of his comments would come back to haunt the company in June 1989, when the DPP announced the outcome of the police investigation. P&O, alongside three of its directors and four of the ferry's crew, were to be charged with manslaughter.

One press report on the P&O prosecution noted that: 'The summons against the company … could make legal history. There is no previous case in English law of a company being convicted of manslaughter.' And while this was indeed correct, it was not for want of trying. There had been attempts at bringing companies to book for fatalities since the early part of the 20th century.

*   *   *

Cory Brothers Limited was the owner and operator of a number of collieries in the valleys of South Wales in the years after the First World War. Its mining empire also included a large electrical plant in the village of Ogmore Vale, which provided power to thirteen of its pits in the local area. Employed at one of these mines was Brynmor John, a sixteen-year-old colliery assistant.

On an August evening in 1926 Brynmor snuck out of his slate-clad cottage on one of the hilly streets of the village and met up with a group of friends near the river, down at the bottom of the valley. A couple of the lads had dogs in tow and one was equipped with a ferret. They set off along the river-bank to hunt rats. When one of the terriers ran off and squeezed through the perimeter fencing of the power station, Brynmor and his friend William Parkhouse followed, crawling through a gap under the wire fencing to retrieve the dog. But their expedition caught the attention of the plant's night watchman, and when Brynmor tried to scarper he tripped and fell against the wire fencing, which was electrified. William tried to help his friend while the guard ran back into the building to switch off the power. But he could only watch as Brynmor lay convuls-ing on the ground, his skin turning a strange yellow colour. By the time the guard returned he was dead.

The inquest into the boy's death heard that the electric fence had only been installed earlier that day, after a spate of thefts of the coal that was stockpiled at the plant to power its engines. The coroner returned a verdict of manslaughter, to much cheering from the local community. Supported by the local miners' union, Brynmor's brother George then launched a private prosecution for manslaughter against the three engi-neers who had installed the fence, together with Cory Brothers as the company that owned the power plant. A change in the law just a year earlier had suggested that the prosecution of a corporation, a non-human entity, for criminal offences was now possible, although the application of this to a homicide offence had never been tried.

The engineers themselves claimed that they believed that the level of electric current was set so low that it would only give any intruders 'a tingle', and that the fence was only ever intended to be a deterrent. This was undermined by the proprietor of a local chippy, who reported overhearing them discussing the fence over a fish supper a couple of days before Brynmor's death:

> We will put a stop to this. We will put something up and I'll switch on the juice and let some of the [expletive deleted] get it in the neck.

The court was not persuaded by the prosecution's case that a company could be convicted of an offence that had personal violence against another at its heart; the manslaughter charge against the company was quashed and the three engineers were all acquitted.

The first attempt to prosecute a non-human entity for homicide had ended in failure. Then, as now, there was no possibility of indicting a company for murder; a corporation could not be sentenced to death or imprisonment and so manslaughter (punishable by, among other things, a fine) was the only option. While the broadening of the law following the emergence of gross negligence manslaughter in the 1920s and 1930s made a case against a company a more feasible possibility, by the time that the manslaughter charge against P&O was announced in

1989 it was still far from clear whether the courts would allow it to proceed.

At an early court hearing P&O argued robustly that manslaughter could only be committed by a 'natural person' (harking back to the language of Sir Edward Coke's historic definition of murder), and therefore a company could not be guilty of the crime. It also pointed to the dismissal of the case against Cory Brothers as a precedent that such an offence did not exist in English law. But the reality was that there had been an exponential expansion in corporate activity over the intervening decades, which had a very real involvement in people's lives. It would be a dangerous anomaly if companies could use their legal status as a means to avoid liability for criminal actions, particularly when these had resulted in someone's death. The law had moved on in other ways as well – the health and safety legislation contained express provisions making corporate bodies liable for criminal breaches of its requirements.

The judgment of the court was clear:

> *Suffice it that where a corporation, through the controlling mind of one of its agents, does an act which fulfils the prerequisites of the crime of manslaughter, it is properly indictable for the crime of manslaughter.*

For the first time in English legal history, a court had confirmed that companies, organisations and other institutions could be guilty of homicide. The case against P&O and the other defendants would proceed.

The trial commenced at the Old Bailey in September 1990. When the number of victims of a single homicide is so huge, the individual tragedies can become lost amid the sheer scale of the horror. Rather than prosecute each of the seven defendants for all of the deaths that occurred on board (which would have totalled over a thousand manslaughter charges), the Crown chose a specimen charge relating to the killing of a single passenger. The story of that passenger, a twenty-seven-year-old north Londoner named Alison Gaillard, would therefore represent and epitomise each person that had died on the *Herald*, in the same manner as the enormous human toll of the First World War is embodied by the single soldier interred in the Tomb of the Unknown Warrior. Alison was travelling on the ferry with her husband Francis. The couple had been married for just eighteen months and had booked the trip to Belgium as a last-minute day out. Alison's body was brought ashore in the initial rescue effort, but Francis was not recovered from the ship until the salvage operation took place weeks later.

The news that the prosecution of P&O for a corporate manslaughter charge was being allowed to proceed was welcomed by the families of people killed in other similar disasters as well. Relatives of the victims of both the King's Cross fire and the *Marchioness* sinking pressured the Director of Public Prosecutions to bring homicide charges against the companies involved in those tragedies as well, with a renewed optimism that they would finally see justice done.

But then, after hearing twenty-seven days of evidence, the judge brought the *Herald* trial to a shuddering halt. The evidence disclosed against the Townsend directors was not, in the view of the judge, enough to sustain a manslaughter conviction. The prosecution had not been able to prove that 'they either gave no thought to an obvious and serious risk or alternatively [that they did but] nevertheless went on to run it'. The judge ordered the jury to return not guilty verdicts against P&O and its directors; the prosecutions against the crew members were to be dropped as well. The first trial of a company for manslaughter in an English court in over sixty years had collapsed.

In allowing the corporate manslaughter prosecution to proceed at the outset, the judge had at the same time strictly limited the circumstances in which it could succeed. The guilt of the company rested on proving the guilty actions of its 'controlling mind'. This rule was known as the 'identification doctrine' and meant that a corporation or other body could only be guilty of manslaughter if it was proved that the cause of the death could be linked to the acts and decisions of the organisation's controlling mind. This required prosecutors to identify a very senior individual within the organisation who had effectively committed the offence themselves.

In practice, only members of the company's board of directors were considered sufficiently high-ranking to have the necessary influence over the business's activities to make them part of the controlling mind. Within smaller companies this link was easier to establish, but the myriad management layers in big companies meant the connecting chain between the decisions of executives and the death was often broken. If the directors were not guilty of manslaughter then it automatically followed that the company was not either. The acquittal of

P&O essentially left the prospect of an English crime of corporate homicide holed below the waterline.

* * *

The failure to hold anyone to account for any of the terrible public disasters that plagued Britain in the late 1980s is a stain on the British legal system that has not yet faded, almost forty years later. But it also opened up wider questions about the law of homicide and its suitability to deal with killings and tragedies that did not conform to the traditional notion of 'murder'.

There had been rumblings of discontent from the judiciary for several years that the concepts that made up the offence of murder required codification and simplification, particularly in cases that raised evidential difficulties with proving an intention to kill. On top of this, the controversy surrounding the convictions of women like Kiranjit Ahluwalia and Sara Thornton had undermined confidence in the law surrounding provocation and how it was applied to victims of domestic violence. And so the shortcomings of the law as applied to corporate manslaughter were now added to the shopping list of homicide reforms that victims, lawyers and campaigners had been pushing for over the preceding decades.

The message from these cases was clear. The overhaul of the law that was so badly required could only come from parliament. The role of the courts in individual cases is to interpret the law as it is, not to make new pieces of law. Sometimes these interpretations can modify or apparently extend elements of the law, enabling it to develop in an almost piecemeal fashion, case by case. But wholesale changes to the very character and fundamentals of the rules can only be made by the government passing legislation. Although the closing years of the 20th century would see some moves from parliament in this direction, this was largely confined to issues on the very peripheries of homicide law.

One example of this was the abolition of the venerable 'year and a day rule', one of those fossilised remnants of murder's archaic origins that occasionally caused legal havoc when it was accidentally excavated. Under the rule, if a victim died 367 days or more after the infliction of the injury that had caused their death, then the killing could not be classed as unlawful. As one academic described it, 'the unfortunate victim lingers in life over the year, the fortunate criminal is free from prosecution for murder'.

The genesis of the rule can be traced back to the murky emergence of the offence of murder in the medieval period. At the time that murder was coming into being as a discrete category of homicide, most prosecutions had to be instigated by the bringing of a lawsuit against the killer. This process was subject to a time limit of one year and a day, outside of which cases were barred. Over time, and for reasons lost to history, this arbitrary deadline ended up being transferred from the commencement of the legal proceedings to the time that the fatal act itself occurred. By the time that Sir Edward Coke set down his definition in the 16th century, the rule was well established and Coke in fact included it within his circumscription of the limits of murder.* The year and a day rule had thus

---

* Coke's definition of murder goes on to state that 'the party wounded ... die of the wound ... within a year and a day after the same'.

become firmly embedded in the canon of homicide law and applied in cases of both murder and manslaughter. But it was a rule that was encountered more often in theory than in practice, which perhaps explains why it was able to survive for so long.

In bygone eras, when pathology was not sufficiently advanced to pinpoint the cause of a death that took place so long after the event, the rule undoubtedly served a useful purpose as a safeguard against injustice. From a defendant's point of view, it operated as a limitation on the criminal process, so that they did not have to live under the shadow of a murder prosecution indefinitely. But by the late 20th century, the continued efficacy of the rule was being called into question. The state of medical science was such that a cause of death could be reliably determined in most, if not all, homicide cases. Modern juries had become accustomed to handling ever more complex scientific issues in criminal trials, particularly since the advent of DNA evidence and other advances in forensic science. MPs were pushed to consider the issue following a number of distressing cases involving victims who had, with medical interventions, kept death at bay for longer than expected and thus inadvertently saved their assailant from prosecution for homicide when they eventually passed away.

The most high profile of such stories was that of Tony Bland. On Saturday 15 April 1989 the football-mad teenager had made the trip from his home in Keighley in Yorkshire to watch his beloved Liverpool play Nottingham Forest in the FA Cup semi-final. The match was being held at a neutral venue – Sheffield Wednesday's Hillsborough stadium. The police force in charge of crowd control at the ground directed more and

so low, the hospital proposed to withdraw the feeding tube and allow him to die with dignity. To Howe's surprise, the coroner informed him that he considered that such action would be unlawful and that the doctor himself could face prosecution for murder if he proceeded.

With the unanimous support of Tony's parents and family, the hospital trust commenced legal proceedings to seek a declaration from the court that the withdrawal of the life-sustaining feeding procedure was in fact lawful.* As Tony himself could take no part in the case, the Official Solicitor was appointed to act on his behalf – the Solicitor is a government department that steps in to represent vulnerable people who are unable to take part in litigation due to mental incapacity. Against the express wishes of those who loved and knew Tony best, the Solicitor opposed the hospital's proposals.

The case would drag on for several years, as the government pursued numerous appeals, up to the House of Lords. In February 1993, upholding the decisions made by both the original judge and subsequently reaffirmed by the Court of Appeal, the Law Lords ordered that the hospital could lawfully withdraw the feeding tube that was keeping Tony alive. He died a couple of weeks later on 3 March, becoming the ninety-sixth victim of the events at Hillsborough almost four years before.

Tony's case was the first time that English courts had had to consider the legality of doctors withdrawing life-sustaining

---

* This was effectively the same legal process used in 2000 by the doctors treating conjoined twins Jodie and Mary to authorise the surgery to separate them.

care or treatment from patients in the knowledge that doing so would result in the patient's death. The key issue for the court to determine was whether or not the feeding process constituted medical treatment; there was persuasive precedent from American cases that it did, and that it therefore could be discontinued if doctors considered that doing so was in the best interests of the patient concerned. This was the basis of the hospital trust's argument in court. The Official Solicitor's stance was that the feeding was not medical treatment, and therefore its withdrawal was a deliberate act that was intended to bring about Tony's death – in other words, murder. Their underlying concern was that a ruling in favour of the hospital would poise the law at the top of a slippery slope that could potentially lead to the legalisation of euthanasia in the UK via the back door.

The exercise undertaken by the courts was in essence a balancing act between the sanctity of life and the right of self-determination; the judges were effectively deciding what Tony would have wanted for himself if he had been able to make the decision. In endorsing the course of action proposed by the hospital, the courts were satisfied that the duty of care owed by the medical team to Tony did not extend to artificially feeding him when it was not in his best interests to be fed. But the House of Lords recognised that there were some inherent contradictions in the ruling they had given. Lord Browne-Wilkinson, one of the bench of five Law Lords that delivered the final decision in the protracted case, observed:

How can it be lawful to allow a patient to die slowly, though painlessly, over a period of weeks from lack of food, but unlawful to produce his immediate death by a lethal injection, thereby saving his family from yet another ordeal to add to the tragedy that has already struck them? I find it difficult to find a moral answer to that question. But it is undoubtedly the law and nothing I have said casts doubt on the proposition that the doing of a positive act with the intention of ending life is, and remains, murder.

While the courts were unwavering that the death of Tony Bland was not and could not be murder, this was not enough for some of the campaigners who had attached themselves to the controversial case. Just a fortnight after Tony died, a Roman Catholic priest from Scotland went to Bingley Magistrates' Court in Yorkshire to try to commence a private prosecution against Tony's doctor Jim Howe for murder. Nicholas Lyell, the attorney general, had already assured Howe that any such attempt would be quashed and the magistrates refused to issue the court papers.

In 1996 the government enacted legislation to abolish the year and a day rule, prompted by the outcry at the risk of injustice for victims like Tony, so there is no longer any limitation on the time period within which a person's death must occur for it to be treated as a homicide. However, in cases where a victim has survived for longer than three years after the act that caused their death, a prosecution must be authorised by the attorney general as the senior law officer of government. It would be years before anyone else would face the prospect of a homicide trial for the deaths caused at Hillsborough, and the bereaved families would join the ranks of relatives fighting for justice for loved ones killed in a catastrophe that should have been avoided.

But the legal controversies thrown up by the stadium tragedy continued to trouble the courts and hit the headlines throughout that time. In 1998 a group of police officers who had been on duty at the ground on the day of the tragedy brought a personal injury claim against their employer, South Yorkshire Police. This was a civil, as opposed to criminal, action, and was a claim for compensation for injuries suffered in the course of their employment. The officers themselves had not been physically harmed (or even at risk of harm) but had suffered psychiatric injuries as a result of the horrors they had witnessed at the stadium; most of the group had been diagnosed with a form of post-traumatic stress disorder.

The recovery of compensatory damages for mental injury by claimants who had suffered no actual physical wound was a relatively recent, albeit controversial, development in the English law of negligence. Early cases used to refer to claims for 'nervous shock' but by the 1990s this term had been replaced by more diagnostically precise conditions. The police officers' claim was based on an argument that the police force had breached the duty of care that it owed to its employees in exposing them to the traumatic situation at the football ground; by this stage in the Hillsborough story, South Yorkshire Police had finally admitted that their actions in allowing the Leppings Lane pens to become dangerously overcrowded were negligent. And for a time at least, it looked as if the claim would succeed. But there was one difficult nuance to the situation that the courts had to confront. Six years before the officers' claim, in 1992, a group of relatives of some of the Hillsborough victims had brought an almost identical claim against the South Yorkshire force – and had been unsuccessful.

The psychological damage experienced by the Hillsborough families made for harrowing testimony in court. Some had been alongside loved ones in the crush; others had been watching the tragedy unfold live on television and had spotted relatives in the crowd. But the court was adamant that the circumstances were insufficient to give rise to a liability for damages on the part of the police. In also rejecting the claims made by the police officers, the court expressly recognised the likelihood of public outrage were the police officers to be compensated while the bereaved were not. The Hillsborough cases helped to clarify the law's approach to psychiatric injury and the rules that they set out are still applied by the courts in similar compensation claims today, just one of the enduring legal legacies of the disaster.

*　　*　　*

In spite of the uproars and the campaigns in the years after Piper Alpha, Zeebrugge and Hillsborough, the body count continued to rise. However, further attempts were made to right the wrongs of the P&O case. In September 1997 a passenger train travelling from Swansea to Paddington ran through two warning signals on its final run in to London and was approaching a red signal. The train's driver had been packing up his rucksack ready for disembarking at the end of the journey and was momentarily distracted from looking at the line ahead. Both of the cab's automated warning systems, which would have alerted the driver to the upcoming signal, had been switched off. A freight train was crossing the line up ahead and the Swansea express ploughed into it at over 80 miles per hour. Seven passengers were killed and over 150 were injured.

Both the train driver and the train operator Great Western Trains were indicted for manslaughter. The prosecution argued that, notwithstanding the individual faults of the driver in missing the crucial signals, GWT should have had better systems in place to prevent such an occurrence, including a failsafe to prevent the manual switch-off of the warning mechanisms. Allowing one of its trains to leave a station in that condition was a gross breach of the company's duty of care to its passengers. But the court was unpersuaded – the prosecution against the train company was dismissed in the same circumstances as P&O's case just a few years before. The court remained adamant that the only way to convict a company of manslaughter was to identify a sufficiently senior person within the company whose negligence had caused the death and, as with P&O, it was not possible to pinpoint a director who could be held accountable. A friend of one of the victims commented bitterly, 'It's Kafkaesque. It's cheaper for GWT to kill people than to install safety systems.' Remarkably, the judge did fine GWT £1.5 million on a separate charge for a health and safety offence to which they had already pleaded guilty, observing that this had resulted from a 'serious fault of senior management', but without commenting on the irony that he felt unable to convict the company of manslaughter on the grounds of the same senior fault.

Public and political anger finally spilled over at the second acquittal of a company for manslaughter in less than a decade. Tony Blair had entered 10 Downing Street just a matter of months before the Southall crash and his New Labour government promised swift action. At the party conference in October 1997 Home Secretary Jack Straw announced that he would look at the introduction of new laws to ensure that companies could no longer escape criminal liability when their activities killed people. Straw's apparently decisive stance begged the question of why it had taken so long for an offence of corporate manslaughter to be countenanced by a British government. It had been over thirty years since Pantglas School had been destroyed in the Aberfan disaster, which saw the NCB escape any criminal liability for the deaths of those killed. But until 1997 there had been no serious attempts by successive UK governments to address this gap in the law. In large part the change in approach had come about on the back of one of the most contentious features in the political landscape in the late 20th century – privatisation.

At the time of Aberfan, coal mining – like many other hazardous industries, such as the railways, gas and electricity – was nationalised. As the ultimate owner of any nationalised company but also as the embodiment of the criminal justice system, the government was essentially both poacher and gamekeeper in respect of any criminal offences committed by such companies. Any fine that was imposed would simply result in the shifting of government money from one department to another. There was no incentive for government to criminalise itself in this manner. But with the scheme of privatising such industries ushered in by the successive Conservative governments under Margaret Thatcher from the late 1970s onwards, this crease in the fabric of regulation began to be smoothed out and a proper law of corporate homicide became a more workable prospect.

But it would take another ten years for Straw's promise to translate into action. Although corporate manslaughter again featured in Labour's manifesto for the 2001 general election, it found itself overtaken by other priorities and it wasn't until 2005 that draft legislation was finally published. It took a further two years until the Corporate Manslaughter and Corporate Homicide Act finally made it onto the statute books, a decade on from the Southall crash that had prompted the government to finally act. The Act created a specific offence of corporate manslaughter,* with the new law aiming to shift the focus away from the 'identification' principle that had proved such a hurdle in the past cases. Attention was now concentrated on the wider concept of the 'way in which [the organisation's] activities are managed or organised by its senior management' by looking at things such as a company's policies, processes and general culture around safety and risk. This was intended to remedy the deficiencies of past approaches and bring the new manslaughter offence into line with the approach taken by the health and safety legislation, under

* The offence is called 'corporate homicide' in Scotland.

which companies had been successfully prosecuted for over thirty years. Almost a century on from Brynmor John's death at the hands of Cory Brothers and its employees, English law had finally recognised that companies can indeed kill.

Corporate crime never has been and never will be sexy. Health and safety prosecutions or corporate manslaughter cases don't capture the public imagination in the same way that serial killers and psychopaths do. But the creation of the corporate killing offence was among the biggest of all revolutions in the law of homicide. It finally recognised that victims and killers don't always conform to the historical archetypes of murder and manslaughter, and that the unintended consequences of institutional laxity can be just as devastating as individual wickedness. Murder and manslaughter had come a long way from their Anglo-Saxon origins, but this historical DNA remains at the heart of the crimes that are part of our law today. The law must constantly reinvent itself in order to punish the deserving and avenge the innocent. As the English law of murder entered its second millennium, there was to be no let-up in this cycle of evolution and revolution.

CHAPTER NINE
MURDER: A PRIMER

'... as society advances ...'

As we enter the third decade of the 21st century, the English crime of murder celebrates its thousandth birthday, give or take a century or so. The last twenty years have seen the most significant efforts to reform and rewrite the law of homicide in its recent history, but the jury is still out on how effective these attempts have been and whether the current law of murder is fit for purpose. At the same time, controversial cases have continued to push at the boundaries of the law as we know it, each of which has the potential to change and transform the law for years to come. The legal definition of murder has not fundamentally altered in the last four hundred years and, if Sir Edward Coke were brought back to life today, he would no doubt be surprised to hear his words still being quoted in English courts. The modern law of homicide bears no resemblance to Edward the Confessor's original *murdrum*, but the varying crimes that sit under that umbrella can all trace their ancestry back to the same ancient roots, which remain at the heart of the law as it continues to adapt to address very contemporary horrors.

What follows is something of a primer on the state of the laws of murder, manslaughter and the other crimes of homicide as they stand in England today, based on the issues that continue to challenge and shape this venerable offence almost a thousand years on from its inception. Let us consider the most recent developments in all of these crimes, along with how and why people continue to commit them, in turn.

*   *   *

As the law stands today, you commit murder if you intentionally kill someone or you deliberately do them serious physical harm that results in their death. This means that, in the eyes of the law, the pub brawler who doesn't realise their own strength is as much a 'murderer' as a hitman who is contracted to kill, or a serial murderer who has carried out an orchestrated campaign of slaughter. As modern courts have wrestled with the task of interpreting Sir Edward Coke's terminology for the modern era, the legal reality of the offence has become far removed from the popular obsession with 'malice aforethought' and premeditation, and does not reflect what springs to mind when most people think of murder.

Like most criminal offences, murder consists of two elements, both of which must be proved to secure a conviction. The first, the *actus reus*, is the killing of another person. It sounds like it should be straightforward but there are a few exceptions, most of which still derive from Coke's definition.

The killing must be 'under the King's peace', meaning it excludes killing of enemies in warfare. This is why soldiers are not routinely up on murder charges for killing on the battle-field. However, there is no like exception for police officers, who are still subject to the same criminal laws as the public they police but will often have a self-defence argument when killing in the line of duty.

The murder victim must be 'any reasonable creature in rerum natura'. This means a human being who has been born before the killing occurs. Babies without an existence inde-pendent of their mother cannot be murdered as they are not a person in being. The crime of infanticide, created at the turn of the 20th century, relates to the killing of a baby by its mother within the first twelve months of its life while the balance of her mind was disturbed by the effect of what we would now term post-natal depression.

The mental element, or *mens rea*, of murder remains one of the most deceptively simplistic in criminal law. The modern courts have interpreted Coke's 'malice aforethought' to mean that the act was done with an intention to kill or commit griev-ous bodily harm. In cases where this intention is denied, the law may infer it if there is an obvious risk of harm created by the killer's actions.

There are not many criminal offences that still rely on a defi-nition written by a lawyer who started his career in Tudor times. From the mid-20th century onwards, the courts had complained that the law's most infamous crime was confused and confus-ing, with proper reform long overdue. Finally, in 2006 the Law Commission published far-reaching proposals to overhaul the law of homicide in England and Wales. This in itself was nothing unusual. The job of the Commission is to keep the country's laws under constant review and make recommendations on reforms to government as and when they consider it necessary. Their past consultations have covered subjects as diverse as poison-pen letters and polygamous marriages. But with the homicide review, the Commission decided to tackle the biggest elephant in the courtroom. They produced the most comprehensive review of the laws on unlawful killing in a century and proposed radical reforms, which, if adopted, would rewrite the English law of murder as we know it.

Part of the problem with the law was that, over three hundred years after his death, judges still deferred to Sir Edward Coke's definition of the offence of murder when explaining the law to juries: 'Even though he successfully prosecuted the gunpowder plotters, Lord Coke's knowledge of the criminal law was patchy and his account of murder contained some bad errors.' The reliance of the courts on such an antiquated definition had no doubt led to injustices down the centuries and, by the turn of the 21st century, the Commission concluded that this had left the law of murder 'a rickety structure set upon shaky foundations'. As the Commission saw it, a comprehensive scheme to rationalise and codify the law, so that it was easily understood and consistently applied, was the only solution.

To solve the perception gap between the myth of murder and the reality, the Commission proposed a new classification system for homicide, along the same lines as in the United States. It can be difficult to generalise when discussing US law, as individual states operate as discrete jurisdictions, with consequent variations in the law that they apply. But in the case of homicide the practice is reasonably consistent across the country. Almost all states distinguish different 'degrees' of murder, which vary according to the killer's culpability and other aggravating factors, such as particularly brutal killings or the use of torture. In so-called 'capital states' a conviction for first-degree murder carries the death penalty.

The new Homicide Act for England and Wales proposed by the Commission would sweep away the decades of judicial fudging and replace it with three straightforward offences: first-degree murder, second-degree murder and manslaughter. First-degree murder would reflect the common understanding of murder as a deliberate and intentional killing. The new crime of second-degree murder would bridge the gap between the crimes of murder and manslaughter under the current law. It would include cases where the defendant intended to cause serious harm but not kill, now classified as murder; but would also cover those cases where a killer was indifferent to the risk of death that they had created, which presently fall towards the top end of the manslaughter bracket. The existing defences of diminished responsibility and provocation would continue to apply to second-degree murder cases. The retention of a separate offence of manslaughter, below the two degrees of murder, would apply to those deaths caused by gross negligence or an unlawful act.

Each offence would be clearly defined in the legislation with the aim of ensuring that only the truly murderous were so labelled, thereby improving justice for society as a whole.

Hurrah, then – surely – for the clear-sighted and pragmatic Law Commissioners and their enlightened proposals. But it was not to be. The government decided not to implement their key reforms and left the law of homicide largely untouched. A report issued by the Ministry of Justice in 2011 confirmed that, after considering the Law Commission's blueprint for a new framework for homicide for several years, the government had rejected the substance of the reforms:

> The Government has given the ... proposals [for a tiered classification of murder] in the report careful consideration. However, it has come to the conclusion that the time is not right to take forward such a substantial reform of our criminal law.

Taking on an overhaul of the most infamous and controversial crime in law is not an appealing task for any government. It inevitably opens up debate around law and order, the labelling of offenders, public safety and sentencing policy. Our response to the word 'murder' is an emotive and visceral one. It is something on which everyone has an opinion, even if murder is not actually as widely understood as it should be. When a concept is so entrenched in society's collective subconscious, any attempt to change it, however legally sound, provokes an instinctive reaction. So parliament decided to let sleeping dogs lie. The reform of murder, which judges, lawyers and victims' groups had been seeking for many years, was once again kicked into the long grass.

*　　*　　*

However, there were some sections of the reform proposals that did ultimately see the light of day. As well as the Corporate Manslaughter and Corporate Homicide Act, long promised by government, which finally reached the statute books in 2007, there were some further amendments to homicide law made during Labour's remaining time in office. In 2009 new definitions of diminished responsibility and provocation, based on the Law Commission's recommendations, were brought into the law, in an effort to update at least some elements of murder for contemporary consumption.

Provocation had of course been an established defence to murder since at least the 17th century, while diminished responsibility had only been created by the 1957 Homicide Act. In cases of intentional killings that would otherwise be classed as murder, a successful defence of provocation or diminished responsibility will reduce the crime to manslaughter. This category of manslaughter is sometimes referred to as 'voluntary', as the killing itself is intentional but the partial defence has mitigated the killer's culpability.

Diminished responsibility had experienced something of a PR problem over the decades since its inception. It was intended to offer a halfway house between a murder conviction and an insanity defence, for those who killed under the influence of some mental impairment but who were not able to meet the threshold for insanity under the law. But the concept, which referred to 'an abnormality of mind' that had impaired mental responsibility for the crime, had long been considered far too vague. Its public image took a further battering in the 1980s, when it was invoked in some of the most horrific cases of the era. Among the controversial cases that came before the courts in the 1980s, Yorkshire Ripper Peter Sutcliffe's attempt at the defence – based on his supposed instruction from God to kill women – was roundly rejected by the jury at his trial; nevertheless, he was subsequently diagnosed with paranoid schizophrenia while in prison. But his case wasn't the only one.

In 1983, two years after Sutcliffe's conviction, police were called to a report of human remains in a manhole at an address in Muswell Hill, deep in the bedsit-lands of north London. The occupant of the top-floor flat, job centre worker Dennis Nilsen, subsequently confessed to killing at least twelve young men, although the true number of his victims is commonly thought to be higher than this. Human remains were found at both the Muswell Hill address and at his former home in Cricklewood, a few miles away. For five years over the late 1970s and early 1980s Nilsen had stalked the pubs and clubs of London, luring his victims back to his flat. They were seemingly never missed, except by their families; but he had hidden in plain sight so successfully that the police did not even realise that they were looking for a serial killer until they caught one.

On trial for six counts of murder and two of attempted murder at the Old Bailey, Nilsen argued that he was suffering from diminished responsibility at the time of the killings. The psychiatrists testifying on his behalf were clear that he was not insane but was suffering from a severe personality disorder that impaired his mental responsibility. As with Sutcliffe, the jury rejected the defence's medical evidence and convicted Nilsen of murder.

The use of the diminished responsibility defence in murder cases had largely supplanted questions of insanity, as it is much easier for a defendant to satisfy the requirements of diminished responsibility than to prove full-blown insanity under the M'Naghten rules, which still remain in force in English law over 170 years since their creation. The courts' powers to deal with defendants who are acquitted of murder on the basis of diminished responsibility include the making of a hospital order, under which a killer is detained in a medical institution as opposed to prison.

The most famous of all such institutions, which, as we have seen, played a significant role in the murder cases that shaped the early development of the law of mental impairment and criminal responsibility, still exists and is the oldest psychiatric hospital in the world. In 1930 the Bethlem Royal Hospital moved once again, from Southwark out to a large, leafy estate in Beckenham on the outskirts of London. The hospital houses a number of specialist units that offer treatment to patients from across the country, including nationally renowned services for anxiety and eating disorders.

From the 1980s onwards, after a 120-year hiatus, Bethlem once again offered facilities for mentally disordered offenders in a new medium-security wing, which takes in patients who do not require the high security-provisions of Broadmoor, Rampton or Ashworth hospitals. The Art Deco hospital buildings are spread across the site like a garden village, a far cry from the traditional images of 'Bedlam' of the 18th and 19th centuries, when visits to the chaos of its wards were a tourist attraction for London's elite. The likes of Daniel M'Naghten and the other notorious criminal lunatics of the hospital's Victorian era are long gone. But there are still some links to Bethlem's mythologised metropolitan past. Although it became part of the NHS in 1948, it still retains the benefit of several philanthropic bequests made to it over the course of its history, including the ownership of a large parcel of land in London's Piccadilly. High-end grocers Fortnum & Mason are the most famous of Bethlem's West End tenants.

The attempts, albeit failed ones, by monsters like Sutcliffe and Nilsen to get away with murder by pleading diminished responsibility did not go down well with the public and, as with so many area of this complex part of the law, for a long time there were rumblings that something needed to change. The updated definition of diminished responsibility, brought into the law in 2010, reduces a murder conviction to manslaughter if the defendant can prove that they suffered from an 'abnormality of mental functioning' that impaired their ability to understand what they were doing, form a rational judgment or exercise self-control over their actions. The abnormality must arise from a 'recognised medical condition', although it is notable that there is no requirement that the medical condition itself be psychiatric in nature – any ailment, physical or mental, will suffice, provided it has impacted on the killer's mental processes. Research by De Montfort University published in 2017 found that the most common conditions cited in diminished-responsibility cases were schizophrenia, depression, personality disorder(s) and psychosis.

The aim behind the new formulation of the defence was to tighten its boundaries and shift the focus to the impacts of the mental impairment claimed by a defendant so that 'what was a test of moral responsibility for the jury's determination under the former regime has become a medical one which will require expert [medical] evidence to resolve'. As they were in the murder trials of Frederick Baker and Richard Archer in the mid-19th century, when the insanity defence was entering its prime, doctors are once again taking centre-stage in courtroom dramas, particularly those that involve complex questions of mental responsibility in uncomfortable circumstances.

* * *

In the summer of 2011 Sally Challen was convicted of the murder of her husband Richard and sentenced to life imprisonment with a minimum term of twenty-two years. At the time of Richard's death the couple had been separated but were exploring the possibility of a reconciliation. Sally had moved out of the marital home in Claygate in Surrey, and on Saturday 14 August 2010 went back there to visit Richard. As he sat at the kitchen table, eating the lunch that she had made for him, she took a hammer from her handbag and hit him hard on the head several times. When she saw that he had stopped moving, she covered his body with blankets, on top of which she left a small note which read, 'I love you, Sally.'

The following morning, police were called to the headland at Beachy Head after a report of a woman standing near the cliff edge at the notorious suicide spot. The woman was Sally. Over the course of a fraught four hours, she told the police what had happened in the kitchen the previous day. She said that she had found out that Richard had been speaking to and meeting other women. This behaviour, coupled with other mistreatment over the course of their thirty-year marriage, had caused her explosion. She finally stepped away from the cliff edge and was immediately arrested for Richard's murder.

Eight years into her life sentence, Sally launched an appeal against her conviction. The basis of her appeal was the availability of new evidence of the coercive control exerted over her by Richard during the course of their relationship, together with medical reports stating that she was suffering from previously undiagnosed personality disorders. Her appeal was successful, and in 2019 her murder conviction was quashed. Although the Court of Appeal ordered that she face a retrial, the Crown Prosecution Service accepted a plea of guilty to manslaughter and she was freed from prison on account of the time she had already served.

In the blanket media coverage of the case and of Sally's release, the watchword of 'coercive control' was seized upon and painted as a new defence to the crime of murder. The Court of Appeal heard evidence that Sally, who had met Richard at the age of fifteen, lived virtually her entire adult life under his sway. He had intimidated, manipulated and dominated her on a daily basis for the entirety of their marriage, and 'these issues were either not explored at all [at Sally's first trial] or were presented to the jury in terms of unhappiness and uncertainty, as opposed to abuse and entrapment'. Coercive control itself had been made a standalone criminal offence in 2015, four years after Sally was convicted, but it was not part of the body of homicide law – and the Court of Appeal confirmed that this remained the case:

> *It is important to remember that coercive control as such is not a defence to murder. The only partial defences open to [Sally] were provocation and diminished responsibility, and coercive control is only relevant in the context of those two defences.*

It was against the background of the history of the relationship – and the new medical evidence that Sally was suffering from bipolar affective disorder before and at the time of Richard's death – that the Court of Appeal concluded that the conviction was unsafe.

Like others before her, Sally Challen's conviction and subsequent appeal involved an intricate entanglement of diminished responsibility and provocation in the context of domestic abuse. The provocation defence, part of English law since the early 18th century, was formally abolished by the 2009 reforms and rebranded as 'loss of control'. Such an overhaul was long overdue, and a belated recognition of the fact that an element of the law of homicide first created to get Georgian aristocrats off the hook for duelling was no longer in step with 21st-century society. A defendant can rely on the defence if they can show that they lost their self-control due to a threat of serious violence from their victim or because of actions or words which 'constituted circumstances of an extremely grave character [which caused] them to have a justifiable sense of being seriously wronged'. There is no longer any requirement that the loss of control be sudden or temporary, as was stipulated under the old law and which proved such a hurdle for women like Kiranjit Ahluwalia to clear in so-called 'slow-burn' provocation cases.

The new law also firmly tackled one of the most pernicious yet enduring myths about the concept of provocation. Back in 1707 when John Mawgridge was on trial for murder, the judges at London's Guildhall had expressly confirmed that adultery was sufficient grounds to reduce murder to manslaughter:

> *When a Man is taken in adultery with another man's wife, if the husband shall stab the Adulterer, or knock out his Brains, this is bare manslaughter, for jealousy is the rage of a Man, and Adultery is the highest invasion of property.*

Down the years, as the scope of the provocation defence became progressively narrowed by the courts, the idea that a cuckolded spouse had a licence to kill largely disappeared from the law. But, whatever the legal reality, the idea had taken on something of a life of its own as an urban legend.

As late as the mid-1940s, newspaper coverage of the trial of Leonard Holmes for the murder of his wife Peggy referred to 'the so-called "unwritten law of the jungle" [that] a confession of infidelity is provocation sufficient to reduce a murder charge to manslaughter'. The case was a sad and faintly wretched one, echoing the worst fears of returning servicemen who left wives at home while they fought in the Second World War. On a November evening in 1945 Leonard and his wife Peggy had been drinking in their local pub in Nottingham, when he saw red over two airmen in the pub who were eyeing Peggy appreciatively. The couple returned home and argued for the rest of the evening; he accused her of being unfaithful while he had been away in the army and she admitted as much. Holmes picked up a hammer from the fireplace and struck Peggy over the head with it.

> *She struggled just a few moments and I could see she was too far gone to do anything. I did not like to see her lying there suffering so I just put both hands round her neck until she stopped breathing, which was only a few seconds.*

He then burned his clothes, made a cup of tea and sat with Peggy's body for the rest of the night. When the couple's children awoke the next morning, he made them breakfast before ushering them out of the house to school; they remained completely unaware that their mother lay dead in the house. Holmes then travelled up to Huddersfield, where he had been stationed in his army days, to renew his acquaintance with a local lady with whom he had been on 'intimate terms'. When Holmes tried to return home a few days later, he was apprehended by police at Retford railway station – his brother had found Peggy's body on the living-room floor when he had called at the couple's bungalow the day before.

Holmes was convicted of murder at his trial in February 1946 and a plea to the Court of Appeal was also unsuccessful. But the idea that an unfaithful wife's confession could incite her husband to kill her was still widely held. Holmes was able to secure a referral of his case up to the House of Lords to consider whether the conviction should be reduced to manslaughter on the grounds of provocation. Holmes's case was the first murder appeal to go to the House of Lords since

Reginald Woolmington's conviction for the murder of his wife Violet was overturned by the Law Lords in 1936. Holmes's legal team included Elizabeth Lane, one of the few female barristers practising in the criminal courts at the time, and the press noted with interest that she was the first woman to appear before the House of Lords in a murder case.*

Holmes's legal team referred all the way back to the categories of provocation set out in Mawgridge's case in 1707 and argued that the question of provocation had not been properly considered by the court at his original trial. But cracks had begun to appear in Holmes' story. He conceded that Peggy had brought up his 'other woman' in Huddersfield in the course of the argument and it may well have been this taunt that ultimately caused Holmes to lose his temper. Evidence from the doctor who had carried out a post-mortem on Peggy confirmed that the head wound itself would not have been fatal had she received prompt medical attention. Holmes had portrayed the strangulation as an act of mercy but it now seemed more likely that he had been callously finishing the job. In one of its more poetic judgments, the House of Lords unanimously rejected the appeal, summoning Shakespeare as they did so:

Even if Iago's insinuation against Desdemona's virtue had been true, Othello's crime was murder and nothing else ... [A] sudden confession of adultery without more can never

---

* Mrs Lane would continue to make history throughout her legal career, later becoming one of the first female QCs and the first woman to be appointed as a High Court judge.

*constitute provocation of a sort which might reduce murder
to manslaughter ... we have left behind us the age when the
wife's subjection to her husband was regarded by the law as
the basis of the marital relation ... as society advances, it
ought to call for a high measure of self-control in all cases.*

But the Mawgridge myth still persisted long after the Holmes
case, typified in the way that courts dealt with men who killed
their partners. In her 2018 book *Eve Was Shamed*, Helena
Kennedy QC noted that many continued to successfully argue
provocation defences based on infidelity and that:

*rather than questioning the deeply gendered and possessive
attitudes which drove husbands to commit so-called 'crimes
of passion', the courts often simply accepted that the red
mist of marital betrayal rendered men less responsible for
their actions. These attitudes were the common currency of
our criminal courts until disturbingly recently.*

Overwhelmingly, in murder cases women are likely to have
been killed by their current or former partner – the ONS homicide figures for 2019 confirmed that almost 40 per cent of
female homicide victims died at the hands of their partners or
ex-partners, compared with just 4 per cent of male homicide
victims. The bleak reality was that abused women like Sara
Thornton, and more recently Sally Challen, were going to jail
for murder, while jealous and possessive men were killing their
partners and getting away with manslaughter. To address this,
the new 'loss of control' concept specifically excluded sexual

infidelity from the scope of the defence. A murderer was now expressly prohibited from relying on their victim's 'betrayal' as justification for killing them. But even following this dramatic change in the law, the practice was somewhat different to the theory.

Jon-Jaques Clinton killed his estranged wife Dawn at their family home in Bracknell in November 2010. The couple had been separated for a short time and he suspected that she had been seeing other men since leaving. Clinton claimed that Dawn had been taunting him about her other relationships and the end of their marriage before he beat and strangled her to death.

At Clinton's trial for murder, as per the new 'loss of control' concept, the judge ruled that any references to Dawn's alleged new relationships be excluded from the evidence and, accordingly, there was no basis for a loss of control defence. Clinton was convicted of murder and appealed. In an eye-popping turn of events, the Court of Appeal decided that this was incorrect and, as Helena Kennedy put it, found 'a way that allows evidence of a wife's adultery in by the back door'. The Court of Appeal's remarkable judgment, which quoted most of Clinton's version of events at the house without question and did not even admit the possibility that his description of the lead-up to Dawn's death may not have been accurate, concluded that Clinton was entitled to cite all of Dawn's behaviour towards him in his defence. Her other taunts could not be separated from the context of her alleged infidelity and therefore must be considered as relevant to his loss of control. Clinton's murder conviction was quashed and a retrial ordered.

But even the defendant himself was apparently abashed by the Court of Appeal's largesse towards him – on the first day of the new trial, and for reasons that he kept to himself, Clinton decided to plead guilty to murder and was again sentenced to life. The Court of Appeal's decision in Clinton's case was an astonishing piece of victim-blaming from a judiciary that had been highly critical of the reforms to the provocation defence in the first place. Lord Chief Justice Phillips, the country's most senior judge at the time that the loss of control defence came into the law, commented that he was 'uneasy' that juries would be prevented from considering infidelity as a possible ground for provocation. Against that background, the prevailing attitudes highlighted by the Clinton case are perhaps not quite as surprising.

*   *   *

Following the prosecution of Dr Percy Bateman for causing the death of Mary Ann Harding during the delivery of her baby, the concept of gross negligence manslaughter had become embedded in the legal lexicon. While the avalanche of prosecutions of doctors prophesised by the medical profession when Dr Bateman went into the dock in the 1920s has not really come to pass, so-called 'medical manslaughter' cases have maintained a prominent position in the development of the law of homicide by gross negligence over the last hundred years. But from its clinical beginnings, rooted in the relationship between doctor and patients, the courts have applied this category of manslaughter in a host of other circumstances and relationships, although cases against doctors whose treatment results in the death of a patient are still an important feature in this area of the law.

When Sean Phillips misjudged the height of a bollard in a game of leapfrog on a day out in the summer of 2000, he can little have imagined how serious the knock to his knee would turn out to become. He had in fact torn his patella tendon, an injury that, although painful, would never usually be classed as life-threatening. He underwent surgery to repair the knee at his local hospital, Southampton General. He was thirty-one years old, and fit and healthy apart from the injury. The operation should have been routine and his discharge from the hospital swift. During his recovery, Sean was under the care of two senior house officers on the orthopaedic ward, doctors Rajeev Srivastava and Amit Misra.

In the days following his operation, Sean developed a particularly nasty strain of infection in the surgical wound. His temperature rose as his blood pressure dropped, and he was struck with bouts of diarrhoea and vomiting. The nursing staff who were caring for him became increasingly concerned, but both doctors failed to recognise the signs of acute infection until it was too late. Four days after the surgery, Sean died from toxic shock syndrome. He left a two-year-old son and a devastated partner. Shortly afterwards, the local coroner received an anonymous phone call blowing the whistle on the failings in care at the hospital that had culminated in Sean's death. The police began to investigate, and three years later Srivastava and Misra were prosecuted for manslaughter by gross negligence.

Like their predecessor Dr Bateman, they were convicted and sentenced to eighteen months in prison. But unlike Bateman, their challenge to the convictions fell on stony ground at the Court of Appeal. The doctors accepted that they had failed to realise the seriousness of Sean's condition but maintained that their treatment of him, while unsatisfactory with hindsight, had not been grossly negligent. Giving evidence for the prosecution, one expert witness said that a third-year medical student should have been able to diagnose the infection from Sean's symptoms and even the average parent would have enough medical nous to recognise the implications of a high temperature. Blood tests should have been ordered immediately and antibiotics prescribed. Had both of these been done, the infection would most likely have subsided and toxic shock syndrome would not have developed. In the prosecution's eyes, this was a clear case of gross negligence that met the Bateman threshold for manslaughter. The Court of Appeal agreed and the convictions were both upheld.

In the wake of the case, the General Medical Council struck off Dr Misra from its register and suspended Dr Srivastava from practice for three years. However, the two doctors turned out to be the tip of a very worrying iceberg. The investigation that was sparked by the anonymous tip-off to the coroner found that the circumstances of Sean's death were indicative of much wider failings at Southampton General Hospital. Misra and Srivastava were merely the ultimate manifestation of poor clinical and ward management practices at the unit. Junior doctors were not adequately supervised and communication between medical staff was extremely poor. Hundreds of patients were found to be at risk as a direct result of the hospital's shortcomings. The hospital trust itself was subsequently prosecuted under the health and safety legislation in respect of Sean's death and fined £100,000.

Away from the medical cases, it was the expansion of manslaughter to cover deaths caused by negligence that ultimately paved the way for a crime of corporate manslaughter, and it provided the grounds for wider accountability for homicide in other circumstances as well. Gross negligence was the basis for the belated prosecutions arising out of the Hillsborough disaster, which finally came to court in 2019, thirty years on from the disaster. The wranglings over responsibility and accountability for the deaths of those killed at the stadium had been almost continuous throughout the intervening three decades. In 1990 the Crown Prosecution Service had concluded that there was no evidence that offences had been committed; the inquests into each of the victims were adjourned while the criminal investigation was ongoing and in March 1991 the coroner recorded verdicts of accidental death in respect of all of those killed in the disaster. In the years following, the Hillsborough families tried unsuccessfully to get the coroner's verdict overturned and the inquests reopened, but they were trapped in a whirlpool of circular legal logic. As the CPS had concluded no crimes had been committed, the inquests' conclusion of accidental death must follow; and if the coroner had concluded that the deaths were accidental, then there was no reason to re-open the criminal investigation. But in 2012, after years of campaigning, the High Court quashed the original conclusions and new inquests were ordered. Finally, in 2016, the process closed with a new verdict of unlawful killing – which opened the door for a fresh police investigation and potential prosecutions.

Following the conclusion of the new investigation, homicide charges were announced in respect of ninety-five of the victims. As previously mentioned, the four years that had elapsed between the tragedy and the death of Tony Bland in 1993 fell foul of the year and a day rule, which was still in force in English law at the time of Tony's death. Moreover, in 2019 David Duckenfield went on trial for the manslaughter of those killed at Hillsborough in March 1989. Duckenfield was the former chief constable of South Yorkshire Police and had been the operational commander at the ground on the day of the match. The Crown's case was that he had owed a duty of care to the thousands of supporters attending the game to keep them safe, and his management of the overcrowding in the stands breached this duty. Duckenfield had already faced a private prosecution in the 1990s, brought by relatives of some of the victims, but this had proved abortive when the jury failed to reach a verdict. The 2019 trial collapsed in almost identical circumstances when the jury was dismissed because it was again unable to reach a conclusion as to Duckenfield's culpability. A retrial later in the year resulted in an acquittal. No one else has ever been convicted of a homicide offence in relation to the deaths of the 96 people killed at Hillsborough.

*   *   *

The ideas behind the diminished responsibility and loss of control defences had been part of the law of homicide in this country for many years, as was the concept of manslaughter by gross negligence. But when it was created in 2007 the new crime of corporate manslaughter was truly radical. It was the first time that a manslaughter offence had been set out in a statute and it was the first time that the law of homicide had been applied to a non-human entity. But, over a decade on from its inception, the legislation has yet to live up to its initial promises, mostly due to circumstance and the lack of headline-grabbing disasters.

The first conviction for corporate manslaughter came in 2011, when Cotswold Geotechnical Holdings Limited were found guilty following the death of an employee. Geologist Alexander Wright had been working for the company at a housing development site, excavating soil samples from a twelve-foot-deep trench as part of ground investigation works, when the trench collapsed on him. The company was fined £385,000.

Like Cotswold Geotechnical, most of the companies that have been convicted since the offence was created have been found guilty of causing the death of an individual employee and have been small- to medium-sized organisations – not the big corporate beasts like P&O that were the catalyst for the change in the law following the catastrophes of the late 1980s and 1990s. While the new law was intended to iron out the difficulties with the identification of the 'controlling mind', which had led to the acquittals of P&O Ferries in 1990 and Great Western Trains in 1997 following mass-fatality transport disasters, the basis for corporate manslaughter under the 2007 legislation still rests on proving wrongdoing or negligence at a senior management level. Although this looks at a broader category of personnel than the statutory directors required by the old law, in practice prosecutions still encounter many of the same difficulties in proving a link between the frontline operations of a large company and the decisions of the upper echelons of its management.

No large company has yet been convicted of the new offence. As the court fines for the crime are based on the turnover of the company in the dock, this has resulted in comparatively low levels of penalties being imposed on conviction. The average fine is around £400,000 and, to date, only one company has received a fine in excess of £1 million for manslaughter; by contrast, in 2017 a water company was fined almost £20 million for environmental offences, the only victims of which were some fish.

As comprehensive as the new offence appeared, there were also some particulars in the small print of the legislation that ensured the controversies around corporate homicide would continue under the new regime. So while there is no blanket immunity from prosecution for bodies such as the police or the military, there are significant restrictions in the Act that prevent them being prosecuted for manslaughter in varying circumstances. In separate incidents in 2013 and again in 2016, a total of four soldiers collapsed and died on Army training marches in the Brecon Beacons, undertaken in sweltering conditions in the height of summer. Despite the obvious risks and the failure to learn lessons from previous incidents, no corporate manslaughter prosecution could be brought against the Ministry of Defence because deaths that occur on hazardous military training exercises are specifically excluded from the offence of corporate manslaughter. Individual homicide charges against the officers who had organised and led the march were considered but not pursued.

This muted impact of the change in the law is also due in part to circumstance. As mentioned, since it came into force there hasn't been a public disaster on the scale of those seen in the preceding decades, no *Herald* or *Marchioness* tragedy into which the offence could sink its teeth. That was until the early hours of 17 June 2017.

When the fire crew first entered Flat 16 on the fourth floor of Kensington's Grenfell Tower shortly after 1 a.m., the source of the blaze to which they had been summoned was quickly identified as a fridge-freezer in the flat's kitchen. The fire safety protocol for the tower, which contained 129 flats spread over twenty-one floors high above west London, stated that any fire would be contained near to its point of origin and so residents should be instructed to stay inside their homes. But within thirty minutes of the fire brigade's arrival, the flames had spread out of the kitchen window and engulfed the entire east side of the block. Eyewitnesses on the streets below could see the flames lick along the panels between flat windows as the fire traced its way up the side of the building.

Grenfell Tower burned for twenty-four hours, with seventy-two people being killed and several families losing multiple members. The blazing panels that people had seen on the exterior of the building were swiftly identified as the root cause of the conflagration – highly flammable cladding that had only been fitted a year earlier during a refurbishment project on the forty-year-old tower. In June 2019, almost exactly two years after the tragedy, the police announced that their investigation into the fire included the possibility of corporate manslaughter charges and that these were still under active consideration. But the Grenfell public inquiry, still ongoing over four years after the fire, has identified a complex tangle of potential liability. Any criminal prosecution will have to be carefully extracted from a complex morass of owners, management organisations, manufacturers, architects, project managers, contractors and sub-contractors, to ascertain where the fault should lie.

The blaze at Grenfell has become emblematic of the type of social injustice that meant hundreds of people were unknowingly risking their lives simply by being in their own homes. It is difficult to imagine that criminal charges won't follow, even if it takes several years. Analysing the potential ramifications for the law, legal academic Victoria Roper observed:

> Grenfell Tower will likely become the most significant test of the [Corporate Manslaughter and Corporate Homicide] Act to date … Can the Act successfully prosecute an organisation which has caused a multi-fatality disaster of the type it was enacted to confront? … If no corporate manslaughter prosecutions are brought, the Act will be regarded as a failure; if prosecutions are brought and fail, the Act will be regarded as a failure … we owe it to the many people who die unnecessarily each year, like those who died in the Grenfell blaze, to strive for nothing less than perfection.

*   *   *

While the creation of the crime of corporate manslaughter was the first entirely new homicide offence to be created in decades, some of the more venerable aspects of the law continue to make their presence felt in courtrooms today.

The aforementioned crime of infanticide was placed on the statute books in the 1920s in an overdue attempt to address the reluctance of juries to convict of murder mothers who killed their infant children while suffering from the mental aftereffects of giving birth. The offence has remained part of the law ever since, although cases are now thankfully rare. But the question of infanticide, mostly consigned to history along with the Victorian slums and moralising that gave birth to it, does still have its part to play in the modern law of homicide.

In June 2017 Rachel Tunstill was convicted of the murder of her baby daughter Mia. Mia had been born, in secret, on the bathroom floor of the Burnley home that Tunstill shared with her partner. Straight after giving birth, Tunstill stabbed Mia with a pair of scissors and hid her body. A couple of days later she told doctors that she had suffered a miscarriage – but they were immediately suspicious.

At her trial for her daughter's murder, Tunstill relied on swathes of medical evidence from psychiatrists. She had been diagnosed with Asperger syndrome several years before her pregnancy and the doctors also concluded that she was suffering from schizophrenia at the time of the killing, as well as experiencing a period of depressive psychosis. The combination of these conditions, along with the 'acute stress reaction' triggered by concealing the pregnancy and giving birth in secret, had culminated in her killing of Mia. This was relied on by Tunstill's lawyers in support of a diminished responsibility defence or, as an alternative, a verdict of infanticide as opposed to murder.

The law around infanticide has been unchanged since the offence was first created almost a century earlier. Tunstill had to prove that she had killed her baby daughter while the balance of her mind was disturbed from the effects of giving birth. The prosecution contested the diagnoses of the medical experts and the judge was unsympathetic; he ordered that an infanticide defence could not apply in the case. Any mental disturbance that Tunstill had suffered had been caused by her pre-existing mental conditions, not the birth itself. She was convicted of murder and sentenced to life, with a proposed minimum term of twenty years.

Tunstill appealed against the murder conviction on the basis of the judge's ruling on the limitations of infanticide. Her legal team argued that the effect of the decision was to place mothers who have a pre-existing mental illness in a worse position than those who do not. The Appeal judges agreed and overturned the conviction – nothing in the infanticide legislation excluded a jury from considering the issue in cases where there was a background of mental-health issues prior to the killing. Tunstill's murder conviction was quashed and a retrial was ordered. But her victory was short-lived and, at her second trial in January 2019, she was again convicted of murder. This time the jury had been given the option to consider a verdict of infanticide, but decided against it. Commenting on the Court of Appeal's decision, lawyers Karen Brennan and Emma Milne observed:

if the position of the trial judge ... had been upheld by the Court of Appeal, then infanticide would be unavailable in precisely the circumstances it is needed most: situations involving vulnerable women and teenage girls who feel compelled to hide their pregnancy and give birth alone.

*   *   *

Unlike the offence of infanticide, which has been unchanged since it was created almost a century ago, the vehicular homicide offences introduced by the road-traffic legislation in the 1950s multiplied over the following decades, to keep up with the spiralling dangers of driving a car or motorcycle, riding a bike or being a pedestrian. Road-safety risks have multiplied considerably since Bridget Driscoll was mown down by a car travelling at the positively stately speed of four miles per hour, and the possibility of sustaining or causing an injury on the roads has come to be accepted as part and parcel of getting behind the wheel. While manslaughter charges have rarely been used in driving cases following the conviction of Wilfred Andrews in the 1930s, there are now seven separate offences relating to causing death by some form of aberrant driving. The most well known are those relating to dangerous or careless driving, but there are discrete offences to cover drivers who kill while uninsured, unlicensed or under the influence of drugs.

Unlike murder and manslaughter, the death by driving offences are tightly defined in the law, making prosecutions easier to pursue and convictions more straightforward to secure. Dangerous driving is defined as:

*[falling] far below what would be expected of a competent
and careful driver [provided that] it would be obvious to a
competent and careful driver that driving in that way would
be dangerous.*

Careless driving, often known as driving without due care and
attention, is defined according to the same barometer of the
competent and careful driver, but at a lower threshold.
Convictions for causing death by dangerous or careless driving
carry lower sentences than for manslaughter, with maximum
jail terms of fourteen and five years respectively. The original
rationale for introducing separate criminal offences for driving
deaths was that juries were often reluctant to convict of
manslaughter in such cases, and, in recent years, history has
repeated itself in respect of other types of traffic fatality.

In February 2016 Kim Briggs was crossing Old Street in East
London during her lunchbreak. Cyclist Charlie Alliston, travelling at around 14 miles per hour on a bike without a
front-wheel brake, collided with Briggs in the middle of the
road. Briggs was knocked to the ground, sustained severe head
injuries and later died in hospital. Had Alliston been driving a
car, the situation would have been straightforward; but the
Crown Prosecution Service deliberated for many months
before eventually bringing a case against him. In September
2017 Alliston was sentenced to eighteen months' custody in
respect of Briggs's death. In order to secure a conviction, prosecutors had had to go all the way back to the Offences Against
the Person Act 1861 to find an offence with which to charge
Alliston. He was found guilty of the antiquated offence of

'wanton or furious driving ... of any carriage of vehicle [causing] bodily harm', which remained a crime under part of the 1861 Act. An alternative charge of manslaughter had been rejected by the jury.

Speaking outside court after the conviction, Kim's widower Matthew summed up the problem that the law faced:

> *This case has clearly and evidently demonstrated there is a gap in the law when it comes to dealing with death or serious injury by dangerous cycling. To have to rely on either manslaughter at one end, or a Victorian law that doesn't even mention causing death at the other end, tells us there is a gap. The fact that what happened to Kim is rare is not a reason to have no remedy.*

This quandary was nothing new; English law had faced exactly the same problem in the mid-20th century when it became apparent that although juries were reluctant to convict of manslaughter in driving cases, the alternative options did not adequately reflect the seriousness of the results when drivers kill. In response to the Alliston case, the Department of Transport commenced a consultation on whether to introduce a new offence of 'causing death by dangerous cycling'. The department proposed that the sentences for the new law should be in line with those for the death by driving offences. The consultation period closed in late 2018 and, as at the time of writing, there have been no further updates from the government.

* * *

For an offence that has not fundamentally altered since it was last defined over four hundred years ago, murder has proved to be a remarkably slippery concept over the course of its long and controversial history. And the macabre fascination that it exerts over us is as strong today as ever. At the heart of the books, films and podcasts that we all love is a deceptively simple crime that we think we know very well. But its real meaning has morphed and shifted over the years, holding up a mirror to society and contorting itself to fit whatever is currently keeping us up at night. It is in an endless race to match the fears and obsessions of each successive generation, from marauding Norsemen, hot-blooded Georgians, sloppy doctors, battered wives or careless companies.

The image of Mackie Messer, or Mack the Knife, that opened this book still exerts a powerful influence on our collective imagination when our thoughts turn to murder – a shadow sneaking around the corner, stabbing an innocent victim and then slinking away. But the truth is darker and stranger than the macabre fiction that we know and love. In real life, murderers include people like Thomas Dudley, who killed Richard Parker in order to survive in desperate circumstances. There's Derek Bentley, who died as a murderer when he had never touched the gun, let along fired the shot, that ended PC Miles's life. Some end up as murderers through dint of circumstances or timing; had Ruth Ellis shot David Blakely just two years later than she did, her crime may well have been reduced to manslaughter on the basis of the new diminished responsibility defence. Russell Shankland was undoubtedly stupid and even reckless when he hurled the concrete block that killed David Wilkie, but he consistently denied that this was enough to make him a murderer. And then there are countless women like Kiranjit Ahluwalia who end up striking the first blow while trapped in abusive relationships, where it is only a matter of time before one party ends up dead.

Fiends like Frederick Baker and the Rippers Yorkshire and Jack, who do conform to the nightmarish image, certainly are real enough, and the rarity of their crimes does nothing to diminish the horror of them. But most of the killers that we have encountered in these pages are ordinary people who have found themselves in extraordinary situations, with fatal results. Their reaction to these situations may have been foolish, rash or badly judged – but seldom straightforwardly wicked. Far from being the monsters of our imaginings, the murderers that have had the most impact on the law are people like us.

Murder, manslaughter and the fault lines between them are never out of the news. But the law relating to them is still often misunderstood and misinterpreted. Its malleability, arising in no small part from the lack of clear definitions of the concepts that make up the offence, can create real and perceived injustices. The terms and crimes involved are so loaded with meaning that we often cannot see past the semantics – a conviction for manslaughter is sometimes seen as 'getting away with murder', rather than a serious offence in its own right. Although life imprisonment can also be imposed for manslaughter, it is the label attached to the crime that is always of primary importance, even if the sentence imposed is the same.

As society has advanced, particularly in the last fifty years, the law has often struggled to keep up. We no longer settle gentlemanly disputes with duels, but the defence of provocation is still more attuned to 18th-century mores than it is to the modern reality of personal relationships. Even the attempt to finally put to bed the dangerous fiction that a victim's infidelity could excuse their murder has been undermined by the courts themselves. It took years for government to recognise that a comprehensive scheme of legislation was needed in order to properly deal with companies who kill their employees or members of the public – and even that isn't perfect. But a similar codification of the rest of the offences under the umbrella of homicide, along the lines proposed by the Law Commission in the early 2000s, is long overdue. Since its inception almost a thousand years ago, through ten centuries of deadly deeds and courtroom dramas, the English law of murder has been in a constant state of flux. Rewriting it to make it fit for the 21st century and beyond will take political courage as well as capital, but it is a bullet that cannot be dodged for much longer. How and why we criminalise those who commit that most biblical of sins will continue to preoccupy us all, in myriad ways, for a long time to come.

SELECT BIBLIOGRAPHY AND NOTES ON SOURCES

N.B. The court judgments in individual cases are listed in the chapter bibliographies below, including their date and the citation for their entry in the Law Reports. Many of these can be accessed online by searching for the case name and citation on the website of the British and Irish Legal Information Institute (bailii.org).

GENERAL

Allderidge, Patricia, *The Bethlem Royal Hospital: An Illustrated History*, 1995, The Bethlem & Maudsley NHS Trust

Arnold, Catharine, *Bedlam: London and Its Mad* (2009), Simon & Schuster

Birkett, Sir Norman (ed.), *The Newgate Calendar* (1951), The Folio Society

—— *The New Newgate Calendar* (1960), The Folio Society

Cooper, David, *The Lesson of the Scaffold* (1974), Allen Lane

Deane Potter, John, *The Fatal Gallows Tree* (1965), Elek Books

Emsley, Clive, *Crime and Society in England 1750–1900* (1987), Longman

Flanders, Judith, *The Invention of Murder* (2011), Harper Press

Grant, Thomas, *Court Number One* (2019), John Murray

Hopton, Richard, *Pistols at Dawn* (2007), Portrait

Horder, Jeremy, 'The Duel and the English Law of Homicide' (1992), *Oxford Journal of Legal Studies*, vol. 12(3)

Kennedy, Helena, *Eve Was Framed* (1992), Vintage

—— *Eve Was Shamed* (2018), Chatto & Windus

Linnane, Fergus, *London: The Wicked City* (2003), Robson

Marr, Andrew, *A History of Modern Britain* (2007), Macmillan

Ormerod, David and Laird, Karl, *Smith, Hogan and Ormerod's Criminal Law* (2017), Oxford University Press

Stephens, Sir James Fitzjames, *A History of the Criminal Law of England*, vol. III (1883), Cambridge University Press

Walker, Nigel, *Crime and Insanity in England*, vol. I (1968), Edinburgh University Press

—— *Crime and Insanity in England*, vol. II (1973), Edinburgh University Press

Wiener, Martin, *Reconstructing the Criminal* (1990), Cambridge University Press

INTRODUCTION: THOU SHALT NOT KILL

Ancient Laws & Institutes of England (1840), The Law Society

Bellamy, John, *The Criminal Trial in Late Medieval England* (1998), Sutton Publishing

Coke, Sir Edward, *The Third Part of the Institutes of the Laws of England* (1817 edn), W. Clarke & Sons

Homicide in England & Wales: Year ending March 2019 (13 February 2020), Office for National Statistics

Lambert, Tom, *Law & Order in Anglo-Saxon England* (2017),
    Oxford University Press
Robertson, A. J., *The Laws of the Kings of England from
    Edmund to Henry I: Part 1 Edmund to Canute* (1925),
    Cambridge University Press

CHAPTER ONE: THE FIELD OF HONOUR

JOHN MAWGRIDGE

The judgment in Mawgridge's trial was reported by judge Sir
John Kelyng in his compendium of famous trials, *A Report of
Divers Cases in Pleas of the Crown* (1708). The details of
Mawgridge's escape and capture in Ghent is documented in *A
Biographical Dictionary of English Court Musicians 1485–
1714*, vol. I (2018), David Lasocki, Routledge.

GIUSEPPE BARETTI

James Boswell refers to Baretti's murder trial in his *Life of
Samuel Johnson* and his own diaries, *The Journals of James
Boswell* (1991), edited by John Wain, Heinemann.

ABRAHAM THORNTON

The British Library holds contemporary reports of the murder
of Mary Ashford, compiled in *Tracts Relating to the Murder of
Mary Ashford* (1818–19), and Sutton Coldfield Library also has
a collection of relevant cuttings. Naomi Clifford reinvestigated
the case in detail in her 2018 book *The Murder of Mary
Ashford* (2018), Pen & Sword.

CHAPTER TWO: THE MADNESS OF BADNESS

ARCHIBALD KINLOCH
The Trial of Sir Archibald Gordon Kinloch (2019), HardPress, contains a reproduction of the transcript of Archibald's trial.

DANIEL M'NAGHTEN
The House of Lords' decision is reported as *M'Naghten's Case [1843] UKHL 16*. Richard Moran explored the case in detail in his 1981 book *Knowing Right from Wrong*, Simon & Schuster.

FREDERICK BAKER
Much of the detail of Baker's horrible crime and his subsequent trial was luridly recounted in *The Police News Edition of the Life and Examination of Frederick Baker* and *The Police News Edition of the Trial and Condemnation of Frederick Baker*.

RICHARD ARCHER
The full transcript of Archer's trial is available on the Old Bailey Proceedings Online website under *Richard Arthur [sic] Prince, Killing – murder, 10th January 1898*.

CHAPTER THREE: OUT OF HER MAJESTY'S DOMINIONS

THOMAS DUDLEY AND EDWIN STEPHENS
The judgment of Lord Chief Justice Coleridge is reported at *R v Dudley and Stephens [1884] All ER 61*. The legal perspective and the history of cannibalism on the high seas is considered in *Cannibalism and the Common Law* (1984) by A. W. B. Simpson (University of Chicago Press). Further detail of the crew's arrival in Falmouth and the initial court hearings is taken from the

contemporary press coverage in the *Evening Standard* and the *Falmouth Packet & Cornwall Advertiser*.

The case of *US v Holmes (1842) (Case No. 15383)* was considered by the court in Dudley and Stephens's case. The modern case of *Re: A (2000) EWCA Civ 254* re-examined the possibility of a necessity defence in the context of medical ethics.

GEORGES CODERE

The National Archives holds files on Codere's trial (HO45/25850), his time in prison (PCOM 8/342) and his release (PRO 30/69/229). The Court of Appeal's judgment in his case is reported at *R v Codere (1916) 12 Cr App R 21*. Some of the detail of the case is taken from contemporary press reports in the *Daily Record* and the *Hampshire Advertiser*.

CHAPTER FOUR: TRUST ME, I'M NOT A DOCTOR

DR PERCY BATEMAN

The judgment of the Court of Appeal in Dr Bateman's case, which provides plenty of grisly detail about Mary Ann Harding's fate, is reported at *R v Bateman [1925] 19 Cr App R 8*. Further background information on the case is taken from contemporary press reports in the *Lancashire Evening Post*, *Gloucester Citizen* and *Western Mail*, and quotations from letters about the case are taken from the *British Medical Journal*.

The explanation of the panel healthcare system was summarised by Anne Digby and Nick Bosanquet in 'Doctors and Patients in an Era of National Health Insurance and Private Practice', *Economic History Review*, 1988, vol. XLI(1). The grim history of infanticide is discussed by A. Hunt in 'Calculations and Concealments: Infanticide in Mid-Nineteenth

Century Britain', *Victorian Literature and Culture*, 2006, vol. 34(1). Dr Michael Powers QC reviewed the emergence of medical manslaughter in his 2005 paper to the Medico-Legal Society, 'Manslaughter – How Did We Get Here?'

REGINALD WOOLMINGTON

The detailed judgment of the House of Lords is reported at *Woolmington v DPP [1935] UKHL 1*. Further detail on the life and death of Violet Woolmington can be found in the contemporary press reports in the *Bath Chronicle and Weekly Gazette*, *Taunton Courier*, *Liverpool Echo* and *Western Morning News*. The subsequent fate of Reg and the strange coincidence of the death of Rose Budd were discussed by Brian Block and John Hostettler in *Famous Cases: Nine Trials that Changed the Law* (2002), Waterside Press.

WILFRED ANDREWS

The details of the fatal crash are taken from reports in the *Gloucester Citizen* and *Leeds Mercury*. The House of Lords' judgment is reported at *Andrews v DPP [1937] UKHL 1*. The circumstances of the death of Bridget Driscoll were taken from the coverage of the incident in the *Croydon Guardian* and *Bury Free Press*.

CHAPTER FIVE: DIMINISHING RETURNS AND CAPITAL GAINS

RUTH ELLIS

Carol Ann Lee's excellent *A Fine Day for a Hanging* (2013), Mainstream, provides a wealth of detail on Ellis's early life and her relationship with David Blakely, and contains a vivid recreation of her murder trial. The case is also covered by

Gordon Honeycombe in *More Murders of the Black Museum, 1835–1985* (1993), Hutchinson. The judgment in the posthumous Court of Appeal hearing is reported at *R v Ellis [2003] EWCA 3556*.

RENEE DUFFY

Much of the detail of the murder of George Duffy, the murder trial of his wife Renee and the public reaction to the case is taken from the contemporary press coverage in the *Manchester Evening News*, *Liverpool Echo*, *Gloucestershire Echo*, *Sunderland Daily Echo*, *Aberdeen Press and Journal* and *Hartlepool Northern Daily Mail*. The court judgment in the case is reported at *R v Duffy [1949] 1 All ER 932*.

DEREK BENTLEY

The Court of Appeal's judgment overturning Derek Bentley's murder conviction is reported at *R v Bentley (deceased) [1998] EWCA Cr 2516*, and much of the detail of the case is taken from the Court's comprehensive discussion of the case in the judgment. The coincidental case of Appleby and Ostler is reported at *R v Appleby [1940] 28 Cr App R 1*.

JOHN CHRISTIE

An abridged version of the report of the 1965 inquiry into the murders at Rillington Place conducted by Daniel Brabin was published by the Stationery Office in its *Uncovered Editions: Rillington Place* (1999). Ludovic Kennedy's extensive investigation into the murders resulted in his book *10 Rillington Place* (1961), Littlehampton. The book argued that Timothy Evans had been the victim of a miscarriage of justice and was instrumental in securing the re-opening of the case that led to the eventual conviction and execution of John Christie.

PATRICK BYRNE

Much of the detail of the investigation into Stephanie Baird's murder and the subsequent arrest and trial of Patrick Byrne is taken from the coverage of the case by the *Birmingham Mail*. The judgment in Byrne's appeal is reported at *R v Byrne [1960] 2 QB 396*.

CHAPTER SIX: HIRAETH

RASPUTIN

The plot to kill Rasputin and its chaotic execution is described in Robert Massie's *Nicholas & Alexandra: The Tragic, Compelling Story of the Last Tsar and His Family* (1967), Sphere.

CYRIL CHURCH

The Court of Appeal's judgment is reported at *R v Church [1965] EWCA Cr 1*. Further details of the case and the original trial were taken from press reports in the *Daily Mirror*, *Daily Herald*, *Aberdeen Evening Express* and *Birmingham Daily Post*.

ABERFAN

The events of the disaster and the investigation into its causes are set out in *Inquiry into the Aberfan Disaster: Report of the Tribunal appointed under the Tribunals of Inquiry (Evidence) Act 1921*, published in 1967.

PETER SUTCLIFFE

The circumstances of Sutcliffe's arrest and the police investigation into the Yorkshire Ripper killings are comprehensively covered in *The Yorkshire Ripper Case: Review of the Police Investigation of the Case by Lawrence Byford Esq. CBE QPM, Her Majesty's Inspector of Constabulary* (1982). Known as the Byford Report, it was only made public by the government in 2006. Further detail was also taken from the *Guardian*'s contemporary coverage of the case.

The case is covered by criminologist David Wilson in his 2009 book *A History of British Serial Killing*, Sphere. Sutcliffe's diminished responsibility defence at his trial is discussed in the judgments of the High Court and Court of Appeal in his sentence reviews, which are reported at *R v Coonan (formerly Sutcliffe) [2010] EWHC 1741 QB* and *R v Coonan (formerly Sutcliffe) [2011] EWCA Cr 5* respectively.

REGINALD HANCOCK AND RUSSELL SHANKLAND

The national press reported extensively on the tragic death of David Wilkie. Details and quotes are taken from reports in the *Sunday Mirror*, *Newcastle Journal*, *Aberdeen Press and Journal* and *Liverpool Echo*. The House of Lords' judgment in the case is reported at *R v Hancock and Shankland [1985] 2 WLR 1014*. Matthew Dyson covered the case, including its wider legal and political context, in his 2015 research paper 'Hancock and Shankland [1986] AC 455', *University of Cambridge Legal Studies Research Paper Series (Paper Number 59/2015)*. Tony Marlow MP's rhetorical question in the Crime debate is reported in *Hansard vol. 82 (4 July 1985)*.

Alistair Moloney and Anthony Cunningham's appeals are reported at *R v Moloney [1985] 1 AC 905* and *R v Cunningham [1982] AC 566*.

CHAPTER SEVEN: LIPSTICK ON THE MIRROR

THE BRIDGEWATER FOUR

Paul Foot's account of the killing of Carl Bridgewater, *Murder at the Farm: Who Killed Carl Bridgewater?* (1986), Penguin, covered the case in forensic detail and was instrumental in securing a referral of the case to the Court of Appeal, which was unsuccessful. The House of Commons debate on the case is reported in Hansard for *28th February 1996 (vol. 272, pp. 819–842)*. The subsequent Court of Appeal judgment overturning the men's convictions in 1997 is reported at *R v Hickey [1997] EWCA Cr 2028*.

THE BIRMINGHAM SIX

The account of the pub bombings is based on the detailed judgment of the Court of Appeal, reported at *R v McIlkenny [1991] EWCA Cr 2*. In an attempt to address the controversies raised by the case, the *Report of the Royal Commission on Criminal Justice (Cm2263)* was published in 1993.

KIRANJIT AHLUWALIA

Much of the detail of the case is taken from Kiranjit Ahluwalia's memoir *Provoked* (2007), HarperCollins, co-written with Rahila Gupta. The Court of Appeal judgment is reported at *R v Ahluwalia [1992] EWCA Cr 1*.

SARA THORNTON

The two Court of Appeal judgments in Sara Thornton's case are reported at *R v Thornton [1991]* and *[1995] EWCA Cr 6*.

CHAPTER EIGHT: THE BODY CORPORATE

PIPER ALPHA

The account of the events in the North Sea is largely taken from the November 1990 inquiry report entitled *Department of Energy: Public Inquiry into the Piper Alpha Disaster (Cm. 1310)*, which includes many eyewitness accounts from survivors of the tragedy. The Commons debate on the twentieth anniversary of Piper Alpha is reported in Hansard at *2nd July 2008 (Column 233H)*. Reference is also made to the report of Anthony Hidden QC into the Clapham Junction rail crash, dated November 1989.

HERALD OF FREE ENTERPRISE

The Department of Transport's Report No. 8074 into the disaster contains a detailed examination of the disaster and its causes. Further information on the aftermath of the disaster and the resulting legal proceedings is taken from the press coverage in the *Aberdeen Press and Journal, Dundee Courier, Reading Evening Post* and *Sandwell Evening Mail*. The decision of the Court permitting the manslaughter prosecution to proceed against P&O is reported at *R v P&O European Ferries Dover Ltd [1991] 93 Cr App R*.

The judgment in the case against Cory Brothers Limited is reported at *R v Cory Bros & Co Ltd [1927] 1 KB 810*, and further detail of the death of Brynmor John is taken from the contemporary press coverage in the *Bellshill Speaker, Sheffield Daily Telegraph, Portsmouth Evening News* and *Derby Daily Telegraph*.

HILLSBOROUGH

The details of Tony Bland's tragic case are covered extensively in the judgment of the court in *Airedale NHS Trust v Bland [1993] AC 789*. The history of the year and a day rule was discussed by D. E. C. Yale in 'A Year and a Day in Homicide', *Cambridge Law Journal*, 1989, vol. 48(2). The personal-injury claims brought against South Yorkshire Police are reported at *Alcock v Chief Constable of South Yorkshire Police [1992] 1 AC 310* and *White v Chief Constable of South Yorkshire [1999] 2 AC 455*.

SOUTHALL RAIL CRASH

The court judgment confirming that the identification principle applied in cases of corporate manslaughter was reported at *Attorney-General's Reference 2/1999 [2000] EWCA Cr 91*. Further detail of the crash and the failed prosecution are taken from the reports on the case in the *Guardian*. The subsequent report of the Home Affairs Select Committee on the draft corporate manslaughter bill was published in December 2005.

CHAPTER NINE: MURDER: A PRIMER

LAW COMMISSION

The Law Commission's proposals to overhaul the law of homicide were discussed in its *Consultation Paper No. 177: A New Homicide Act for England & Wales?* and its subsequent *Report No. 304: Murder, Manslaughter & Infanticide*. The government's rather cursory response was contained in the Ministry of Justice's *Report on the Implementation of Law Commission Proposals* dated 24 January 2011.

DIMINISHED RESPONSIBILITY

The reforms to the defence of diminished responsibility were discussed in R. Mackay and Barry Mitchell's article 'The New Diminished Responsibility Plea in Operation: Some Initial Findings', *Criminal Law Review*, 2017, vol. I.

SALLY CHALLEN

Much of the detail of the case is taken from the judgment of the Court of Appeal, reported at *R v Challen [2019] EWCA Crim 916*.

LEONARD HOLMES

The account of this case is based on the contemporary press coverage in the *Nottingham Evening Post*, *Nottingham Journal*, *Lancashire Evening Post*, *Lincolnshire Echo*, *Daily Herald* and *Derby Daily Telegraph*.

JON-JAQUES CLINTON

The judgment in this case is reported at *R v Clinton [2012] EWCA Crim 2*. Lord Chief Justice Phillips' comments on the reforms to the provocation defence were reported in *The Independent* (7 November 2008).

RAJEEV SRIVASTAVA & AMIT MISRA

The judgment in this case is reported at *R v Srivastava & Misra [2005] Cr App R 328*.

CORPORATE MANSLAUGHTER AND CORPORATE HOMICIDE ACT 2007

The impact of the new corporate manslaughter offence is discussed by Victoria Roper in her article 'The Corporate Manslaughter and Corporate Homicide Act 2007 – A 10-Year Review', *Journal of Criminal Law*, 2018, vol. 82(1).

RACHEL TUNSTILL

The judgment in this case is reported at *R v Tunstill [2018] EWCA Cr 1696*, and the case was considered by Karen Brennan and Emma Milne in 'Infanticide: Guarding against Harshness', *New Law Journal*, 2019.

CHARLIE ALLISTON

The detail of this case and the government's response to it was taken from the Department for Transport's 2018 *Cycle Safety Review Report* by Laura Thomas, together with additional comments from reports in the *Guardian*.

GLOSSARY

Actus reus: In English criminal law, the prohibited act which, when combined with the guilty mental state (see *Mens rea*), establishes the commission of a criminal offence. The *actus reus* of all homicide offences is the unlawful killing of another person.

Appeal of murder: A legal doctrine dating from Norman times, under which the family of a murder victim could bring a further prosecution against someone who had already been acquitted of the murder at a trial. Little used and long believed to be defunct, the appeal process was formally abolished in 1819 following the trial of Abraham Thornton.

Assizes/Assize Court: The periodic court sessions held by judges touring the country to try serious crimes in different counties, usually twice a year, from the Middle Ages onwards. The Assizes were abolished and replaced by Crown Courts in 1972.

Bedlam (*see also* Bethlem Royal Hospital): The historic nickname for the Bethlem Royal Hospital, which became a generic name for asylums and psychiatric institutions. The term subsequently passed into the English language to describe situations of general chaos or uproar.

Benefit of clergy: The practice of excusing members of the clergy from criminal offences that carried a death sentence, including murder. Over time it was extended to noblemen and anyone literate (this being accepted as prima facie evidence of a religious calling). The use of the benefit helped to shape the early differentiation between murder and manslaughter.

Bethlem Royal Hospital (*see also* **Bedlam**): The world's oldest psychiatric hospital established in 1247 in Bishopsgate, London. Now in Beckenham, Greater London, the hospital has also been based at sites in Moorfields and Southwark during its history, and housed so-called criminal lunatics in specialist wards following insanity verdicts. Hospital clinicians were often called as expert witnesses in 19th-century murder trials that involved questions regarding the defendant's sanity.

Beyond reasonable doubt: The threshold to which a jury must be satisfied of a defendant's guilt, in order to convict them of a criminal offence. In modern English law, this equates to virtual certainty of guilt.

Bloody Code: The name given to the series of statutes issued during the 18th and 19th centuries that imposed the death penalty for many criminal offences, including many minor crimes.

Bot (see also *Wergild*): Under Anglo-Saxon law, the requirement for a killer to pay compensation to his victim's relatives, calculated according to the victim's individual *wergild*.

Broadmoor Hospital: Opened in Berkshire in 1864, Broadmoor is a high-security psychiatric hospital. It was purpose-built as the first state-run asylum for criminal lunatics.

Central Criminal Court (*see also* **Old Bailey**): The Crown Court building located on London's Old Bailey. The court hears criminal trials for the Greater London area but is also used for major criminal trials from across the country, particularly when a defendant may not receive a fair trial at their local court or the trial requires a higher level of security.

Coroner (*see also* **Inquest**): A judge appointed to investigate unnatural or unexplained deaths, as well as any death occurring in a state detention facility (such as a prison), and make a finding as to the cause of death.

Corporate Manslaughter and Corporate Homicide Act 2007: The statute that introduced the crime of corporate manslaughter into UK law. Under the Act, a company is guilty of the offence if the way in which its activities are managed or organised causes a person's death, as a result of a gross breach of a duty of care owed by the company to the victim.

Court of Appeal (*see also* **Supreme Court**): The second-most senior court in England and Wales. In criminal cases the Court hears appeals against convictions and sentences passed at trials by the Crown Court. The decisions of the Court of Appeal can be further appealed up to the Supreme Court (formerly to the House of Lords).

Court of Crown Cases Reserved: Established by parliament in 1848, the Court of Crown Cases Reserved was the only mechanism to review and overturn a criminal conviction. Cases could only be referred to the Court if the original judge chose to do so; the defendant had no right of appeal to the Court. The Court was replaced by a new Court of Appeal for criminal cases in 1908.

Criminal Cases Review Commission (CCRC): The statutory body established in the 1990s to investigate potential miscarriages of justice and refer cases to the Court of Appeal if appropriate.

Criminal Lunatics Act 1800: The statute that enabled the indefinite detention of defendants found not guilty by reason of insanity. The Act was passed in the wake of the trial of James Hadfield for the attempted assassination of King George III in 1800.

Death by dangerous driving: A vehicular homicide offence relating to deaths resulting from driving that falls far below the standard expected of a competent and careful driver. The offence was first created under the Road Traffic Act of the 1950s.

Diminished responsibility: A partial defence to a charge of murder, based on the killer's abnormality of mental functioning, which diminishes their responsibility for their actions. If accepted by a jury, diminished responsibility will reduce murder to voluntary manslaughter.

Director of Public Prosecutions (DPP): The head of the Crown Prosecution Service and the most senior prosecuting lawyer in the country, with ultimate oversight of all criminal cases. The DPP reports directly to the attorney-general, the government's chief lawyer.

First-degree murder (United States): The highest classification of homicide in most US jurisdictions. It generally relates to intentional killings.

Gross negligence manslaughter (*see also* Involuntary manslaughter): A category of involuntary manslaughter, where a death results from the gross breach of the duty of care owed by the killer to the victim.

Health and Safety at Work Act 1974: The piece of legislation that imposed statutory duties on employers and other companies to ensure the health, safety and well-being of their employees and members of the public. The Act also created the Health and Safety Executive, the statutory

322

body that regulates and enforces health and safety in this country.

Her/His Majesty's Pleasure: An indeterminate custodial sentence that is reviewed periodically. It is used in cases where the imposition of a straightforward life sentence is not appropriate, such as for minors or mentally disordered offenders. In such cases the defendant will be ordered to be detained until 'Her Majesty's pleasure be known'.

HMP Holloway: The prison in Holloway, north London. Built in the Victorian era, for much of its life it was a women's prison, and inmates included Ruth Ellis, who was executed there in 1955. It closed in 2016.

Homicide: Generic term for the unlawful killing of a human being.

Homicide Act 1957: The statute that reformed the law of murder in the middle of the 20th century. It codified the defence of provocation and created the defence of diminished responsibility, together with reforming the application of capital punishment in murder cases.

House of Lords (*see also* Supreme Court): Until 2009, the House of Lords also acted in a judicial capacity as England's highest appeal court and could hear cases referred up to it from the Court of Appeal. This function was then given to the newly created Supreme Court.

Infanticide Act 1922: The piece of legislation that created the offence of infanticide. This homicide offence applies only to women who kill their own child under the age of twelve months, while the balance of their mind is disturbed from the effect of giving birth. The Act was intended to mitigate the harsh effects of sentencing such women to death for murder.

Inquest (*see also* Coroner): A court hearing to consider evidence on a death that is under investigation by a coroner.

Insanity defence (*see also* **M'Naghten rules**): The plea of not guilty to a criminal charge on the basis that the defendant is insane. A finding of insanity will result in detention at Her Majesty's Pleasure in a psychiatric institution, rather than a prison. The test for determining criminal insanity is based on the M'Naghten rules.

Institutes of the Laws of England: A legal textbook written by Sir Edward Coke in the 16th century.

Involuntary manslaughter: An unintentional homicide, where a death has been caused by the wrongful act or gross negligence of a killer.

Joint enterprise: The legal doctrine under which a person who assists another to commit a crime is treated as being guilty of committing the offence, to the same extent as the person who has directly done so.

Loss of control (*see also* **Provocation**): A partial defence to murder, in cases where a person has killed another due to a loss of self-control. The loss of control must have been caused by either a fear of serious violence or other circumstances of extremely grave character that caused the killer to have a justifiable sense of being seriously wronged. The defence was introduced into law in 2009 and replaced the long-established defence of provocation.

Manslaughter: The secondary classification of homicide in English law, below murder. It includes killings that were unintentional (involuntary manslaughter) and deliberate killings that are subject to a partial defence (voluntary manslaughter)

***Mens rea*:** The guilty mind that must be proved alongside the *actus reus* in order to establish the commission of a criminal offence. For murder, the required *mens rea* is an intention to kill or cause serious harm.

M'Naghten rules: The test applied by courts to determine whether a defendant can rely on an insanity defence. The rules require a defendant to prove that they were afflicted by a disease of the mind that meant they did not understand what they were doing or, if they did know what they were doing, they did not realise it was wrong. The rules are named after Daniel M'Naghten, who was acquitted of murder on the basis of insanity in 1843.

Mord/Mordor: The earliest classification of a category of homicide in English law, which referred to a secret killing.

Murder: The most serious homicide offence in English law. A person is guilty of murder if they cause the death of another person, and either intended to kill them or to cause them serious physical harm. A conviction for murder carries a mandatory sentence of life imprisonment.

Murder (Abolition of the Death Penalty) Act 1965: The statute that suspended the death penalty in murder cases (by then the only capital crime) for a period of five years. The suspension was made permanent by parliament in 1969.

Murdrum: The ancient homicide offence referred to in the laws set down during the reign of Edward the Confessor. It related to secret killings, which were punishable by death, as opposed to payment of *bot*.

Offences Against the Person Act 1861: The statute that governed most crimes of personal violence, including homicide. The Act restricted the use of the death penalty to murder only.

Old Bailey (*see also* Central Criminal Court): The London street, running between Fleet Street and Ludgate Hill, on which the Central Criminal Court is located. The court itself is also commonly referred to as the Old Bailey.

HMP Parkhurst: The high-security prison on the Isle of Wight. Former prisoners include Canadian soldier Georges Codere.

Prerogative of mercy: The convention under which a monarch could pardon a person convicted of a criminal offence. Prior to the abolition of the death penalty, this extended to commuting a death sentence to one of imprisonment. In modern times, the exercise of the prerogative has been delegated to the home secretary.

Provocation (*see also* Loss of Control): A partial defence to a charge of murder based on the killer's sudden and temporary loss of control, occasioned by their victim's behaviour towards them. It was replaced by the new statutory defence of loss of control in 2009.

Rampton Hospital: A high-security psychiatric hospital in Nottinghamshire. The hospital opened in 1912 and was the second purpose-built state institute for the criminally insane, following the opening of Broadmoor in 1864.

Road Traffic Acts: The series of statutes from the 1950s onwards that regulate all aspects of driving and road use, including vehicular homicide offences such as causing death by dangerous driving.

Self-defence: A defence based on the killer's use of force to defend themselves against physical threat. If proven, self-defence is a complete defence to murder, but the defendant must show that the force used was proportionate to the threat involved and it was reasonable to use such force in the circumstances.

Supreme Court (*see also* House of Lords): The highest court in England, which was created in 2009. It hears appeals against the decisions of the Court of Appeal and replaced the judicial function previously exercised by the House of Lords.

Voluntary manslaughter: An intentional killing that would be classified as murder, but for the fact that the defendant can rely on a partial defence of diminished responsibility or provocation/loss of control.

Wager of battle: The ancient right of a defendant in a criminal trial to opt to be tried by battle or combat, instead of arguing the case before a judge and jury. A defendant who outfought his accuser would be acquitted of the crime. The concept heavily influenced the practice of duelling, which was popular in both the UK and across Europe from the 16th until the 19th century. The option to elect for wager of battle was abolished in 1819 following the trial of Abraham Thornton.

HMP Wandsworth: The men's prison in Wandsworth, south London. Previous inmates include Derek Bentley, who was executed there in 1953.

Wergild (see also *Bot*): In Anglo-Saxon law, the price at which the life of an individual was valued, which in the event that he was killed had to be paid in *bot* to his family by his killer.

PICTURE CREDITS

Page 2, bottom: Courtesy of the author
Page 3, bottom: © *British Library Board*
Page 4, bottom: Courtesy of the author
Page 5, top left: © *Western Mail/Reach PLC*
Page 5, top right: © *Liverpool Echo*
Page 5, bottom: Courtesy of the author
Page 6, top left: © *Birmingham Mail/Trinity Mirror*
Page 6, top right: © *Birmingham Mail*
Page 6, bottom left: Photo by Keystone/Staff/Getty Images
Page 6, bottom right: John Twine/ANL/Shutterstock
Page 7, top left: PA Images/Alamy Stock Photo
Page 7, top right: PA Images/Alamy Stock Photo
Page 7, bottom: PA Images/Alamy Stock Photo
Page 8: Roberto Pfeil/AP/Shutterstock

ACKNOWLEDGEMENTS

I still haven't decided if 2020 was the best or worst year in which to write my first book. The enforced time at home meant fewer distractions, and most of the book was written from my attic study, with only a little dachshund for company. In the spring I feared that my plan for a long summer of research trips and library visits was scuppered entirely. But it was put back on track in no small part thanks to the staff of the British Library and the National Archives, who were without exception helpful and friendly, even from behind a facemask. Thanks also to the staff of Wolverhampton Libraries, Sutton Coldfield Library and the Law Society Library. The patience of the staff at the Library of Birmingham in explaining, demonstrating and then re-explaining how to use a microfiche machine was also much appreciated.

I am grateful to several people for answering my questions on various cases in the book. Jane Hurst provided insight into the story of Fanny Adams, and David Green was very generous with his time regarding his work on the case for his own book on the trial of Frederick Baker. David Luck of the Bethlem

Royal Hospital gave me valuable assistance in tracking down Daniel M'Naghten's records and Sophie led me on a fascinating tour of the hospital's thought-provoking Museum of the Mind. I must also thank Howard Watson for casting his expert eye over the sections on corporate manslaughter and providing very helpful feedback. All mistakes are, of course, my own.

This book would never have come into existence without my fantastic agent Euan Thorneycroft, who 'got' the book from the very beginning and has steered me expertly towards publication. Thanks also to Bill Hamilton, Jessica and the rest of the team at A.M. Heath. At Mudlark and HarperCollins, my brilliant editor Joel Simons has worked tirelessly on the book, always with the deftest of touches and an unflagging enthusiasm for the project from our very first meeting. Holly Macdonald did a wonderfully macabre job on the cover design, and Isabel Prodger and Julie MacBrayne masterminded great publicity and marketing campaigns. I'm grateful to Sarah Hammond for bringing the whole thing to life and into production, and to Mark Bolland for his meticulous copy-editing. Thanks also to Fionnuala Barrett for producing the audio version.

Thanks to my friend Tiara, who provided moral support in the form of frequent café trips, as well as impromptu German translation services, and to Dan McClane for the author photo on the jacket. To my parents Sue & Tony – thanks, as always, for everything, especially for encouraging a love of reading books that finally made me have a go at writing one of my own. Thanks to the rest of my family for their interest and support: Charl & Andrew; Steve & Julie; Bec, Glenn, Aoife & Fin; and the glamorous grans Freda, Nancy & Mabel.

ACKNOWLEDGEMENTS

Finally, to my wonderful husband James – for cooking dinners, walking the dog, driving home from Aberystwyth and back again so I could work by myself by the sea, making endless cups of tea, as well as checking my drafts, photographing, critiquing and telling everyone he meets that his wife's writing a book – thanks, bab.

INDEX

Bentley, Derek 156–60, 164, 166, 173, 174, 175, 176, 212, 215, 235, 302, 311, 327

Bethlem Royal Hospital ('Bethlehem') ('Bedlam') 52–3, 61–2, 68, 70, 71, 73, 77, 82, 83–4, 278–9, 305, 319, 320

'beyond reasonable doubt' concept 17, 320

Bible 49

Birmingham Six 212–14, 216–18, 231, 234, 236, 237–8, 314

black people, murder statistics and 8

Blair, Tony 267

Blakely, David 18, 147–50, 152–5, 173, 175, 176, 212, 225, 302, 310

Bland, Tony 259–64, 292, 316

Bloody Code 9, 162, 320

boiling in oil 161

Boswell, James 28–9; *Life of Samuel Johnson* 25, 28–30, 307

bot, or compensation 11, 320, 325, 327

Bouche, George 151

Brady, Ian 71

Brecht, Bertolt 1–2

Brennan, Karen 298–9, 318

Bridgewater, Carl 208–11, 231, 233, 234, 314

Bridgewater Four, The 208–11, 212, 219, 231–4, 236, 237

Briggs, Kim 300–1

Briggs, Matthew 301

Brine, Daisy 128–9, 136

British army training marches, Brecon Beacons 294–5

British Medical Journal 125–6, 144, 309

British Secret Service 180

Broadmoor Hospital 70–2, 83, 278, 320, 326

Brooks, Edward 86–95, 101

Brown, Charlotte 145–6

Brown, Margaret 168–9, 172

Browne-Wilkinson, Lord 262–3

Budd, Burt 129, 136–7

Budd, Rosalind 129, 136–7, 310

Burgundy, Kingdom of 31

Burke and Hare killings 54

Burton, John 88–9

Byrne, Patrick 169–73, 176–7, 312

cannibalism 84–102, 111, 113, 308

capital murder 166–7, 170, 176–7

capital sentence *see* death penalty

Carter, Godfrey 137

casuale (accidental) 13

Central Criminal Court (*see also* Old Bailey) 320–1, 325

Challen, Richard 280–2

Challen, Sally 280–2, 286, 317

chance-medley/'hot blood' 15, 38

Channon, Paul 250

Charles II, King 32

Cheeseman, Robert 86, 87, 88, 89, 90, 130, 131

Chesham, Richard 235–6

Chesham, Sarah 235–6

Christie, John 160, 166, 173, 215, 311

Church, Cyril 182–6, 199, 204, 312

Clapham Junction rail crash (1988) 242, 244, 315

Clarke, Kenneth 219, 231

class prejudices, justice system and 34, 37, 39–40, 161, 163, 282

Clinton, Dawn 287–8

Clinton, Jon-Jaques 287–8, 317

Cnut, King 12

Codere, Lieutenant Georges 104–11, 216, 309, 326

coercive control concept 281–2

Coke, Sir Edward: *Institutes of the Lawes of England* 13–15, 16,